The
GODFATHER'S
DAUGHTER

HAY HOUSE TITLES OF RELATED INTEREST

All of the above are available at your local bookstore,
or may be ordered by visiting:

Hay House USA: **www.hayhouse.com**®
Hay House Australia: **www.hayhouse.com.au**
Hay House UK: **www.hayhouse.co.uk**
Hay House South Africa: **www.hayhouse.co.za**
Hay House India: **www.hayhouse.co.in**

The
GODFATHER'S
DAUGHTER

An Unlikely Story of
Love, Healing, and Redemption

Rita Gigante
with Natasha Stoynoff

HAY HOUSE, INC.

Carlsbad, California • New York City

London • Sydney • Johannesburg

Vancouver • Hong Kong • New Delhi

Published and distributed in the United States by: Hay House, Inc.: www.hayhouse .com® • *Published and distributed in Australia by:* Hay House Australia Pty. Ltd.: www.hayhouse.com.au • *Published and distributed in the United Kingdom by:* Hay House UK, Ltd.: www.hayhouse.co.uk • *Published and distributed in the Republic of South Africa by:* Hay House SA (Pty), Ltd.: www.hayhouse.co.za • *Distributed in Canada by:* Raincoast: www.raincoast.com • *Published in India by:* Hay House Publishers India: www.hayhouse.co.in

Cover design: Amy Rose Grigoriou • *Interior design:* Tricia Breidenthal
Interior photos/illustrations: Courtesy of the author, except where noted

Library of Congress Cataloging-in-Publication Data

Gigante, Rita.
   The godfather's daughter : an unlikely story of love, healing, and redemption / Rita Gigante ; with Natasha Stoynoff.
      p. cm.
   ISBN 978-1-4019-3880-2 (hardcover : alk. paper)
   1. Gigante, Rita, 1967- 2. Gigante, Rita, 1967---Family. 3. Gigante, Vincent, 1928-2005. 4. Children of criminals--New York Metropolitan Area--Biography. 5. Mafia--New York Metropolitan Area--History. 6. Organized crime--New York Metropolitan Area--History. 7. Italian American families--New York Metropolitan Area. I. Stoynoff, Natasha. II. Title.
   HV6452.N7G54 2012
   364.1092--dc23
   [B]
                                        2012018133

Hardcover ISBN: 978-1-4019-3880-2
Digital ISBN: 978-1-4019-3882-6

15 14 13 12   4 3 2 1
1st edition, September 2012

Printed in the United States of America

SUSTAINABLE
FORESTRY
INITIATIVE
Certified Chain of Custody
Promoting Sustainable Forestry
www.sfiprogram.org
SFI-01268

SFI label applies to the text stock

To all the souls
on Earth and in spirit.

CONTENTS

PREFACE

I write this memoir with much love in my heart for all the people who have crossed my path in the past, who are with me in the present, and who will appear by my side in the future.

My memories are based upon actual people, conversations, impressions, and events in my life to the very best of my recollection. Although they are my truth, they may not be the same truth as someone else's. I share them here to further my own spiritual healing—and also, hopefully, to help those I love and those I don't even know to embark on their own healing paths.

All names and most nicknames have been changed, except for family whose names are already public record and people who have agreed to be named. At the request of certain family members, references to, photographs of, and events concerning them have not been included here unless crucial to my personal story.

Confronting one's past can be difficult, but to stay in a state of fear and denial keeps one from moving forward and truly living. To me, sharing truth is the ultimate expression of love and hope for a better today and tomorrow.

INTRODUCTION

A Space of Grace

When the images finally surfaced, they were as disjointed and broken as they were vicious and cruel.

It was January 2012, and I was in my healing room at home in the middle of a session with my client Marina, who had come for help with her persistent back pain. The session started out like any other: I lit the room with candles and rubbed drops of essential oil of lavender between the palms of my hands. The vibration in the room was calm, and the air smelled warm and sweet.

This was Marina's second visit, and I suspected that the nagging back injury she'd had since her teens was connected to an emotional trauma she'd experienced at that age—an upsetting event she'd been holding on to that we needed to get to the root of and expose. It was the only way for her to release the pain.

Marina lay down on her stomach on my table, and I shut my eyes and held my hands over her lower back. I could feel a swirl of energy surge from the top of my head down through my arms, shooting out like moonbeams from the tips of my fingers to Marina's back. I began to see images of my client in my mind. I saw a shadowy image of her as a child crouched beneath an old wooden table, playing alone.

"What happened under the wooden table, where you played as a child?" I asked her. I could feel my energy opening up to the universe and my hands getting hot.

"I'm not sure what you mean," she said. "I don't remember playing under a wooden table."

A new scene flashed before me: The same little girl was under the same table, and Italian music was warbling in the background—a woman with a beautiful voice was singing on an old radio. Suddenly, the song was interrupted by the harsh voices of angry men stomping into the dining room. The men didn't notice the little girl in her spot beneath the table, but she was afraid anyway, so she scooted further into the shadows, trying to disappear. I could feel the girl's growing panic.

"The Italian music, the angry men, when you were about five years old?"

"I don't understand what you're describing, Rita. I don't remember any angry men. And we're not Italian, so . . ."

Then it hit me like a tidal wave. This wasn't for her; it was for *me*.

Before I truly understood what was happening, I was jolted back in time and found myself sitting under my grandmother's table in the dining room on Sullivan Street.

> *From where I am sitting, I can only see the legs of the men, from their knees to their shoes. Their yells get louder and louder until they're cut off by my father's voice. Dad's gravelly whisper is so low it's hard to hear, but so powerful that nobody dares to speak over it.*
>
> *He says only five words—hard and sharp, like rough, unfinished metal.*
>
> *"Don't ever fuckin' disrespect me."*
>
> *His sentence ends with a smacking thud, like the sound when my Gram tenderizes the veal chops with her stainless steel meat mallet. Then a man I've never seen before is on the floor facing me, looking into my eyes as blood gushes from his*

nose onto the floor, flowing toward me like a little red river across the black-and-white tiles.

Then I see a fist smashing into the man's face. The ring on the fist's pinky finger belongs to my father. I follow the ring with my eyes as it flies up out of sight above the table, and then comes down again into the man's cheekbone. It pumps up and down, again and again, until the man's face is ripped and shredded. Then my dad's shiny shoe stomps on the man's head three times before everything goes quiet.

"I'm done with him," Dad whispers. "Get him out of here."

The man's body is pulled away, and a few minutes later I am alone in the dining room. I can hear the beautiful music once again. Then the little river of blood reaches my toes and pools around my feet. In that moment, I make a connection between the blood, my father, and me: If I don't do as I'm told, Daddy's going to hurt me, too. I want to scream, but instead I slap my hands over my mouth and whimper softly until I hear my mother looking for me. I crawl out from under the table.

"Oh my God, Rita. Have you been sitting under there this whole time?"

She scoops me up into her arms and hugs me, trying to stop my body from shaking.

"It's okay . . . shhh. Daddy just got angry. Don't worry. Put it out of your mind."

And that's exactly what I did, for almost 40 years.

Those few minutes comprised one of the earliest and most traumatizing memories I have of my father, Vincent Gigante. Even though I was only five, I understood that I had to bury what I'd seen into the depths of my consciousness to keep from facing the horror of it. There I locked away the memory, where it would take root and fester—along with countless other experiences that were too horrific to face.

The trauma from those experiences would emerge in other ways throughout my childhood and into my adulthood as illness, anxiety, depression, violence, and obsessive-compulsive behavior.

I hid the memory of those minutes and the ensuing years of confusion, betrayal, and family secrets so deep in my body, heart, and soul that it would take years of counseling, medication, and spiritual healing to dredge them out of the darkness and into the light, where I could finally confront them. Where they would have no more power or hold on me.

I now make my living as a healer, and healing is all about faith and a belief that we are already healed, already whole. There is a moment that happens between a healer and a client that I call "a space of grace." It's an instant of stillness when I can feel a great, benevolent energy—some, like me, call it "God"—connect with the energies of my client and me to create a surge of healing. In that moment, I am just a vehicle for this energy to do its wonderful work.

With this book, too, I am a vehicle to pass along a healing energy that is grander than all of us. And I hope what I'm about to share with you will encourage a healing space of grace for you as well.

Every day in my work I try to teach people how to connect with a universal light, clarity, and truth—words never uttered or understood in my family while I was growing up. Because, as the daughter of Vincent Gigante, my world was smothered beneath a cloak of darkness, violence, and confusion.

My father and I lived secret, tangled, double lives. It took us a lifetime and one death to untie and unite them.

PART I

IN THE DARK

CHAPTER 1

HOME SICK

I had a split childhood. One half was spent growing up with my mother and siblings in the quiet, leafy suburb of Old Tappan, New Jersey. Our rambling, spacious home had a swimming pool in the backyard, along with a majestic weeping willow that had long, drooping shoots that swayed lazily in the wind.

The other half of my life unfolded across the Hudson River in my grandmother and father's dark, ground-floor apartment in Manhattan. I'd step over the dead mice and dodge cockroaches that made their way up from the basement below us, and enter Gram's warm kitchen, where she'd be at her place by the stove. My father would be sitting silently in the next room, with big men who had funny nicknames whom he'd order around.

Shuffling between these two worlds was like having a dual personality: suburban Jersey girl and Manhattan street kid. And I'm not sure I felt I belonged on either side of the river.

FROM THE TIME I WAS SIX MONTHS OLD, the house in Old Tappan was our main family home. Our street was in a typical New Jersey neighborhood, which, in the early 1970s, still offered the illusion of safety and innocence.

My friends and I would race our dirt bikes after school, having skin-scraping adventures on the winding trails tucked behind the rows of houses. The trails led us to Sunden's Stone Pointe Farm a block away, where we'd park our bikes and fish out quarters from our pockets to load up on Gobstoppers and Jawbreakers and Good & Plenty. We'd sit on our bikes by the farm's store out front, gorging on our sweets in the sunshine, until our mothers came out from our homes, screen doors slapping behind them, yelling out, *"Dinnnnnerrrrr!"* Our area was mostly Italian-Catholic and Jewish, with a little Irish mixed in for luck. So come dinnertime, we'd all disperse and scatter home to stuff ourselves with latkes or lasagna.

I say my neighborhood offered the *illusion* of safety and innocence because even as a child—*especially* as a child—I sensed that violence lurked just under the sunny, happy surface of our daily lives.

For example, I remember waiting by the curb for my mother to pick me up after school when I was in second grade, and a strange man pulled up to me in his car. "I know your mom," he said with a smile. "She wanted me to pick you up."

"But I have to wait for her."

"No, no! She wanted me to come and get you! I'm going to take you right home. I have some candy in here . . . "

I don't remember being taught as a kid to never get into a strange man's car, even if he was smiling and had candy. But my gut knew something horrible would happen if I did, so I ran into the school, yelling back at the man: *"No!* I'm waiting for my mom!"

Nothing was as it seemed—even in the so-called safety of my own home, with my own family, who were far from being "strangers."

BY ALL APPEARANCES, WE COULD HAVE PASSED for a regular Italian-Catholic family like any other on the street. There were a lot of us, and we ate and argued boisterously, and then we went to church on Sundays to pray and ask for forgiveness.

My mother and father were each the product of an Italian-immigrant success story. Their parents had come across the ocean from Naples (where they hadn't known each other), settled a block away from each other in lower Manhattan, and had children in the new country. Their mothers—Grandma Yolanda on Dad's side and Grandma Rose on Mom's side—came to know each other quite well, and their young kids played together.

By age 12, my father already had other plans for my mother, who was one year his junior. He asked her to go for a walk through Washington Square Park with him, and as soon as they sat down on a bench, he leaned over and planted a shy kiss on her lips, a first for both of them.

My mother, Olympia Grippa, was a vivacious beauty among her six sisters and one brother. As a teenager, she drew portraits, danced the Lindy Hop, and stole the hearts of all the soldiers one year at a block party when she stood up on a truck and crooned Ella Fitzgerald ballads. She could have done anything with her talent, but she only wanted to be a wife and mother (it's what she was taught to want).

My father, Vincent Gigante, was a handsome young man with impeccable manners, my mother noted. She appreciated that he never cussed around her, and she adored his slicked-back dark hair, heavy-lidded eyes, and full mouth—he was a combination of a young Brando and Elvis, Italian-style. "He was yummy," Mom once said to me, about Dad in his youth. For her entire life, she would love him like a starstruck teenaged girl.

Dad learned how to box at a young age and started fighting in the ring as a light heavyweight at age 16, even fighting at Madison Square Garden. It was the time of Rocky Graziano and Jake LaMotta, and my father was a fierce contender—winning 21 out of his 25 fights over a three-year period.

In between bouts, he wooed Mom, driving past her one day in his uncle's borrowed car. "Wanna go for a ride?" he called out as she was walking down the street.

"Sure!"

They drove a bit, parked, and "mushed it up," Mom described with a laugh. They were officially smitten and going steady.

One day during Sunday Mass, Dad produced a ring from his suit pocket and whispered a solemn proposal in Mom's ear as they sat next to each other in a back pew. As she later told me, "I looked up and smiled at him, and gave him a kiss on the cheek."

That was that. My parents were married in 1950 and began raising a big family in Grandma Yolanda's old, cramped, West Village apartment on Sullivan Street. Dad gave up boxing and took any job he could find. As my mother later said, "If it snowed, he'd go out and shovel snow. Or he'd load boxes. At one time, he worked for a trucking company. And although it was menial labor, I was proud of him. He finished high school, but he didn't have a trade to speak of so he had to make money any way he could to support us."

Their firstborn was Yolanda—we all call her "Yo"—named after Dad's mother. As a child I was mesmerized by her beautiful black hair that cascaded down her back. It was so thick and shiny she once won a contest for it. She was smart and strong, just like Gram, and dreamed of becoming a doctor one day. As the eldest, she was in charge of all of us as we arrived one by one. From the moment I was born, she even took me under her wing as if I was her own baby.

Next in line was my sister Roseanne—"Ro"—named after Mom's mother. She had big doe eyes and was sexy, smart-mouthed, and the fun family rebel, often getting in trouble with my father for mouthing off or disobeying him. When I was 14, Ro would let me drive her car, and we'd stay up all night laughing and dancing and making pancakes.

Then came the first son, Salvatore—"Sal"—named after Dad's father. Sal had our father's charm, along with his temper. My brother looked up to Dad and yearned for his approval but, like the rest us, rarely got it. When the family moved to Jersey and Dad later moved back to the city to live with Gram, Sal became the man of the house, a job he certainly wasn't prepared for since he was only 12 years old. Dad wanted Sal to become a lawyer, but at heart Sal was an artist, like Mom, and excelled at playing the guitar and building with his hands. He married his high-school girlfriend, Janet, soon after they graduated and was out of the house by the time I was in kindergarten.

Next came another son, Andrew, who was named after Mom's father. He was the youngest member of the family until I arrived, ten years later.

Before I was born, my siblings tell me that their days were carefree, and at night, they'd wait for Dad to come home with special presents. One night just before Easter, he showed up with a four-foot-tall chocolate bunny, which they ate ear-first. Another time when the chicken pox had invaded our home, Dad arrived with a box of real baby chicks to make them laugh.

This was how life was until Dad had to go away to the Army for five years in 1959. They missed him, but he'd write colorful letters telling them all about kitchen-patrol duty and being promoted up from washing the floor to chopping the vegetables.

Or so my siblings were told. One day my supersmart and sleuthing sister Yolanda found a box of papers in a closet with Dad's name on them. They were trial transcripts.

As they were going to bed that night, she broke the news to Roseanne: "Ro . . . Daddy wasn't in the Army."

"Yes he was."

"No, he wasn't." She pulled out the papers and showed them to her.

"Daddy was in *jail!*"

The early good times, and a first loss of innocence for my sisters about my father, happened before I was born, and I wouldn't know about any of it until decades later.

I was the true baby of the family, and soon became known as the weak and sickly one who played alone. By the time I was six years old, three of my four siblings had gotten married and left home. So in a very real way, I grew up like an only child, even though I was born into a big family.

Today, when I look at the old family photos, I see the smiling faces of my big brothers splashing me in the swimming pool and holding me up as I kick my little toes in the water . . . or me surrounded by a group of teenagers as I blow out pink birthday candles and sit in my smiling father's lap . . . or me at age five at my sister Yolanda's wedding, looking lost and bewildered. I'm sure I was distraught because I was losing my sister, but that's also around the time I witnessed my father smash his fist into that man's face under Gram's table.

I see the images of older kids playing with me—this chubby, earnest little child with big, dark eyes like my father—but the images feel foreign. I want to remember these happy moments, but it's as if they happened to someone else. By the time I was old enough to start forming memories, most of my siblings had moved on, and I was left home alone with my mother.

I ENTERED THE WORLD ON JANUARY 24, 1967, with great promise, as evident by my very naming.

It's tradition in an Italian family to name your children after the grandparents. But since my parents already had two girls and two boys, all the important names had been taken. So my mother asked my grandmother Yolanda to do the honors. Gram, the family matriarch, was a devout Catholic and had no hesitation when choosing.

"I name you for Saint *Reeeta*," she liked to remind me, in her broken English, whenever I scurried after her with her wire cart on Saturday-morning errands to pick up fresh mozzarella (*"mutz"*), roasted peppers (*"pep-puhs"*), and veal from Joe's Dairy and Pino's Meat Market down the street from her apartment.

It didn't matter that Gram had lived in New York for 50 years; she always looked as though she'd just stepped off the boat from Naples. She had long silver hair that she braided and coiled up into a bun, along with an Old World beauty and upright bearing from another era.

Saint Rita, Gram explained, was an Italian nun born in 1386, who prayed to Jesus to let her suffer as he had. As the story goes, a thorn fell down from a figurine of Jesus one day and wounded Rita on the forehead. The wound was deep and emitted a terrible stench and never healed, causing her great suffering and isolation from the other nuns for the rest of her life. But on the day she died, the odor from the wound became a beautiful scent of roses. Rita is the one to pray to in order to resolve impossible situations, she told me.

"I name you after her," my grandmother continued, as I trailed behind her, "because she is Saint of the Impossible! And one day, Rita, you too will do the impossible."

Gram always spoke with such conviction and certainty, you couldn't help but believe that what she said was the absolute truth. Maybe that's because among our family and friends, she was famous for having a direct line to heaven. Saint Rita was one of Gram's favorite saints, yes, but Gram was also on intimate terms with and completely devoted to someone even higher up in rank.

Gram loved to tell the story of the time she was a young mother in her early 30s and had been admitted to the hospital with serious blood poisoning.

"She's not going to live another day," the doctors assured my grandfather. "You should start making arrangements."

As she lay in the hospital bed, semiconscious, she could overhear her two sisters-in-law hovering over her bed, arguing about how to split up Gram's five little boys—Pat, Mario, my father, Ralph, and Lou. The idea that her boys were going to be divvied up like puppies tore at her heart. Gram had already endured two family tragedies in her life, and she didn't want her boys to suffer as she had done.

Back in Naples when she was 13 years old, her father, Pasquale, a well-respected and well-loved pharmacist, witnessed a crime committed by a member of *La Mano Nera* (or "the Black Hand")— a Mafia-like extortion racket that infiltrated the city in the early 20th century. Gram's father was subpoenaed to appear in court to testify against the Black Hand, but he feared for the lives of his wife and children if he did. Great-grandfather Pasquale saw only one way out. Before the trial, he procured the poison strychnine and ingested it to save his family, dying an agonizing, slow, choking death. Gram cried for years over her father's heroic but senseless suicide.

The second tragedy happened during a trip back to Italy when Gram was a young woman. Friends in Naples were cooking dinner when her 18-month-old son, the first Vincent, tugged at a pot of boiling water and it fell, dousing him. He was in the hospital for two weeks before he died. "I sat with him in my arms, and his eye fell right out of his face," Gram said. She never recovered from losing her first Vincent, and my grandfather blamed her for it for the rest of his life. Gram named her next baby—my father—in memory of her other lost son.

So as she lay there in her hospital bed, the idea of losing her other sons, and of them losing each other, was too much for her. As she tells it, she began praying to the Virgin Mary to spare her life. A moment later, she saw Mary's placid, beautiful face at the foot of her bed.

"I plead with her, 'Pleeeease, you must let me live for the sake of my children! You are the mother of all mothers, you must understand! If you do this one thing for me, I will endure any hardship you give me for rest of my life, I no complain!'"

Gram thought surely that, speaking mother to Blessed Mother, her request would be granted. And sure enough, it was. Gram had a "miraculous" recovery, and two weeks later was rolling out lasagna noodles with a broom handle on her well-floured kitchen countertop.

So when my grandmother used to tell me that I'd grow up to do wonderful, impossible things in my life, I wondered if I could really believe her.

And yet, as a child, every little thing seemed so impossible to me.

BY THE TIME I WAS A TODDLER IN THE LATE '60s, my father had moved out of our New Jersey home and back in our old apartment with Gram. At the time, I didn't know why. Their apartment was a few blocks west of Little Italy and a block south of Washington Square Park. The site where Mom and Dad shared their first kiss was now crowded with peace-loving hippies and mind-altered NYU students who were doing a lot more than kissing, I'm sure.

During those first few years after my father moved out, my mother's effervescent personality dimmed. I remember waking up early on a Sunday morning, padding downstairs in my pajamas, and not finding her in her usual spot at the kitchen table having coffee. I went roaming about the house, taking my favorite pink rubber ball with me and bouncing it along the walls, searching for Mom. I found her sitting in the den with the shades drawn and the lights out. She was facing the wall, rocking back and forth in the black swivel chair.

I stood at the doorway, afraid to speak, and bounced the ball into the den to get her attention. It rolled to her feet, but she still didn't look up.

"Mom?" I whispered, inching toward her. "Are you sick?"

She looked over at me and covered her face with her hands. "I'm okay," she said, choking between her tears. "Just give me a minute . . . "

As soon as I was old enough to understand that other dads lived at home while mine only visited us in Jersey every so often, Yolanda sat me down on my bed to have a sister-to-sister talk. I had been asking questions, and it was her job to try to explain the odd things going on in my family to me. Either that, or she was sent to shut me up.

I dove into my menagerie of stuffed animals on the bed and waited happily to hear what my big sister had to tell me. She began by assuring me that just because Daddy didn't live with us, it didn't mean he didn't love us. Dad had moved away because he didn't feel well. "If anyone asks you where Dad is, you tell them he's sick," Yo instructed me.

"What's Daddy sick with?"

"It's his heart."

I looked up at her, quizzically. "But he doesn't *look* sick."

"He is. But it's nothing you need to worry about, okay?"

I nodded.

Those were the kind of conversations I usually had with my family. The kind where I was told something and that was The End. I shifted my position on the bed and looked up at my sister from my zoo of animals. Yolanda was the only one in the family who gave me information—or, more often, she told me about the things she wouldn't tell me. But at least she talked and paid attention to me. She was my only hope to get more details about what was going on with the mysterious adults who populated my world.

I tugged on the edge of her fringed corduroy sleeve and cleared my throat. "Um, Yo . . . what's Daddy's job?"

She sighed and patted my cheek. "He's sick, that's all."

"Oh. Is being sick a *job?*"

This time, Yo laughed at me.

"Ri, go and watch *The Jetsons*, okay?"

OUR EXCHANGE MAY HAVE BEEN FUNNY to my sister, but I couldn't laugh with her because my throat was tightening up. I was learning pretty quickly that to survive in my family, you were supposed to keep your mouth shut and not ask questions.

I went outside and sat under the willow tree in the backyard and thought about what Yolanda had said. I decided that if I had any questions about my family, I would stuff them back down my throat so that I wouldn't make a sound. That was a good plan, I thought. The only problem was that when I did this, I could feel myself start to choke ever so slightly.

And I didn't have a plan yet for dealing with the world outside my front door and the brutal preschool set. One afternoon I was sitting cross-legged on my friend Linda's burnt sienna shag carpet in her living room. She and I were happily slurping Kool-Aid with another little girl while we passed around crayons and coloring books. Somehow, the topic got onto daddies.

"My daddy's a pilot," said the girl, "and he flies people across the ocean! What does your daddy do?"

Linda and I ooohed and ahhhhed. Linda went next. "My daddy's a teacher," she said, "and he teaches 'rithmetic."

The other girl and I nodded, in confirmation. They both looked over at me, waiting, Crayolas poised midair.

I kept my gaze down, concentrating on the outline of Dr. Seuss's Cat in the Hat on the coloring book in front of me. Then I looked up with a big grin. "My daddy works in a hat company!" I told them, breezily. "He makes hats!"

"Ohhhh," they both cooed, in unison. "You're so luckeeeee . . . "

One of my siblings had told me about the hat company once, going so far as to say that Dad had showed them a business card. Even at four and a half, though, I knew it was bullshit. But my playmates were satisfied—impressed, even—and we went back to our work. It was a strange moment for me. I realized that I had figured out a way to deal with my big "problem" of not knowing what to tell my friends about Dad's job, and it felt good to give them an answer that more than worked—it dazzled them.

Yet after I said it, I felt my stomach twisting up along with that choking feeling. I coughed and sipped my Kool-Aid, staring at the bizarre Dr. Seuss creatures in front of me. *Linda knows exactly what her daddy does; he teaches math. That other girl knows exactly what her daddy does; he flies planes. I know my daddy doesn't really make hats; I made that up.*

My stomach twisted some more, into a big, painful knot. Lying to my friends and not knowing what my father did made me sick. Knowing that he *was* sick, and that Mom might be sick, too, made me feel even worse.

The next morning, I woke up and could barely speak. I thought about the snake I'd seen in an old Tarzan movie a week earlier, and I imagined it coiling itself around my neck, squeezing the air out of me. I stayed home from school with a sore throat and lay on the living-room couch all day, watching TV. Then I had a sore throat the next day. And then again the day after that. The days turned into weeks, and the sore throats continued, becoming ear, nose, and throat infections and mysterious stomach ailments and on-and-off fevers.

"She must be catching every virus out there," the doctors told Mom. "She's a very *susceptible* child."

Mom quarantined me at home while the other kids on the block went to their first day of kindergarten toting neon-colored lunch boxes. I spent my September days on the couch or in Mom's bed, swaddled safely from the outside world, bundled up against whatever badness may be lurking around me, inside and out.

BY THE TIME I FINALLY MADE IT TO KINDERGARTEN, I was an emotional basket case. If anyone at home noticed, they didn't say anything. Yet if they didn't notice, my teacher, Mrs. Rosa, sure did. She didn't call my parents, though—she must have known that wasn't the way to go.

Yo was picking me up one day when Mrs. Rosa took her aside. My teacher was a big, soft lady with a sugary voice, and Yolanda knew her well because she had dated her son a few times. Mrs. Rosa sat me down at a little table with a paper cup of apple juice and a package of animal crackers, then pulled Yo a few feet away behind the cubicles.

"Rita is not coping well in class," Mrs. Rosa reported. "She sits in the classroom all day long with her face in her hands, crying, saying that she wants to go home. She has no interest in any activities. She's not socializing with the other kids properly . . ."

My sister was a little surprised—she knew I'd cry whenever one of my family members left me at school, but she didn't think my sobs lasted all day. She asked Mrs. Rosa a few more questions, then thanked her and came to fetch me. As we drove the few blocks home, we had another one of our sisterly talks.

"Rita, why are you crying in school? Is someone bothering you? Is someone hurting you?"

I shook my head. I felt a lump in my throat and my stomach turned somersaults. I couldn't answer Yolanda's question: I didn't know how to explain my predicament. I only knew I was afraid. I was afraid to be away from home, I was afraid to talk to the other kids, I was afraid of being left somewhere and forgotten, I was afraid of something I couldn't quite put my finger on. I hated myself for feeling afraid, and then I hated myself even more for crying in front of the other kids at school who stared at me like I was from another planet.

We arrived home and went to look for Mom in the kitchen to tell her about my eventful day. Instead, we found her in the den, crying. Yolanda ushered me into the kitchen and brought me cookies and milk. It was my second stay-quiet-and-keep-out-of-the-way cookie bribe of the day.

"Stay here," Yo said. "I need a few minutes alone with Mom." She then disappeared into the den, closing the door behind her.

From my spot at the kitchen table, I could hear my mother's muffled tears and the sound of Yolanda's voice talking to her, soothing her. A few minutes later, my sister emerged from the den and made a beeline to the bathroom. I trailed behind her and leaned against the bathroom doorframe, watching her rummage through a bunch of pills in the medicine cabinet.

"Why's Mom crying?"

"She's sick."

"What's she sick with?"

"She has a headache."

"I want to help."

"There's nothing you can do. Don't worry, she'll be okay."

Yolanda disappeared again into the den, taking a bottle of pills with her.

An hour or so later, Mom and Yo emerged from the den and joined me in the kitchen, where I'd stayed put per my sister's orders. Mom had stopped crying and seemed very, very relaxed, so I guessed she was better. Better from what, I didn't know. It was just another unmentionable subject on the growing list of unmentionable subjects that wreaked havoc on my stomach and throat. I didn't ask Mom what was the matter, and neither she nor Yolanda offered any explanation.

That night, Mom and I both laid in her bed next to her statue of the Blessed Mother, beneath the wooden rosary that hung from the wall. The rosary had beads the size of cherries.

We picked up our smaller rosaries from her night table and did our Hail Marys. When we were done, I slipped under Mom's covers

onto Dad's empty side of the bed. It had become understood somewhere along the way that when Dad was gone, which was most
of the time, I was to sleep with my mother. I'm not sure if it was
more for her benefit or mine—we were both in need of comfort
and didn't want to be alone.

I snuggled up next to my mother and put my head on her
chest. I guessed she had taken another one of those relaxing pills
from the bottle Yolanda had given her earlier because now she was
breathing deeply and fell asleep quickly. It was strange to be so
close to her physically yet still feel so far away. At the same time,
I could feel her emotions so deeply that it confused me—I never
knew if my feelings were hers or mine. I looked at her face and
wondered what was happening to us.

I could see the image of Mom and me, clinging to each other
on that bed, as if I were watching us from above. We looked tiny
and disappearing, not life-size at all, like I was looking from the
wrong end of a telescope.

Then I looked out the window, at the weeping willow sway-
ing in the breeze. I hoped Gram's good and blessed friend Mary
had heard our prayers. Because on days like this, with Mom crying at home and me crying at school, we needed a divine family
intervention.

I didn't realize it, but my mother was falling apart before my
very eyes. She didn't realize it, but I was falling apart before hers.

I wondered where my father was and what he was doing, and
if he was thinking about us at all. I wished I could call out to him
to come and help us, but what good would that have done?

I didn't have a voice, and he wouldn't have heard me anyway.

CHAPTER 2

DUNGEON AND DRAGONS

By the time I was seven years old, the weekend routine I'd follow for the next ten years was more or less established. Every other Saturday morning, I'd wake up, inhale a bowl of Cap'n Crunch, watch Bugs Bunny, and go visit Dad in the dungeon.

In the late '60s and early '70s, the West Village was the hippest place in Manhattan, which made it the coolest spot in the world. In 1974, the journey to get there from New Jersey was magical. Mom and I would climb into her forest green Cadillac and head for the George Washington Bridge, that magnificent structure that joins New Jersey with Upper Manhattan. As we crossed the bridge 212 feet above the Hudson River, I'd press my face against the car window and gaze at the city sprawled out in front of us. The morning sun would hit the water and skyscrapers so that they sparkled like ornaments.

I was both excited and nervous. Crossing that bridge, my mother and I entered another state and another world. More specifically, we crossed over to my other life.

MOM AND I WOULD ZOOM SOUTH DOWN the west side of Manhattan, with the Empire State Building and the Twin Towers ahead of us. Then we'd shoot into the city off an exit ramp, to see, hear, and smell Manhattanites waking up to bagels, coffee, and stylish department-store windows. Once downtown, we'd zigzag through the cobblestoned streets of the West Village, packed with coffeehouses and musicians, until we reached Gram's six-story walk-up at 225 Sullivan Street.

After she buzzed us into the main front door, though, all the light and magic would end.

The gray, bleak hallway that led to Gram's parlor-floor apartment was so narrow that my cousins and I would slide our feet up against the walls on either side and move down the hall like Spider-Man. This particularly came in handy when we saw cockroaches and mice. Gram used to live on the third floor, but moved downstairs after Grandpa died. She called this lower apartment *il basamento* (the basement); I christened it the dungeon.

The dark and dreary two-bedroom apartment was once a lively place. Until I was a toddler, my whole family lived there while Gram was in another apartment upstairs—all seven of us, plus two giant German shepherds named Spike and Jiggs, using one tiny bathroom. And a couple of closets the size of a cupboard. How we all squeezed in there without killing each other, I'll never know.

As Mom and I neared the door of Gram's apartment, my heart would begin to race. I knew my father was on the other side of that door, and my feelings were mixed about seeing him. I loved him and wanted to be with him, but at the same time, I never knew what torture awaited me in the dungeon.

Yet as my mood plummeted, Mom's lit up like the Christmas tree at Rockefeller Center. She was so excited to see my father that her vivacity returned, full force. Any sad part inside of her stayed back in New Jersey. After hours primping and plucking and sitting under the hair dryer in curlers that morning, she would arrive at the dungeon looking as pretty as a '40s pinup girl. My mother was head-over-heels, truly-madly-deeply, heart-thumpingly in love with my father.

Her arms would be loaded with goodies for Dad—homemade cookies and apple pie, plus all the laundry she'd taken home on the last visit. Over this, she'd pile dozens of shirts, perfectly and lovingly ironed and starched—she'd even iron his underwear and socks!

Gram would answer the door, wiping her hands on the ever-present apron over her housedress. She'd already have dinner cooking in the kitchen: macaroni with meatballs; pasta fagioli; or roast beef with her famous fried zucchini with garlic, oil, and vinegar. Gram used to make handmade ravioli the size of a deck of cards (we used to call them "lead bombs"). The scent of her food smelled like love . . . intermingled with the scent of mothballs, old smoke, and mustiness rising up from the cellar.

When we'd enter the apartment, my eyes would blink for a minute to adjust to the lack of light. Gram and Dad would only turn on a few dim bulbs from the three lamps in the entire apartment. My father enforced a strict no-light policy: he was paranoid that someone might look in from the outside, even though three of the five main windows faced a brick wall next door and the other two looked over a tiny courtyard in back. All the windows had iron bars on them like a jail cell, and they were covered by thick shades that blocked any sunlight from getting in.

Gram's dozens of hand-crocheted doilies were the only color dotting an apartment that was swathed in chocolate browns. She churned out those doilies at a rapid pace, like an assembly line, to keep her hands busy and her mind occupied. Gram grew up wanting to be a pharmacist, like her father, but she quickly realized she wasn't allowed to have that dream. Instead, she took care of her family, and she knit until her hands were tired and thoughts of lost dreams and lost loved ones left her head.

As the apartment door closed behind me, I'd feel sucked into a dark vortex in space. For the next two days, I wouldn't know if it was day or night.

WHEN I'D ACTUALLY BE PRESENTED TO MY FATHER was always a mystery. After I'd walk in, Gram might say, "*Shhhh* . . . keep-a quiet, your father's asleep; he was working all night!" (*Working? But at what, Gram? Please tell me.*) The phone would stay off the hook until he awoke in the afternoon, and I'd have to pretty much stay mute until then.

If Dad was awake when he arrived, he'd be sitting at the dining-room table eating breakfast in his underwear. Against the darkness, his clothes were shockingly bright—bleached white T-shirt, boxer shorts, and socks. He'd be eating the same breakfast he ate every day —Shredded What with yogurt and fruit. He was careful about what he ate ever since he was diagnosed with a heart condition that stemmed from having rheumatic fever when he was a baby.

My father didn't used to eat so healthy; he used to eat like your typical Italian mama's boy and grew up a pudgy kid like me who loved his sweets. Yolanda told me that before I was born, Dad would come home early in the mornings after "working" all night (*at what?*) and cover the kitchen table with boxes of *zeppole* and *cannoli*, and he'd nudge Yo awake to come eat the pastries with him.

After the doctors told Dad that his heart was not good, he changed his diet drastically. He'd eat big salads and send his buddies to fetch fresh fish or buffalo steak from the market or butcher. Mom used to cook him a rice dish with vegetables and Muenster cheese melted on top; along with another favorite that had lentils, rice, red onion, and tomatoes dressed with olive oil and garlic. If you look at pictures of my father, you can see his weight trajectory go from lean-and-mean boxing days to pudgy married man back to fighting weight.

When he wanted to be, my dad was the most disciplined man I knew. The only sweet treat he'd allow himself was frozen yogurt, because it was low fat, or Mom's low-sugar shortbread cookies and apple pie, which she'd make with whole-wheat flour.

Dad never ate Gram's cooking, but we kids inhaled it—even the one Christmas when she baked a 12-inch fork right into her lasagna. We all sat around the table waiting hungrily for Mom to cut in and dole out the brick-sized pieces, when the knife hit the barbecue fork in the middle of the *mutz*.

At that time, I was becoming the family clown, so I started making sounds—*meeaeeeeh-meeaaaawwwwww!*—like the talking birthday cake on an episode of *The Little Rascals*, and we all lost it. Gram was in the kitchen and didn't hear us laughing, but my father was right there. He gave us "the look," which he was famous for. It meant *Don't mess with me*.

"Eat it!"

We shushed and ate the metallic, fork-laden lasagna.

Even if Dad was just sitting there in his underwear, the man dominated the room and exuded power. While eating his break-fast, he'd give me a nod to come to him. I'd go give him a hug and kiss on the cheek. He'd stay sitting, but grab me and give me a big strong hug and kiss back. This two-minute exchange would sig-nal the commencement of our father-daughter quality time that weekend. After the hug, I'd sit down and he'd ask me questions. The questions were always the same, and so were my answers.

"So, how are you?" he'd ask, in his low whisper.

"I'm okay."

"You taking care of your mother?"

"Yeah."

"How's school?"

"Good."

"I love you."

"I love you, too."

And that was that. After our soul-baring chat, I'd be dismissed until further notice. Period. We'd all eat dinner together—with the grown-ups talking among themselves, often in Italian—then Mom and Dad would go be alone. I'd be left with Gram for the rest of the night, and conversation was difficult due to her limited

English and my nonexistent Italian. Thank God I had football to watch, and she had knitting to do.

For the next day and a half, I'd mope about the four-room apartment, trying in vain to amuse myself. If he had been a different kind of a father, like the dad on *The Brady Bunch*, maybe I would have been able to ask him what I was dying to know: *What's your job, Dad? Are you really sick? How do we afford to live in a big house in New Jersey when you're sick? How come, even at Christmas, we only see you for a few hours and then you go somewhere else?*

But he wasn't that kind of dad. And I knew not to ask him anything real during our weekly father-daughter session. No one told me not to, but the rule was understood and woven into our family's fabric of being. It was an unspoken rule given in an unspoken language that everything was to remain unsaid and all questions were to remain unanswered.

THE "DON'T ASK" RULE WAS A GOOD ONE in one way, because the last thing you wanted to do was say something to make my father angry.

He could be very affectionate and loving when he wanted. If I was sitting next to him on the couch and I didn't feel well, I'd lean over and lay my head in his lap, and he'd make me feel better by rubbing my back. For a former boxer, my father had very soft, gentle hands. His fingers were long—like a surgeon's, my grandmother used to say. And his touch was so soothing that after 15 minutes of massaging my back, whatever pain I felt eased. He wouldn't say anything; he'd heal me with his hands somehow. The man had a healing gift.

I loved when he'd do that, because it was one of the few moments in my childhood where I felt he loved me. I knew that underneath his dominating, frightening exterior, he had a big heart. I'd be in the kitchen with Gram, for instance, and we'd hear a knock on the door. A neighbor would walk in, looking for Dad. He'd see Gram first, and ask, "Mama Yolanda! *Come stai?!*"

Gram would wipe her hands, hug and kiss the person, then lead him through the dark to Dad's makeshift "office" in the dining room. I'd follow and watch the next scene unfold from a few feet away in the living room, peering over the couch.

"Thank you for seeing me," the man would say, and kiss Dad's cheek.

Dad would wave him to sit down, then turn the radio louder.

"It's about Angelo, the butcher," the neighbor would say.

"What's the problem?"

"He can't pay his rent . . . he's going to lose his store."

"I understand."

My father and the man would talk some more in Italian, then Dad would nod and the man would leave. I found out later that Dad helped a lot of people in the neighborhood, especially the old and sick ones who couldn't buy food or were facing eviction from their homes. As Mom later told me, "He paid that Angelo's rent for years."

All of us kids loved my father deeply and desperately wanted his approval and attention, but there was no set recipe for how to get it. I could do something silly like dance around in the living room wearing my grandmother's hat, mink coat, and black shoes with the hole in them, and he'd laugh and say, "I'm proud of you." (But Gram would say to me, "*Tu sei pazza!* You're crazy!")

Yet you never knew if he was going to snap your head off the next minute for doing something else. He was like Dr. Jekyll and Mr. Hyde, so we were always on guard. He was the toughest on my brothers and Roseanne—if they did something he didn't like or disagreed with him, his big heart shrank.

"You're stupid!" he'd yell. "You don't know what you're talking about!"

I think he was easier on me because of my anxieties and illnesses. But I have to wonder now, so many years later, if I might have willed myself sick to keep his anger at me at bay and bring out the other, loving side.

After Dad and I would have our father-daughter "talk," he and my mother would go lie down in the bedroom and hold hands like teenagers, talking about us kids and whatever else was going on.

Sometimes I'd tiptoe in while they were talking and curl up in bed next to my parents to feel the tenderness passing between them.

As they talked, I'd gaze at Dad's collection of religious items on his nightstand. He had a figure of Joseph, the patron saint of fathers; a statue of the Blessed Mother; a statue of Jesus; two crucifixes; several rosary beads and religious medals blessed by a priest; a bottle of holy water; and a booklet on how to pray the rosary. Not that he needed it—he'd been reciting the rosary every day since he was a kid. He was his mother's son, after all.

Dad's little religious collection had to be just so. With his graceful hands, he'd place each icon or blessed object in a specific spot, angled a certain way, as if the nightstand held a glass menagerie or Nativity scene. If you accidentally bumped the table and moved anything out of place, you'd be in big trouble.

His relationship with religion baffled me. I knew he was Catholic and that he believed in God. I'd seen him sit in his recliner and pray the rosary, over and over. I could count on one hand the times I'd actually seen him step foot in a church, and yet it really upset and worried him to find out one day that his name was left out of our "family rosary." Mom had excitedly pointed out to us that the first initials of all our names—Roseanne, Olympia, Sal, Andrew, Rita, and Yolanda—spelled out the word R-O-S-A-R-Y. She considered it a sign from God that our family was blessed.

"Hon, where am I?" Dad asked her. "I'm not there! Why is my initial not there?"

She rushed to soothe him. "Hon, don't worry . . . you have the 'V' for Vincent, which stands for the five decades of the rosary!"

My favorite of his religious objects was a painting of Saint Rita, my namesake, which hung on the wall facing his bed. I studied it so intently, I could draw it from memory: She wore a black robe, her hands were crisscrossed against her chest, and a big thorn was sticking out of her head. Above her, a beam of light shot toward her from heaven as little angels danced around the light.

I'd lie in bed next to my parents and stare up at her for hours. *There's that Saint Rita again, always doing the impossible,* I'd think. The dungeon made me so tired, so dragged down by whatever dark energy permeated the air. *She does the impossible, and I can barely get through the weekend.*

In that cloak of darkness, Mom would have to tell me when it was bedtime. She slept with Dad in his room, and I was sent to the lumpy pullout couch in the living room, next to the picture of Christ hanging on the wall.

With all my aches and pains and assorted anxieties, sleeping well anywhere, under the best of circumstances, was a challenge for me. Trying to get a decent night's sleep at the dungeon was impossible. The mattress was so thin that the coils poked up against my ribs. After tossing and turning for a while, I'd turn on the little black-and-white TV with its measly seven channels, and it gave off the most light I ever saw in that place! When I couldn't find anything good to watch—and who could at 2 A.M. in the '70s with no cable?—I'd turn it off and lie back on the stabbing coils and think.

Once I turned my imagination on, I couldn't turn it off. I'd look around the oppressively dreary room, and everything appeared ugly and scary to me. The garbage cans bumped against each other in the alley outside the window, and I imagined a pack of rats making their way up the brick wall outside, into the living-room window, and jumping under the blanket with me. I worried about cockroaches marching across the floor, plotting to attack me. But worst of all was the creature under the bed, waiting for one of my feet to hang over the edge so he could pull me under and into the abyss.

SOME SATURDAYS, I'D ESCAPE THE DUNGEON WALLS and play with my cousins Vinny and Lisa—Uncle Ralph's kids—who lived a block away on Bleecker. We'd slip out Gram's back door and play Wiffle ball behind the apartment, on the tiny patch of cement Gram called a backyard. It was dirty and disgusting, but what did I care? I was outside! I could see sky!

When we got tired of Wiffle ball, we'd go to the candy store. But this was no regular candy store: In that narrow entrance hallway of Gram's apartment, there was a secret door just for us kids that led to our own Willy Wonka–style paradise. The door from the hall led us directly through a long curtain and into a barren, backroom candy store with a counter stocked with all-we-could-eat Tootsie Rolls, Snickers and Hershey's bars, Bubblicious and Big Red gum, 3 Musketeers and Milky Ways. And the best part was, the candy was free because my father owned the store. Or at least, I *think* he did. *(So . . . was this Dad's job, then?)* The store had no name or sign out front, and the only person who worked there was Mary Milk.

Mary was a short and heavyset Italian granny in her 70s with tight, curly black hair and a voice like the sound of bike tires popping against the gravely path behind my house in Jersey. She lived in the neighborhood, and her brother Petey Dark was a friend of my father's. Petey Dark wasn't his real name, just a nickname my father called him. Then again, Mary Milk wasn't her real name, either. We had no idea what anyone's real name was, and we didn't care.

"Hey, Mary!" we'd yell, charging in from the hallway.

"Hey, what are you kids up to?"

"We want some candy!"

"Okay, pick whatever you want."

"I want that one, and that one, and . . . "

"Ahh, don't go ruining your dinner!"

Mary joked around with us, but sometimes she could be a bit of a hard-ass. We liked it, though, because it made us respect her.

She'd waddle to the front window and put up handmade signs listing the sundries she sold: CANDY, SODA, NEWSPAPERS, ICE CREAM, DOG FOOD. We'd laugh at her because, as far as we knew, she had no other customers besides us. Yet we never wondered why. It was our hangout, that's all we really cared about.

When my cousins weren't around and Dad was busy—you know, selling hats or something—Mom and I would set out on our own West Village adventure and visit her sisters.

Dad's family grew up on Sullivan and Mom's a block away on Thompson, and most still lived there or steps away. In a three-block orbit I had an entire solar system of aunts, uncles, and cousins surrounding me so the streets felt like home, especially in the summertime.

Every June, we helped out at Saint Anthony's Feast: a ten-day smorgasbord of food, music, and carnival rides. The feast ran all the way down Sullivan, and my brothers and I worked in the little food stands chopping onions for the sausage and peppers or deep-frying the *zeppole*—little Neapolitan doughnut balls sprinkled with sugar. Behind the stands in the parking lot, Dad would sit in a tent and eat with his buddies under a string of lights. Behind them, the Ferris wheel went round and round, and the Tilt-a-Whirl spun until all the kids got sick and threw up. It was great.

On the Fourth of July, we'd line up tables along the sidewalk outside of Arturo's, one of our favorite restaurants, and everyone would come to eat, drink, and laugh all night. My brothers rigged our own fireworks on the roof across the street, and we'd watch the sky light up. To this day, these remain some of the most magical moments of my life.

Mom and her siblings all had funny nicknames for each other: one sister, Vincenza, was nicknamed "Chubby"; another was named Amelia but called "Millie"; Aunt Camilla was "Peppermint" because she chewed peppermint gum; Uncle Emmie was known as "Donkey Ears" because, well, that was self-explanatory. They called my mother "Dancer" because she loved to dance, and her other nickname was "Wini Shaw," after a singer-actress in the '30s famous for the hit "Lullaby of Broadway" in the Busby Berkeley movie *Gold Diggers of 1935*.

They all lived across from each other on the same street for years, so they never used the phone. They just opened up their windows and yelled, "Hey! Do you have a cup of sugar I can borrow?" When Mom and I visited, I'd yell up from the street, "Aunt Camilla, we're coming up! Open the door!"

We'd sit in their kitchens and talk, eat, and laugh for hours. Aunt Jo made fried vegetables dipped in egg and breadcrumbs, and Aunt Carmella made *mozzarella in carrozza*—two pieces of bread with mozzarella in the middle, dipped in egg, fried, then smothered with marinara sauce. It's no wonder I was a chubby kid.

And then Sunday mornings were reserved for Gram and church. The closest was the Shrine Church of Saint Anthony of Padua, where Dad donated a lot of money. Gram's favorite church, Our Lady of Pompeii, was a few blocks away on Carmine Street.

She went to church every day, not just on Sundays—believing that you could never get too much of a holy thing. Dad's brother Lou was a priest, and she was proud to have a man of the cloth in the family. I think sometimes that Dad was jealous of Lou and his other siblings and the attention Gram gave them when they came to visit. To Gram, having a priest in the family gave us gold stars in the eyes of God. "God is everything, Rita . . . you *must* pray," she'd tell me sternly, as she clipped her carrot-colored support hose to her girdle and smoothed down her black dress.

I loved my grandmother, but sometimes, between her broken English and her Neapolitan intensity, she scared the hell out of me. Once, when I accompanied her to church, I was mortified as she began to recite the Mass out loud and in Italian. The entire congregation was silent, but there was Gram, giving the Italian translation with the drama of a Fellini film star, center stage and front pew, emoting to the rafters.

"Shhhhhh, Gram!" I whispered, embarrassed.

"*Shuddduppppp!*" she said to me, not in a whisper.

And I surely did. But in my mind, a new nickname was born for my one-of-a-kind, delightfully off-center grandmother: "Gram Crackers."

As I said, Dad wasn't a churchgoer. So we'd come home from Mass and he'd still be snoring away in his white boxers. Gram didn't want him to be a bad example to me, so when he finally got up and appeared in the kitchen for an espresso, she'd do a little more acting for my benefit.

"Vinchennnzzze!" she'd say to him, pouring the coffee, but looking directly at me. The steam from her chipped espresso machine, imported all the way from Milano, wafted across her eyes, making her gaze all the more dramatic. "Did you go to early Mass today?"

"Yeah, Ma . . . sì, sì," Dad would say.

"Ah, good, gooooood."

Then she'd sternly rhyme off a string of Italian words to him that I didn't understand, as if she were taking him to task. *"Ascolta la tua bella mamma . . .* listen to your pretty mother!" she'd say, clasping his arm.

"All right, all right," Dad would reply. "Now let me drink my coffee, the both of you."

At 5'11", Dad towered over Gram, who was a foot shorter. She scolded him like a good Italian mother—and like a good Italian son, he took it and took care of her. Every week, as she stood at the stove stirring her gravy with a wooden spoon, he'd come up behind her and slip a roll of bills, her weekly allowance, into her apron pocket.

"Grazie, Chinzee," she'd say, and he'd lean down and plant a kiss on the top of her head. Gram had called him "Chinzee" ever since he was a boy and she had to call his name out the window to tell him to come home for supper. "Vincenzo" was too long, so she shortened it to "Chenzo," which begat "Chinzee"—and finally, to his friends and his boxing-ring opponents when he got older, just "Chin."

WHEN DAD'S FRIENDS CAME TO VISIT, the apartment looked like a Francis Ford Coppola casting session. First came the Doms: Big Dom was a short, beefy guy with salt-and-pepper hair; Skinny Dom was tall and scrawny with thin strips of hair on the sides of his head like a skunk; Domenick the Tailor wore suits and hats. (There were a few other Doms in there . . . I lost count.) Then there was Frankie Stunad, who had a shock of white hair and thick glasses that made his eyes bug out twice as big as normal eyes; and Jerry Bulldog, who, as you might guess, had a flat face and waddled when he walked.

They'd show up wearing button-down shirts and slacks and kiss Gram, Mom, and me on our cheeks. Then they'd sit down at the dining-room table with Dad, who had changed from his underwear-undershirt ensemble into a similar slacks-and-shirt outfit.

I'd be in the living room with one ear cocked to the cartoons and the other tuned in to the men. As Gram poured coffee, here is the scene I'd routinely witness:

Dad would start by motioning to one of the men to turn on the radio before they began whispering to each other.

"Tell this to the guy," my father might whisper to a Dom, scribbling a few words on a little bit of paper and handing it to him, "and don't come back until you do."

Dom would read it, nod, then pull out his cigarette lighter and burn the tiny piece of paper in the ashtray. After he was sure it had disintegrated, poking it around with his finger, he'd leave.

Petey Dark would be there, too, and he'd scribble a bunch of numbers on his bit of paper and pass it to Dad.

"That's good," Dad would say, then give him a nod. Petey would take back the bit of paper, rip it up into smithereens, and take the fragments to the bathroom and flush them down the toilet.

They'd continue on like this for half an hour—passing notes, drinking coffee, nodding, whispering, and flushing. I'd watch from my perch on the couch in amazement and confusion.

What game were these grown men playing?

I kept my mouth shut, like a good girl. But I had eyes and ears, and I saw and heard everything.

CHAPTER 3

GIRLFIGHT

I was nine years old when I first realized that peanut butter was going to kill me.

It wasn't that I'd developed an allergy to the stuff, far from it. I loved peanut butter and always did. It was my favorite food as a kid. I'd heap it on bread and top it off with a mound of Welch's grape jelly. But one afternoon during the summer after third grade, I went downstairs for lunch and it hit me: peanut butter was out to get me.

My mom wasn't feeling well that day and hadn't prepared the big meat-and-potatoes feast that usually greeted me. Instead, she presented me with a "treat." "Here you go," she said with a smile, sliding a plate across the table. On the plate was my version of a perfectly balanced meal—Wonder bread with a slab of peanut butter and jelly. Normally I would have grabbed it and gobbled it down, but when I reached for the sandwich this time, I halted.

You can't eat that. Something bad will happen if you do.

It was a little voice in my head that suddenly knew something very important: if I ate even the tiniest taste of peanut butter, disaster would strike. Either I would die on the spot or someone else in my family would. I envisioned my father being run down by a car or my sister Yolanda falling down a flight of stairs or my mother choking to death on one of her pills. I had no idea why I knew that peanut butter was dangerous, or how—I just did.

I looked at the Skippy jar on the counter. This was ridiculous. I reached for my sandwich.

You want a bite? Go ahead, take a bite . . . go ahead, kill your father, kill your sister! Why not take two bites and kill your whole family while you're at it?

"No thanks, Ma," I said, pushing the plate away. "I'm done with peanut butter."

THE PEANUT-BUTTER EPISODE WAS THE FIRST TIME I made a bargain with myself to keep my family and me "safe." It was nutty, I know. But after the initial back-and-forth struggle, I discovered that it felt surprisingly good to deny myself for such a worthy cause. It gave me a sense of comfort and control when my life felt so unknown and uncontrollable.

Denying myself peanut butter made me feel strong, and before long I was passing on my other favorites: pizza and ice cream. No one in the family seemed to notice, care, or fully appreciate that I'd stopped eating certain foods to save us all from a terrible fate. Had I tried to explain it to them, I don't think they would have understood that my dinner-table sacrifices were for our greater good.

But then, the voice didn't stop at food.

One morning as I was getting ready for school, I found myself staring at the row of colorful pants, shirts, and blouses (and the one lone dress) in my closet, unable to move. Usually I'd have no trouble picking an outfit, but on this day I was paralyzed. Suddenly, such a simple decision was filled with danger.

What's safe to wear?

"Ri! You're going to be late for school!" Mom called from downstairs. "Hurry up and get dressed!"

"All right al-readddddy!"

I took a deep breath and reached for my blue jeans and my *Charlie's Angels* T-shirt.

Forget it, you can't wear that. Somebody will get hurt if you wear that.

All right, I reasoned with myself. *How about the red shirt and the cutoff shorts?*

No. Red is bad today. You can wear the gray one. Gray is okay. Yes to the shorts.

Done. (Heavy sigh of relief.)

So it became a new morning ritual, rifling through my closet until I found my safe clothes for the day. Some mornings the bargaining took longer than usual, and I had to be clever about talking to myself. Or talking to the voice. We were one and the same, anyway.

Listen. I really wanna wear the red shirt. How about I give up ice cream for a day instead? No? Okay. How about I give up ice cream for a week? Okay? Okay. Done. Deal. Done deal. What the fuck am I doing? My brain feels like a Ping-Pong ball bouncing back and forth against the walls of my head. Ah, screw it.

I didn't have time to figure out the logistics of what was happening to me. I only knew that it made me feel better and safer, so I kept doing it. If I accidentally wore something "bad," I wouldn't be able to think straight for the rest of the day. I did wonder, as I debated longer than usual one morning, if one day all clothes and food would be off-limits and I'd have to go to school starving and naked.

Then another weird twist happened: while some clothes had become evil, others now had superhuman powers. For instance, I never had any doubt what I needed to wear when I played softball—I had to wear my Levi's overalls. I *had* to. I wore them once during a game when I made a diving catch in left field and then nailed another runner racing for home. Ever since then, it didn't matter if they were ripped, stained, or too small; I couldn't wear anything else. But wearing the "good" clothes came at a price, too.

"Hey, Gigante! Are you playing in the same old dirty clothes again?" Josh Gold, a kid at school who hated me, would yell out.

He used to laugh at me in kindergarten when I cried, and now he and his friends liked to taunt me from the sidelines at the baseball diamond.

I shot him a look from the outfield that said, *I'm gonna kill that motherfucker someday.*

SOON, FOOD AND CLOTHING STRATEGIES WEREN'T enough to maintain my sense of equilibrium, so I was forced to turn to physical objects around me—doorways, tabletops, and silverware.

On days when I was more anxious than usual, I couldn't just walk into the kitchen. No, I'd have to walk in and out of the kitchen doorway several times before I could remain in the room. I never knew how many times it would take because it varied, depending on my stress level at the moment. Monday, it might be 4 times; Wednesday, it might be 20. I kept going until I was "done" and felt a calm, soothing click in my head that told me everything was going to be all right. And once again, I felt I had structure, order, focus, and control in a world where I otherwise felt powerless.

The more stressed I was, the more complex the ritual needed to be. One Sunday night, after coming home from a confusing, nightmare-filled weekend at the dungeon, I had this feeling that I needed to take my world apart and put it back together again, anew.

I rushed into the garage looking for something to break apart and fix, something I could get my hands on—a lawn mower, an old clock, anything. And there it was: my beautiful bike, a fire-engine-red chopper.

I grabbed a wrench and went to work.

An hour later, I had little towers of washers, nuts, and bolts stacked up in neat piles beside me. In front of me, in their own little piles, I'd placed the wheels, the gears, the brakes, the banana seat, and the custom steering wheel that I used instead of handle-bars. Just like Dad and the placement of his religious icons, I was very methodical in my madness. I'd just put the wrench down and was wiping the grease off my hands when Mom walked into the garage. She looked at me and my array of bike parts and shook her head.

"Rita, come to bed."

"All right, Ma, I'll be there soon."

I picked up the wrench, reassembled the bike in 20 minutes, and stood up to admire my re-creation. I had accomplished something. I had started and finished something. For a moment, I was master of my universe.

ALL OF MY IMAGINED CONTROL AND POWER WENT OUT the window when Dad visited us in Jersey.

When we didn't go to the dungeon, Dad came to us. His visits were inconsistent and usually a surprise. If we were lucky, we'd get a heads-up from somebody a few hours ahead of time, and that would launch Mom into a mad flurry of cleaning, cooking, and beautifying herself.

First, she'd put her hair up in big, fat curlers and draw on her eyebrows. Then she'd rush around the kitchen, pulling out pots and pans to make my father's favorite lentil-and-brown-rice dish. Once it was simmering on the stove, she'd put me to work slicing the apples for his pie, while she vacuumed and mopped and cleaned until the house sparkled. After the house, the food, and her face were perfect, Mom would lay out Dad's pajamas at the foot of the bed.

Meanwhile, I looked at her like she was crazy. Why was she doing all this shit for someone who came to visit only when the mood struck him? She still was and always would be that adoring, 16-year-old girl, under Dad's charming spell. When he came home, any attention usually focused on me went to him, like I had disappeared.

After we'd gone to sleep, we'd hear his car come up the driveway (usually around 3 A.M.) and the door open and slam shut. My mother would jump out of bed, as excited as a kid hearing Santa's sleigh landing on the roof.

"He's here, Rita, he's here! Get up! Let's go say hello to your father."

We'd go downstairs and hug and kiss him hello, then I'd be kicked out of Mom's bed and sent to my real bedroom. I wasn't used to sleeping alone in Jersey, so on those nights Dad came home, I rarely got any rest. I'd lay awake listening to my parents' muffled voices through the wall, talking for hours.

What could they possibly be talking about for so long when he and I only managed the same ten words?

The next morning, Dad would still be asleep when I left for school and would wake up just before I returned home. By age ten, I was walking home from school on my own. It was one of the few things I felt comfortable doing by myself, and I cherished that feeling of independence. Walking up the driveway when Dad was there, however, was not a good feeling. My stomach would tighten as soon as I saw the closed drapes. I was never allowed to bring friends home after school when he was visiting—no one told me not to, it was just understood. Whenever Dad came to visit, he took all the light out of the place.

As much as I hated the dungeon, at least there my father and I had a well-established, if unspoken, agreement as to how to communicate with each other. It wasn't much—those same ten words—but it was our routine and we relied on it.

Here on my home turf, I was never sure how to approach him, and I'd feel even more ill at ease than usual. Mom was always busy in the kitchen when I'd get home from school, so when I arrived, it would be just me and Dad alone—a rare happening. In the dungeon, Gram was an ever-present buffer, and my father's buddies like the Doms would be in and out a lot.

I'd arrive to find Dad sitting in the living room on the U-shaped couch, with his legs up, dunking Mom's shortbread cookies into coffee and wearing his usual outfit of boxers, T-shirt, and slippers. Now that he was here, the house was "dungeon-ified" —Mom would draw the drapes before he even arrived, and he'd keep the TV on as a constant hum in the background.

I'd go to him on the couch and give him the usual hug and kiss hello—he wouldn't get up. And, like in the dungeon, we wouldn't have anything to say to each other. It's not like Dad suddenly became a great conversationalist once he crossed state lines. He'd sit there waiting for me to say something, and I'd stand there waiting for him.

After a few minutes of awkwardness, we'd resort to the tried-and-true dialogue we knew so well.

"How's school?"

"Okay, Dad."

"How you feeling?"

"Good."

"You taking care of your mother?"

"Yeah, Dad."

And that was it. I'd be dismissed until I was called for an early dinner at 4:30. After he finished eating, Dad would change into street clothes and leave a pile of dirty laundry in his wake. Whenever my father left, I was relieved . . . but he took all the light out of my mother.

My very first full-blown anxiety attack occurred hours after one of Dad's Jersey visits. It was the middle of the night and I was sleeping next to Mom, having the same recurring black-and-white nightmare I'd been having all year. In the dream I was standing in the basement looking out the window, watching a violent tornado sweep around our house, uprooting trees and sucking up all the water from the pool, destroying everything in sight.

I woke up shaking and sweating, gasping for breath, wondering if it was real or not and feeling like I was dying. I got up and looked out the window and saw the trees and swimming pool were intact. Mom slept through my attack, and I didn't want to wake her. But I was so upset that I headed downstairs to watch one of my taped episodes of *The Love Boat* to calm my nerves. Cruise director Julie McCoy had such a perky yet soothing voice.

Mom found me asleep on the couch the next morning. "What happened, you couldn't sleep?"

"I had a bad dream." I didn't want to worry her too much.

Relief from self-torture and inner-dungeon doldrums would also arrive in the forms of Vinny and Lisa. Every summer for years, my cousins would come stay with us for and we'd have a pisser of a time. Along with our usual Wiffle ball, we'd laze around in the swimming pool all day and spend nights watching movies on Mom's big-screen TV or shooting pool and playing pinball and Pac-Man in the basement.

We'd stay up all night playing gin rummy and eating home-made concoctions of Cheerios drizzled with honey and covered in nuts. (Later on, we were certain we were the ones who invented Honey Nut Cheerios.) With my cousins around, my mood lifted like one of those strongman games at a carnival, when you hit the lever with a mallet and the puck shoots up to bang the bell.

Mom was so happy to see me more extroverted and less troubled that she let us have the run of the house—and we always took it too far. One time, we painted her car tires eggshell blue, just for the hell of it. Well, we got our asses handed to us. When she saw what we'd done, she took off her slipper and clocked us with it from clear across the front yard.

For a petite, girly type, my mother had an arm like Sandy Koufax and could hurl a slipper across the house if she wanted to. Later on when I started playing softball, I knew my throw from the outfield got its oomph from Mom's "slipper arm" rather than Dad's "right-hook arm."

Mom let us get away with murder because those sweet, dog-day afternoons of summer when we the relatives came over, it gave us both such a lift. Mom bloomed, too, especially when her sisters and their kids came for the weekend.

Dad's side of the family could be serious and moody. But Mom's family were born life-of-the-party types, and when they showed up it was a never-ending whirlwind of games, card playing, jokes, music, and tons and tons of food. When the relatives were over, we were like a happy, normal family.

Sometimes I just couldn't feel safe, though. There was a menacing presence in my life, a malicious undercurrent I couldn't escape. And that menace followed me no matter where I went, even under a clear blue sky on a beautiful autumn day.

As I mentioned, I liked to walk home from school. Strolling along the leafy streets gave me a much-needed feeling of independence. On the street, alone, I had two blocks and five minutes where I felt carefree.

All that changed on this day, just a block from home.

As I waited to cross the street, I looked up and gave the crossing guard a smile. He was a kindly old Italian man, and a longtime neighborhood fixture. Mom and I passed him hundreds of times when we stopped at the intersection on our way to the grocery store. Mom would roll down her window and they'd exchange a few pleasant words in Italian.

I'd just reached the other side of the street when I felt a pair of arms reach around from behind and grab hold of me. It was the crossing guard. He pulled me against him and—with his scratchy, whiskered face so close to mine I could smell garlic and wine on his breath—murmured something in Italian. Then he dropped his red stop sign to the ground and pawed at my breasts with his ugly hands.

I froze. It wasn't as though I had much there, barely two bee stings. But that didn't seem to matter. I looked down and saw his yellowed, nicotine-stained fingers all over me—and then it was over as quickly as it began. He let go and I bolted, running as fast as I could all the way home. I hoped my mother wasn't locked up in the den, crying. I needed her now. I burst through the kitchen door and saw her at the stove cooking.

"Mom!" I cried out.

She spun around. "What happened? What's the matter?"

"The crossing guard grabbed me. He rubbed his hands all over my chest."

I burst into tears and told her what had happened. After I'd calmed down, she put something to eat in front of me and sat down across from me, looking serious. I thought maybe she was going to call the police. Instead, she said, "Rita, we're not going to tell anyone about this, especially your father. Okay? You understand?"

"What?" I asked her, completely confused.

"If we say anything to your father, he's going to do something horrible to that old man."

"But, Mom. That man . . . he touched me!"

"I know. But it's better this way."

"But, Mom . . . "

"Forget about it. We're going to pick you up from school again or someone will come and walk with you."

My heart sank. Even about this ugliness, my voice was silenced. Just another little trauma I was ordered to forget. On top of that, I was losing one of the few freedoms I had, too.

I said okay, but what I wanted to tell her was: "Why are you punishing me when that dirty old man hurt me? He's the one who should be punished! Daddy *should* do something to him! Isn't anyone going to tell the crossing guard what he did was wrong? Don't I matter?"

There was no point in complaining. Like other times when I was in pain or confused, I swallowed the emotions and buried them. I'd been sexually assaulted a block from my own home, and my father, who always asked me how I was, would never know about it. If my parents couldn't make me feel safe, who could?

I turned away from my mother, walked into the garage, picked up the wrench and started taking my bike apart.

Two weeks later, I came down with a raging upper respiratory infection and a cough so horrendous that I hacked up blood. Mom carried me into the doctor's office, and the doctor was so alarmed when he saw me that he immediately shot me with a double dose of penicillin. He had no idea what was wrong with me. But I knew.

"Mom?" I asked weakly, as she tucked me in on the couch when we got home.

"Yes, Ri?"

"Am I dying? I'm dying, I know I am."

"No, don't talk like that. Nobody's dying!"

We went to see a throat specialist the next day, and he got to the bottom of it—turns out I had leftover scar tissue from when I had my tonsils out a few years earlier, and it had become infected.

The doctor stuck a giant Q-tip down my throat and swabbed it with iodine to shrink the scar tissue, then prescribed three weeks of couch rest at home with plenty of TV watching. Yet another three weeks of school missed.

Hanging out on the couch all day always gave me time to think, and this time I was thinking about that damn crossing guard. I was tired of being sick and weak. I was pissed off that people hurt me and nobody—myself included—did anything about it. I'd kept my mouth shut and played nice, but what good had that done me?

That's the frame of mind I was in when I walked past Josh Gold in the hall my first week back at school. Josh had been picking on me for years now—he was a classic bully, and I was his favorite prey. He continually (and loudly) made fun of my hair, my clothes, and the way I walked. He tormented me about my naturally low voice, and for that reason I tried not to talk when I saw he was nearby.

This day, as I headed down the corridor, I passed Josh standing in the hall with his buddies. I picked up my pace in the hopes that he wouldn't notice me.

I was almost at the exit door when he yelled out, "Yo, there's Gigante. She acts like a boy! She dresses like a boy! She even has a boy's voice!"

I couldn't hear if his friends were laughing at me or not. All I could hear was the blood pounding in my ears. *You motherfucker.* I walked outside into the crisp, cold afternoon air and leaned up against the school's brick wall and waited.

Something deep inside of me had snapped. When Josh walked out toward the street with his friends, I followed closely behind, measuring his speed and matching the length of his footsteps with my own. My anger didn't muddy my thinking; it made me acutely aware of my surroundings.

I knew I was going to take Josh Gold down, and I knew exactly how I was going to do it.

I sped up and grabbed the collar of his jacket and yanked him back. *Now you're gonna feel the way you make me feel, asshole,*

I thought. He hit the ground so hard I heard the wind rush out of his lungs in one big whoosh.

And then I was on top of him, whaling away at him with both hands. I wasn't slapping or scratching at him like a girl—I was pounding the living shit out of him with my fists. I hit him in his face as hard as I could, and then hit him again, and again, and again. My fists pummeled his eyes, nose, and mouth. I wanted to knock his teeth right down his throat and shut him up forever.

A group of schoolkids circled us, and started yelling, "Fight, fight, fight!" But their chanting was short-lived. When they realized how viciously I was beating Josh, they fell silent and someone ran to get a teacher. They saw I was trying to kill him, but no one dared to interfere.

Josh was screaming in pain, but I couldn't hear him. Everything around me shut off.

"You're not so funny now, are you?!" I yelled, hammering him as hard as I could a few more times before a teacher finally pulled me off him. I think it was a teacher. I was so numb and pumped with adrenaline that I didn't notice or care. I stood up and watched Josh whimper as he lay on the ice.

"I'm done with you," I said. Then to the others: "Get him out of here."

I walked away and left him bleeding in the snow.

I didn't wait to get picked up from school that day. Obviously, I could fend for myself now. I ran home exhilarated, drunk with a sense of power that I never wanted to end. I made an example of Josh Gold that day and sent a message out to my other classmates: *From now on, don't fuck with me.*

Word of my KO on the school playground reached home before I did. Yolanda was standing at the door when I came up the driveway.

"What happened?"

"I beat the crap outta Josh Gold. "

"What's the matter with you? You can't go around beating up other kids like that!"

"That little shit's been picking on me since kindergarten. He deserved what he got, and he got what was coming to him."

"*Jesus*, Rita."

I walked passed her and into the house. I wasn't going to let anyone rain on my parade: I wanted to enjoy my moment of triumph a little bit longer.

Two days later, I was sitting in the office of the school shrink. I grudgingly planted myself on the fake leather sofa in her office, not understanding why I had to be there. Sure, maybe I shouldn't have beat up Josh. Hitting people was wrong; I got that. But what was this whole therapy deal? In my house when someone did wrong, the thing to do was shut up about it. You didn't go around sharing your feelings.

Now I was sitting in front of this foreign lady with kinky hair and a confounding accent as she interrogated me. Yeah, right. Like I was really gonna open up to her.

"So. Rita. Why don't you tell me what's going on in your head?"

"Nuthin'."

"All right, Rita. Why don't you tell me how you're feeling?"

"I feel okay."

"How are you doing in school?"

"Okay," I said, realizing this sounded just like my conversations with Dad. I knew how to play this game.

"How are things at home?"

"Okay," I said.

And that was the end of my first therapy session. I had to go a few more times, but the sessions were all brief because I wouldn't talk. For ten years I'm repeatedly told not to say anything, and now I'm supposed to spill my guts? Within a couple of weeks, my mother told me I didn't have to go to therapy anymore since I didn't feel comfortable talking to that lady. I think Mom was even more relieved than I was; the family seemed nervous about what I might reveal about them.

Even though I'd triumphed in the schoolyard, I rapidly sank into a depression at home. The more I thought about it, the more the rage I unleashed on Josh that day scared me. I hated violence. What was wrong with me? A couple of weeks later, Gram came to stay in Jersey while my mother went to the city on her own to see Dad. Gram found me lying in a semicatatonic state in Mom's bed, clutching my pillow. She brought me a plate of food and placed it next to me, but I rolled away.

With a sigh, my grandmother sat down on the edge of the bed and brushed the hair away from my eyes with her strong, knobby fingers—from all that furious knitting, I guess. And then she said something that still echoes in my mind to this day.

"They *ruined* you," she said. "I told them I want you to live with me, but they no listen. You would have been good if I took care of you. I would have raised you right and you wouldn't have such problems. But instead, they kept you, and they ruined you."

I lay in bed staring out the window at that looming weeping willow in the backyard once again. Her words slowly sank deep, deep into the core of me. She was right. I was no good. I was ruined.

The next morning while Gram was still asleep, I went downstairs, pulled the calendar off the kitchen wall, and randomly placed my finger on a date.

This is the day I'm going to die.

CHAPTER 4

WALK LIKE A MAN

I wasn't planning to kill myself.

I thought about it, especially on the worst of days, but I'd been around enough Catholic teaching to know that suicide was a sin—one of those really bad, go-straight-to-hell types. So unless I purposely ate peanut butter or wore a "bad" shirt, I wasn't going to die by my own hand. I didn't really want to die, anyway.

Yet Gram's proclamation that I was ruined filled me with a sense of impending doom. I became certain that if I was that damaged, there was no way I would survive in the world. I was convinced God would come down, gather my soul, and take me back to heaven. Surely He would scoop up such a broken girl for fixing.

I wasn't sure exactly *how* it was going to happen, but I kept thinking that I could predict *when*. That was my new obsession. I'd stand in Gram's kitchen on Sunday mornings and stare at her calendar, waiting to see if I'd be pulled toward a certain day that would be my day to die. I'd slowly scan the week, waiting for the "death day" to pop out at me.

The 5th? No. The 15th? I don't think so. The 20th? Yes, I think there's something there. Oh, the day before Easter, that's when it will happen. So that's it. I'm a dead girl then.

As the death day approached, I'd pace frantically in Gram's kitchen or in my bedroom at home, whipping myself into a frenzied state of hysteria, barely eating or sleeping, wondering if I'd be alive the next morning.

Once, after marking a new death day on the calendar with a pencil, I absentmindedly poked my finger with it, and a chunk of lead stabbed me. I held my finger up and looked at the deadly little triangle of blackness beneath my skin, certain it was fatal. *Oh, so that's how it's gonna happen? Lead poisoning!*

I would be wrecked until the death day came and went. Since I was still alive when the date passed, I figured I'd miscalculated— a simple math mistake. Missing a death day didn't diminish my conviction that the next death day would actually be the one that would bury me six feet deep. So I kept making those dates with the Grim Reaper, pacing back and forth.

In a strange way, selecting and then obsessing about my death days was actually healthy for me; it gave me something much grander and more dramatic to focus on than my little, everyday worries. And the more insane my world became—beating Josh Gold to a pulp, hearing Gram's words, meetings with shrinks— the bigger the tool I needed to cope. My food and clothing fixations weren't enough to distract me from my confusion and give me a sense of purpose. Death days were an extra-strength, heavy-duty method of self-rescue. If I couldn't control my life, at least I could focus on my death. As crazy as it sounds, planning my death days helped keep me alive.

I knew I needed more than that, though. And floating just underneath the surface of my terror of impending death, I could still feel the exhilarating adrenaline high after beating up Josh Gold. My new reputation at school was born that day—that of a kick-ass, no-bullshit girl that no boy could fuck with. It gave me a feeling of strength, a taste of power, and a sense of control not easily forgotten. I knew, as Yolanda said, that I couldn't go around bloodying every kid who bothered me. But I wanted to maintain the sense of fear I instilled that day so I'd never be messed with ever again. I needed, in a way, to kill "weak Rita" and be full-time "powerful Rita."

I needed to create a new, tough-guy persona, and I didn't have to search far for inspiration.

When I looked around at my family, I could see that the power belonged to the men; that was clear. The women were expected to do as they were told and trained—cook, clean, churn out babies, and have no say in any matter whatsoever. I watched my mother and sisters do this for years, and I couldn't stand it.

When I watched my father, on the other hand, I saw that he entered a room and was instantly respected and feared. When he walked into the café, the men sat up at attention and were at his beck and call. If he was in a good mood, they smiled; if he was in a bad mood, they'd shut up and get out of his way. I wanted to walk into the classroom that way, so the Josh Golds of the world would leave me alone. I wanted to walk down the street that way, so the crossing guards of the world would keep their hands off me.

Yes, the men were in charge. I remember once when I was seven years old, I was having a particularly upsetting weekend visit with Dad at the dungeon. I snuck away into the bathroom and shoved a big wad of toilet paper down the front of my pants. You know how girls stuff their bras to make their boobs look bigger? I stuffed my undies. *You want to have a pissing match? I'll give you a pissing match.* Freud would have had a field day.

Yet I knew deep down even then that it wasn't about penis envy or wanting unnecessary control. At that young age, I could already see that in my family the males had privileges, self-power, and respect—even though when I looked around me, I could see that the females in our family were smarter, stronger, and harder working. The hierarchy structure made no logical sense to me.

So I began a transformation I was only half-conscious of. I began modeling myself after my father, imitating the way he walked, dressed, and acted. Josh Gold had already teased me for dressing like a boy, but I dressed that way to be comfortable and have the freedom to run and play and get dirty—it's not so easy to climb trees and hang upside down in a dress. Mom, too, was used to my so-called boy clothes. She was curious why her little girl, who was approaching puberty, didn't like party dresses the way her other two daughters did. But she chalked it up to my being a tomboy.

"You're the easiest child to dress," she'd say to me, unaware of my self-torture in front of the closet each morning.

Now it became more about projecting an image. As I chose my day's wardrobe each morning, I had an updated filtering system. Not only did the item have to be *safe*, it also had to make a statement. It had to exude the same message my father did when he looked at you: *Mess with me and you're dead.* So I threw in a few accessories—like baseball caps and football jerseys—to pump up my usual ensemble of jeans, a T-shirt, and a pair of Adidas.

I looked in the mirror and turned my baseball cap backward. *There, that oughta do it.*

MY NEW PSEUDO-MALE DEMEANOR fit in perfectly over at Dad's café, where I was able to pick up invaluable lessons on how to be tough and one of the boys.

By the time I was 11, I had graduated from hanging around with the kids at Mary Milk's candy store and was allowed to go to the café, Dad's hangout at 208 Sullivan—just a half block from Mary's and Gram's. I'd tag along with my father when he went to play cards with his buddies. Like Mary's place, I assumed Dad owned the café. And also like Mary's place, I never saw another soul enter the café for a cup of coffee except for Dad, his brothers, and his friends. It didn't surprise me that this so-called café had no real customers; I accepted it as normal, just like all the other things in my life that were out of the norm.

From the outside, the café looked so inconspicuous, you'd miss it if you were walking by and didn't know it was there. The front door and windows were painted black, so passersby couldn't see inside, and there was no sign out front. The only sign of life outside was Jerry Bulldog, who sat in a fold-up chair on the sidewalk smoking a cigar and scaring away the rare potential customer—usually an unsuspecting tourist—with his flat, round, pug-nosed face. To those who lived or worked in the area, Jerry was a friendly neighbor. To strangers, he was a gruff guard dog. To me, he was as sweet and soft as a marshmallow.

My macho makeover didn't go unnoticed by his sharp eyes. When I strutted down Sullivan Street next to my father, I looked like a midget doing a half-assed impression of Tony Manero in *Saturday Night Fever.* Jerry was quick to approve. "You two look like twins," he said, as I greeted him at the door with a kiss on the cheek.

The café, which had an exclusive club membership of 12 guys at most, was the dingiest room you'd ever seen. The furnishings consisted of three old rickety tables; a sink; a counter with an old-style cappuccino machine; a fridge filled with Manhattan Specials, Cokes, and pastries; a recliner with the stuffing coming out; and a TV balanced on a shelf across from the bar. Everyone except my father chain-smoked cigars and cigarettes; the black-and-white floor tiles were so stained that they had no white left.

I used to love walking into that room with Dad. He'd come in the way he came into any room—like he was king and this was his castle. And as far as father-daughter activities went, this was pretty much it for me, so I ate up every second. Inside, his friends would be sitting around the table waiting for him and getting the cards ready for pinochle.

Behind the bar, Mack the bartender brewed coffee—he was older than the rest of them and he had a patch of silver hair. Mack rarely spoke, which suited his job and the others just fine. They played for money, and Dad was a really good card player and won a lot. But even if he lost, he didn't care—he simply loved playing the game with the guys. It was one of the few times I'd see him at ease and enjoying himself. It never lasted long, though.

Invariably, in the middle of a game one of Dad's friends would enter the café, walk over to him, and whisper something urgent in his ear. Dad would tense up. If I was sitting next to him, my whole body could feel the change in his. My stomach would knot up as I worried what would happen next.

Dad would get very serious, nod, and whisper something back. A minute later he'd whisper some more: "What are you waiting for? Go do it."

Even if I was sitting beside him, I could barely hear his voice. If someone whispered something in his ear that he didn't like, Dad could go from relaxed to enraged in two seconds, giving the messenger a look that could kill. The room would get really quiet, and everybody held their breath.

To command respect, I realized, *you have to make people fear you.*

WE KIDS KNEW THE CAFÉ AS THE MEN'S HANGOUT, but I was slowly discovering that it was somehow my father's place of business. Sometimes when I was visiting and couldn't sleep, I'd hear Dad come and go in the middle of the night and assume that he was going over there for some kind of business meeting. I still didn't know exactly what type of business he was in, but as I grew older I began wondering more and more.

As in the dungeon, the men in the café whispered secretively and even communicated in their own secret sign language. At one point, it occurred to me that I'd never once heard any of these men speak my father's name out loud—even his nickname, Chin. Years later, my friend Carlo told me that instead of using my father's name, the men who knew him would silently point to their chins or call him by another nickname, "the man on the West Side." Whatever they called him, it was obvious that Dad was in charge.

But how is he in charge if he's supposed to be sick? He doesn't look sick. Something doesn't add up here.

It was around this time that I started to notice that my family was different from other families. It started with little things, like when Mom and I used to pull into the parking lot beside Gram's apartment. Everyone else had to line up and pay, but we didn't. Then, on special occasions when Dad took the whole family—my siblings and their spouses and the growing brood of grandkids— out to eat at Joe's Restaurant down the block on MacDougal Street, we never needed a reservation, even on Christmas day.

One of my brothers would call the restaurant before we left Gram's and tell Tony, the maître d', how many to expect. There was never a question if there would be a table for us. When we arrived, Enzo the waiter would be waiting by the back door in the alley to escort us to a private room in the rear of the restaurant. Then we'd spend the next five hours being waited on hand and foot, ordering anything and everything we could possibly want on or off the menu.

"Hey, Yo," I asked once when we were there, "does Dad own Joe's?"

She shook her head.

When we were done, we'd leave by the back door as well. Why the back door and not the front door, like other people?

"Hey, Yo, why do we use the back door at Joe's?" I asked another time.

She shrugged.

We were different, but nobody would tell me why. It was like trying to put a jigsaw puzzle together with most of the pieces missing.

BACK IN JERSEY, I put my newly learned macho muscle into practice. By the time the new kid moved in across the street, I was in full-blown bully mode. The new kid's name? Josh Gold. Yep, he had the same name as the other Josh I had pummeled the year before.

But this Josh was a cute, sweet kid—a skinny little *malink*, as my Mom used to say. I never heard anyone else use that word, but I figured out what she meant by context; if you blew on him, he'd be down in three seconds easy. Next to him, I looked like a giant. By fourth grade, I was taller and stockier than most of my classmates—everybody thought I'd soon be towering over Yo if I kept growing like that. (I didn't. I stopped growing two years later, and watched all my friends shoot up heads and shoulders above me.)

Because Josh lived across the street, it was easy for us to hang out together—riding dirt bikes, watching TV, swimming, and playing football on the street. He was such a nice kid that I nicknamed him "*Good* Josh" as opposed to the other "*Bad* Josh." But even though he was good, I still pushed him around. I had my new rep to consider.

"Yo, Josh! The ball went into the woods. Go get it!" I'd say. (I sounded just like Dad.)

He'd do as he was told and fetch the ball.

"Yo, Josh! Sit here and don't move until I say you can move."

He'd wait. Sometimes I'd keep him waiting for an hour, just because I could. It felt good, this power thing.

The few times he tried to speak up, I didn't listen. And if he hesitated too long before doing what I told him to do, I'd rough him up a bit—shove him or punch him hard on the arm. I was a chip off the ol' block. Had I been a boy, Dad might have been proud watching me take over my own turf.

He might have also been proud to know that, just like him, I maintained a spot in my heart for the underdogs. If I ever saw a kid making fun of another who was physically or mentally challenged in any way, I was in their face in an instant.

One of the neighborhood kids, Jake, was left with brain damage after falling into his backyard swimming pool one summer. To keep up appearances, I ordered him around a bit when we hung out on the street. But like Dad paying Angelo the butcher's rent, I was also Jake's loyal, fierce protector when he needed me. Maybe kids like him reminded me of myself—underneath my tough exterior, I felt weak. I wondered if my father ever felt that way, too.

I'm glad to say my tyrannical reign with Josh lasted only a few months. He got tired of being picked on, reached his breaking point, and called in the big guns—his mommy.

ONE AFTERNOON JOSH AND I WERE SWIMMING in his backyard pool when Mrs. Gold waved me into the kitchen to have a little chat. She was a very nice woman, and sweet like her son. She had pale blue eyes set in a heart-shaped face, like paintings I'd seen in Gram's books of the Blessed Mother.

Mrs. Gold handed me a towel as I stood in the doorway dripping chlorinated water on the linoleum, and guided me toward the kitchen table to sit. I had no idea what was happening, or what to expect. This sort of request was unprecedented. I'd been summoned to my first sit-down!

Mrs. Gold took a seat next to me and with a concerned look, came straight to the point. "Rita, please tell me . . . why are you bullying my son?"

She graciously gave me a list of all the cruel things I'd said and done to Good Josh. Her words were so heartfelt that I sat there with my mouth open, not believing that this conversation was happening. I wasn't shocked because she was telling me how badly I'd behaved—I knew I'd mistreated Josh, and on purpose! The shocking part was *how* she was telling me.

Mrs. Gold was talking to me with kindness and respect, like I was a human being. She was talking as if she believed I was capable of hearing her, capable of expressing myself, and would want to share my thoughts and feelings with her on this important subject. No one had ever, *ever* talked to me like that before. My mind was reeling.

I looked out the window and saw Josh splashing about in the pool with his mask and snorkel, pretending to dive for treasure. He was so innocent, that kid, it killed me. If I had been his mother, I would've beat up a crummy person like me for harming him. Yet here was Josh's mother protecting her son and also teaching me. She was being mother to both Josh and me, and it was the kind of mother I couldn't grasp, had no experience with.

Not that my mother didn't care or love me—she did, very much, I knew that. But there was something about her depression and the secrets between us and in our family that prevented the two of us from having what Mrs. Gold and Josh had.

As I watched Josh do a belly flop off the diving board, I felt both awful and so damn happy. It was one of the most pivotal moments in my life because I'd just learned a truth outside my family dynamic: Making people afraid of you, like Dad did, did not earn you respect. It made you a tyrant.

I looked up at Mrs. Gold and said, from the bottom of my heart, "I'm so, so sorry I hurt Josh. I hope that you and he will forgive me?"

She put her hand on my cheek. "Of course we will, sweetheart."

I went home that day and promised myself to be a better person, and a better friend to Josh. No more bullying, I vowed. I was ashamed of myself. Mrs. Gold had held a mirror up to my face and showed me the monster I had become, and it made me sick—literally.

Looking back, of course, I can see the obvious connection between my emotions and my illnesses. But I had no idea then that every time I buried pain and confusion, it found another way to come to the surface. Soon after my enlightening sit-down with Josh's mom, for example, I came down with an upper respiratory infection that wouldn't go away. We tried antibiotics, we tried humidifiers, and I drank gallons of liquids . . . and still I lay in bed like a wilted piece of lettuce, barely able to breathe and not eating a morsel.

Then the cough arrived. When Mom took me to the doctor, he said, "Her lungs are clear, Mrs. Gigante," and sent me home.

Two days later I was in the bathroom, and I started coughing and couldn't stop. Mom ran in and found me sprawled across the white floor tiles and hanging on to the bathtub, soaked in blood— it was spouting from my nose and gushing from my mouth like a horror movie.

"Oh, my God, Rita!"

The look of terror on her face meant just one thing: *That's it; this time I'm really dying.*

I don't know how she did it, but she got me dressed and into the car, and drove me to the hospital. X-rays showed pneumonia, and doctors hooked me up to an IV. Mom and my Aunt Chubby stayed with me all week, but they were also tending to their sister Millie, who was very ill and expected to pass away any day.

One night they'd left me alone and I was petrified. I had to pee so bad that I got up and weakly tried to walk to the bathroom, trailing my IV tubes behind me. Before I reached the bathroom, I had a coughing fit so violent that a giant golf ball of phlegm dislodged from my lungs and shot up my throat. It was so dense that it gagged me and made me throw up. Man, was it gross—and I was waking up the entire floor.

That's when Nurse Ratched walked in. "Look at what you did —you made a big mess, and now I've got to clean it up."

Lady, if I had an ounce of strength in any part of my body . . . oh, the beating you'd get.

But I knew it was my bullying, coming back to bite me in my sorry karmic ass.

AFTER MY ILLUMINATING EXPERIENCE WITH JOSH'S MOM, I tried to remember the lesson she had taught me. I must admit, though, that there were times when I wondered if the Gold family was a freak of nature. How could a mother be so gentle, attentive, and understanding? Soon after that, I experienced another kind of father, too.

In sixth grade, Mom hired Mrs. Russo as my after-school tutor for reading comprehension and math. I was naturally a good student, but because I'd missed a lot of classes from being sick, I'd fallen behind and always hovered within the C and D range. It was more than that, though; I had trouble finishing anything. If I started a book or tried to do homework on my own, I couldn't stick with it. So far the only task I could handle from beginning to end was taking my bike apart and putting it back together.

Mrs. Russo lived two doors away, so I'd go over twice a week after school and work with her. They were Italian, like us, and had three daughters, like us, but that's where the similarities ended.

When I went over there, it was like visiting another planet. I watched their alien ways one night when I stayed over for dinner. My first surprise was that their father sat down at the table with all of them, every night. My second shock was that during dinner, he talked to his children. He asked them about their day, he was interested in their answers, and he asked follow-up questions.

Mr. R knew what each of his daughters was studying, the names of their teachers and friends, and if they were taking dance class or choir. I had never seen this before, even with my uncles and their kids. For seven years, my own father had asked me weekly how school was; I don't think he ever heard my one-word response.

I looked around the Russo dinner table in awe as the kids shared their day and their lives with their dad. *This is a real father,* I thought. *This must be what other fathers do! This is how a father talks to his daughters.* I looked over at Mr. R, smiling from across the table. *I respect this man.*

Then Mr. R passed me the scalloped potatoes and asked me a question that nearly made me fumble the bowl. "So, Rita, I hear you're a real Joe DiMaggio at bat. Who's your favorite baseball player?"

He paused eating and looked at me, eagerly awaiting my response. So did the others.

"I, ummmm . . . I like . . . "

It was such a simple question, and I knew my answer. I stammered because it was my first time doing this sort of thing.

"I like that Sweet Lou," I said, cautiously. "Lou Piniella, the outfielder for the Yankees."

Mr. R smiled, then pitched me a follow-up, which I answered as well. And then we did it a third time. I was getting the hang of it. Soon enough we were tossing words back and forth like a friendly game of catch, having what was commonly known among other families as regular, everyday, father-daughter talk. I'd seen it on *The Brady Bunch*, but never in my own dining room. Yeah, it was with a man who wasn't my own father, but beggars couldn't be choosers.

It was the first time I'd ever been asked my opinion on anything, and it felt spectacular.

CHAPTER 5

EDUCATING RITA

News of my Yankee Clipper talents on the baseball diamond traveled fast.

I'd always been able to throw and hit any ball faster and better than most of the boys on the street when we played impromptu football or baseball, but I'd never displayed my athletic abilities in any official capacity.

Until one day, on a muddy baseball field in the fall of '78, when I pulled the ace out of my sleeve. I was strong and fast, and, as most of the kids in the neighborhood knew after the incident with Bad Josh, I had balls. But after my important lessons learned with Mrs. G and Mr. R, I was looking for a healthier way to empower myself that didn't involve bloodying a kid's nose. Since I'd always had a knack for sports, I joined the town softball team that spring to see if it would be a good fit.

At one of our first games, the bases were loaded, and I was sent to the outfield. Home plate was so far away that the batter looked like a tiny action figure. But I could still hear the crack of the bat and see the fly ball hurtling toward left field. My teammates figured we were goners, but I sprung into action.

I tore across the field at lightning speed and dove for the ball, sliding through the mud and stretching my arm as far as it would go until I heard the solid *thud* of it landing snugly in my mitt pocket. I was on my feet instantly, sending the ball like a laser-guided missile to the catcher's glove, hovering inches above home.

Whooosh! Thud! Out, out, out!

My play won us the game, and the crowd (my 11-year-old teammates) went wild. When I jogged in from the soggy field, splattered with mud, they surrounded me and were jumping up and down, patting me on the back.

The next day I delivered a repeat performance, only this time I was at bat. The pitcher—a sweet girl with a bouncy blonde ponytail—stared me down and lobbed the grapefruit-sized ball at me.

Crack!

It sailed up in a high arc into the big, blue sky, and kept sailing until it dropped on the other side of the fence. I made an easy victory run around the diamond to the echoing cheers of my new admirers.

That was it; I was hooked. That year, I played ball wherever and whenever I could. The men might rule at home, where I had to stand on the sidelines and be quiet, but on the field I was the star of the big show. I played football at recess, softball after school, and Wiffle ball or football after dinner.

At night I'd lie awake in Mom's bed, excited about my new life and glorious future. I dreamed about being on the high-school football team. How could I not? Every time I ran across the end zone hugging the pigskin, the cheers from my teammates washed over me like a tidal wave of love, a wave that washed away all past hurts and sorrow. And best of all, they temporarily pushed down thoughts of death days and food rules and evil clothes that threatened to destroy my family and me.

If any ugly, painful memory did surface, I was able to squash it. Like the time I cut my hand so deeply on the jagged edge of a tin can at home. Sal carried me down the stairs and into the car, and he and Mom rushed me to the emergency room. The nurses tried to give me a needle to numb my hand before the doctor could sew me up, but I was squirming so wildly that they had to strap me down to keep me still. On the table, they bound my chest and wrists using thick rubber belts and I began howling like a trapped animal. I didn't howl because of the straps; I howled because of what they made me remember—the disgusting arms of the crossing guard crushing against my chest.

Sports helped me push away ugly moments like that. The adrenaline rush I got from playing ball had to do with its freedom and its simplicity. Sports were real and honest; there was no secret keeping. The team worked together like the parts of my well-oiled bike, like the functional family I wished I had but did not. And it gave me a new sense of my self-identity. At home, I was pegged the weak and sick one by my family, as that was what they saw. On the field, I was strong and capable to my fellow athletes. Once I got high on the healthy drug of sports, I never had to take my bike apart ever again. Sports became my passion, my escape, my first love, and my saving grace. Sports saved my life.

MY STATUS AS A STAR ATHLETE and no-bullshit tomboy helped me make a lot of new friends, mostly boys. I had girls as friends, too, but I was never into dolls or trying out the new flavor of Bonne Bell Lip Smacker. I had more of an affinity with the boys. They'd come home with me after school and dive into our basement, which was stocked with bootleg videos and full-size arcade games like Pac-Man —I always had cool stuff other kids didn't have, and I loved to share it with them.

Then, just as I was getting some control over my life, Mother Nature threw me a curveball. One day walking home from school, I felt one of my old stomachaches coming on. Or so I thought. By the time I got home, I felt like I had wet my pants. I went to the bathroom, pulled down my jeans, and saw blood.

"*Mooooooooom!*"

She came running. Mom had told me about monthly periods only two weeks earlier, but had assured me I wouldn't be getting them for another year or two, and then—gush!

"You got it!" she said. "I can't believe it!" She was smiling from ear to ear.

I could feel my mother running girly-girl scenarios in her brain. *Today, my baby became a woman. Now she'll finally act like a girl. Now she'll wear dresses. Now she'll get crushes on boys.*

All I was thinking was, *What a pain in the ass!* What came next was a very uncomfortable lesson on how to use a big, bulky Kotex pad that came out of a pink box with an image of windblown dandelions on the front. I hated it. I was always afraid at school that I'd bleed through and look down to find red splotches staining my white Adidas.

Once I had fully entered puberty and hormones began pumping through my body, I lay awake at night fantasizing about more than being a football star. My fantasies took on a whole new context . . . they weren't about sports, and they weren't about boys.

I remember quite clearly the night I put up the red-bathing-suit poster of Farrah Fawcett-Majors on the wall above my bed. On nights when Dad stayed over in Jersey and I was sent to sleep in my own room, I'd look up at Farrah and have all sorts of decidedly unangelic thoughts and feelings about her.

I never had one singular "Aha!" moment when I knew I was gay. It's more a feeling that was always a part of me, for as long as I can remember. From a very early age I was attracted to girls in a more-than-friends way, and I liked to be close to them. Up until now, I had hidden my feelings from others and even to myself. Beaming Farrah helped bring them to the surface.

Like most of the male population of the world (and some women) in the '70s, I'd had a crush on Farrah from the moment I first laid eyes on her on *Charlie's Angels*. I never missed an episode. If anyone was looking for me on a Wednesday night at 10, they knew where to find me—glued to the tube watching my favorite blonde beauty fight crime in high heels. After the show I'd go to my room and stare at the poster, certain it was my destiny to meet her.

That belief was my first experience in manifesting my own reality.

You see, a few months after I'd put up her poster, I was walking to Joe's Restaurant with my cousins to meet my family there for dinner when we bumped into Uncle Ralph a block from the restaurant.

"You will never believe who's eating at Joe's right this minute!" he said, excited.

"Who?"

"Farrah Fawcett-Majors!"

"No!" I could barely breathe. "I don't believe it!"

"She's there! She's sitting at the first table when you walk in. Hurry!"

I raced to the restaurant with my cousins trailing behind, my heart thumping so hard I thought my ribs were going to break. The back door was unlocked for us, and I ran in, flushed and out of breath. I made a beeline straight for my father, who was about to attack his dinner.

Dad wasn't the kind of man who liked to be interrupted, certainly not while he was eating, and definitely not by *me*. But I was so worked up that none of the usual rules applied. I wasn't sure if he knew I loved Farrah or if he knew I had her poster on my wall, or even if he knew who she was. Uncle Pat, who worked in the entertainment industry, had brought around Steve McQueen and Ali MacGraw to dinner with us at Joe's, but Dad wasn't overly impressed just because someone was a celebrity. But this was a momentous, unparalleled occasion, and I needed help—and he was the only one with the power to help me.

"Dad! Dad! Uncle Ralph said Farrah Fawcett-Majors is in the front room! Dad, can I get her autograph?!"

He put down his fork and knife and looked at me. Then he smiled.

"Tony!" he called out. The maître d' came running.

"Tony, do me a favor."

Tony looked worried.

"Go get an autograph for Rita from this Farrah person." Dad paused, looking at my face. "And take Rita with you."

Tony looked relieved. "Of course, yes, of course! Right away!"

I followed Tony through the inner doors to the front room, where Farrah was sitting with her manager at the table across from the bar. I took once glance at that unmistakable flash of white teeth and blonde hair, then ran scared to the bar to wait while Tony approached her. He leaned over and whispered to Farrah, then pointed in my direction. Farrah looked up, shot me a smile that would have lit up the entire dungeon, and waved me over.

I don't know how I made it the ten feet from the barstool to Farrah, but I did. She wrote her autograph on a scrap piece of paper and handed it over to me, with another smile. It felt better than hitting a grand slam. I floated back to the other room and showed off my autograph to each person, one by one, going down the long table until I reached Dad.

"Are you happy?" he asked.

"Yeah," I said, grinning. It was one of the few times my father ever came through for me.

Farrah was my first fantasy crush. My first real-life crush was Mrs. Weiss, my softball coach my second year with the town league. She was a tall, slim brunette with pretty brown eyes and a soft energy about her. (By sixth grade, I was already sensing people by their "energies" before I knew what I was doing.) You might say that she was more the Jaclyn Smith type than a Farrah, but that was fine with me.

Every game, she cheered us on as she paced up and down the third baseline in jeans, T-shirt, and liberally applied frosted blue eye shadow. "All right, girls, let's go! We need some muscle out there!"

I could feel myself showing off in front of her, trying to impress her with how fast I could run or how far I could throw the ball, hoping to hear her compliment me—which she always did. If I performed an exceptionally difficult maneuver, like catching a fly ball before it went over the fence, or making a double play as shortstop, she'd pat me on the shoulder and say, "Good job, Rita! Great play!" She gave me the attention I craved and saw my potential, and it lifted me up.

Yolanda came to most of my games and always cheered me on from the stands. She'd bring Mom with her when she could, but Mom never came alone. I didn't question why; I just assumed it was because she didn't feel very well.

By THE TIME I WAS 12 YEARS OLD, I'd come to accept that I liked women. My strong attraction to Farrah and Mrs. Weiss further confirmed what I already knew to be true: I was gay, no question in my mind. I just didn't know what to do with this information.

We never talked about sex in my family. My brothers could do whatever they wanted as long as they didn't get a girl pregnant. My sisters and I were told, "Don't let boys touch you—get married and have kids." But there was always this silent added warning to me of, "Don't let boys touch you, but letting girls touch you is even worse." I don't know if it was because they sensed I was gay, or because I had an uncle who was gay—Dad's brother Pat—and they were worried I'd inherited the gay gene.

In our world, men were men and women ironed. If you were anything in between you were *finocchio* and ran the risk of being mocked, beaten up, or worse. It's no wonder that Uncle Pat, who was gay for as long as everyone could remember, never officially "came out" to the family. We kids loved going to his beautifully decorated house in Long Island where he and his boyfriend, Jay, would whip up lamb stuffed with apples and other gourmet concoctions foreign to our Italian-only taste buds.

Uncle Pat was like Felix Unger in *The Odd Couple*—lean, neat, fashionable, and fabulous. He was nothing like his manly brothers, and he and Jay would serenade us with Italian love ballads and show tunes. He had his own business in the entertainment industry, and we loved how fun and exciting he was. It was understood he was gay and I guess I knew he was, but it was something no one talked about in front of us.

"It's not normal, it's not right," I'd hear the grown-ups say when they thought I was out of earshot.

I'm not sure what my family would have considered a worse tragedy—for one of their sons to be gay or one of their daughters. Italian men are notoriously macho, and my dad and his other brothers (even Lou, who was a priest) were the epitome of that stereotype. You'd never catch my dad singing "That's Amore" with Uncle Pat and Jay. But I know Dad loved his brother. Apparently, Uncle Pat was Gram's protector growing up. As the eldest, he'd go up against my grandfather if he ever raised a hand to Gram Crackers, and Dad remembered that and respected him for it. But my father and his brothers were also old-fashioned and homophobic.

"What did that faggot say?" I heard Dad ask once, when he was watching TV and thought someone on the screen was gay.

So in our family the verdict was clear. Being gay was very, very bad. And in Dad's lifestyle, it was a disgrace. I wondered how Uncle Pat dealt with the family's reaction to his being gay and made a mental note to ask him about it, if I ever got the nerve. Until then, it became just another secret I was going to have to put in a box and bury in the backyard until I knew what to do with it.

SECRETS WERE HARD TO KEEP BURIED, THOUGH, as I was soon to discover. By the time I started seventh grade, I had unearthed one of my father's big ones.

I was still in the dark about what Dad's job was, or if he had a job at all. The last time I'd asked my mother, maybe a year earlier, how we paid for our big house, swimming pool, big-screen TV, pool table, and video games, she said, "Your brothers help out with the expenses because Dad's sick."

Okay, okay. He's sick. I finally accepted that he was really sick because I'd seen doctors coming in and out of the dungeon and witnessed Dad acting strange in front of them. But I was reaching that age where I started asking questions again, so the family must have thought it was time to toss me another bone.

Once again, it was Yolanda who was elected to do the tossing. She came over to the house one day after school and sat me down in the living room.

"Look, you keep asking what's the matter with Dad. Well, he's got paranoid schizophrenia. It's a mental illness. If anyone asks, that's what it is. You understand?"

I wanted to ask her what "paranoid schizophrenia" was, but I knew better. It was the most information I ever got from anybody about my father during the first 12 years of my life, so I didn't want to push it. Besides, Yolanda's tone told me the conversation was over. At least I finally knew what Dad's mystery illness was called. I wasn't too worried, because no one in the family seemed to be making a big deal out of it.

But the next day, my curiosity got the better of me and I went to the school library after class. I pulled down a thick medical encyclopedia from the shelf and thumbed through the paper-thin pages until I found it:

> Paranoid schizophrenia: A psychotic disorder characterized by loss of contact with the environment . . . deterioration in the level of functioning in everyday life . . . persecutory or grandiose delusions or hallucinations. Genetics play a very important role in the development and progression of schizophrenia.

Holy shit! *This* is what Dad had?

But . . . this described me! My brain went into overdrive, and I felt a panic attack coming on.

Is this why I act differently from other people? Did I inherit this from Dad? Is this why I like girls? Is this why I have panic attacks and depression and they had to send me to the school shrink? Am I going to start hearing voices? Is this why my clothes are dangerous? Am I doomed to spend the rest of my life in the dark dungeon with Dad and Gram?

Gram's voice echoed in my head. *They ruined you.*

I checked out every book I could find on the topic, stuffed them in my backpack and rode my bike home. When I got there, I took the stairs two at a time up to my room and hid the books under the bed so my mother wouldn't see them.

I was quieter than usual during dinner, upset by what I'd read. Mom asked me if anything was wrong, and I told her I was tired and going to my room to watch TV. I went upstairs, dragged the *American Medical Association Complete Medical Encyclopedia* from beneath my bed and started carefully rereading one of the pages I'd turned down.

Genetics play a very important role in the . . .

I slammed the book shut.

What the fuck was wrong with Dad? What the fuck was wrong with *me?* I needed to think about it all, sort it out, and I needed the space to do it. I went to Mom's bedroom, noticing that she was already in her nightgown and under the blankets waiting for me to turn in with her. I sat down on the bed next to her.

"Ma, I really need to start sleeping in my own bed now. I feel like I need my own space."

She looked surprised, and sat up a little. "Is everything okay?"

"Yeah, everything's fine. It's just time for me to grow up a little."

"Okay," she said. But I could see she was hurt.

I felt bad saying it because growing up with all her sisters and then moving in with Dad and Gram, it would probably be the first night in her whole life that Mom slept alone in a bed. Maybe it would be good for her, I tried to convince myself.

For myself, there was no question it was the right move. As soon as I'd said it, I was engulfed by a wave of freedom. I went back to my room and got into bed, clutching the encyclopedia to my chest. I looked up at smiling Farrah, who didn't have a care in the world.

It was time to have my own life now, yes. I wasn't sure exactly what that life would be, but I had taken my first baby steps toward finding out.

CHAPTER 6

STRAIGHT
TO HELL

By the time I was 13, going to confession had become unbearable.

My weekly visits to the "penalty box" had slowed down after I realized I was gay. Now they had dwindled to near nothing, and for good reason: I was in a gridlock with God.

More specifically, my heart, head, body, and soul were at war with the Catholic Church. I was a mixed-up mass of emotions—confused, frustrated, afraid, and hurt. I knew from my weekly catechism classes in preparation for my upcoming confirmation exactly how the Church felt about people like me: homosexuality was contrary to the "natural order" God ordained for the universe, and Church doctrine labeled people like me "disordered." Disordered? How many disorders can one person have? Apparently, if I acted out on the thoughts and feelings I had, I was doomed to hell.

Maybe I *was* disordered. Sometimes, I felt like I was going out of my mind. But I sure didn't want to hear about it over and over again in the confessional. Gram had already told me I was ruined, and her words were as official in our home as if they had come from the Pope himself.

I had worked hard to pick my spirits up after she had made that devastating pronouncement. It had taken two years to fully banish my death days, and they were finally behind me. So the idea of crawling into that coffin-like box to listen to a faceless man —a man of God, especially—tell me I was made all wrong was not high on my fun-things-to-do list.

I tried to practice what I'd say to him if I had the nerve, and it didn't go well, even in my imagination.

Forgive me, Father, for I have sinned.

What have you done, my child?

Oh . . . I've had impure thoughts.

What thoughts, my child?

Well, Father. You know Charlie's Angels?

My dear, what kind of impure thoughts could you possibly have about the angels?

Ah, well . . . no . . . it's not . . . you see . . . ah, fongool.

I carried my terrible dark secret inside of me instead, and I carried it right past the confessional. Skipping confession meant that I couldn't take Holy Communion—a big deal in the Catholic Church. I was taught that receiving the Eucharist was receiving "the body of Christ," and it made you cleansed and new again, free of sin.

At some point, my avoidance of the box and the priest became so apparent that my mother asked, "Ri, have you been to confession lately?"

"No."

"Why?"

"Because I don't believe I have to confess my sins to a man in church when I can talk to the Man Himself directly."

"But, Ri! The priest was chosen by God to absolve you of your sins!"

"Ma, I don't feel comfortable with it. I talk to God all the time. I don't feel I need to go to church for Him to heal me."

"I don't know what I'm going to do with you. At least say the Act of Contrition with me."

Oh, my God . . . I am heartily sorry for having offended Thee, and I detest all my sins . . . because I dread the loss of heaven, and the pains of hell . . .

Before long, the belief that I was going to hell became a whole new fear to occupy my mind. I'd hear an angel on my left shoulder telling me I was going to heaven, and the devil on my right saying I was going to hell. Or was it the angel warning of hell, and the devil promising heaven?

One night I was helping Gram with dinner. As I made the salad dressing, lost in thought about heaven and hell, the bottle of olive oil slipped from my hand and crashed to the floor. Gram heard from the kitchen and came rushing in with a box of salt in her hand.

"Oh, no, no, *noooooo!*" she wailed. She immediately began crossing herself and tossing pinches of salt over her left shoulder, then sprinkling it on the pool of glass and oil spreading on the floor.

"When you spill oil, it means som-a-body has a terrible fate. Maybe som-a-body's gonna die! The salt takes away the back luck!"

It was one of those nutty, medieval superstitions that Gram had smuggled through customs and imported from the Old Country. I couldn't think of anything more ridiculous than foretelling someone's death by knocking over the salad dressing. And yet, it scared the hell out of me, so to speak.

Maybe one of my death-day predictions was rearing its ugly head now and threatening to come true? Maybe I was the one to die? I got down on the floor and joined Gram, who was now on her knees in prayer position, to help her toss salt and mop up the oil spill. I started throwing the salt everywhere—over both my shoulders, on the mop, on the oil—anywhere it was needed to turn our fate around.

Oh, my Jesus, save us from the fires of hell . . . and lead us all to heaven . . .

TWO WEEKS LATER, THE SUPERSTITION didn't seem crazy at all. My favorite uncle, Pat, had visited Gram on a wintry January morning for a cup of coffee on his way to his midtown office, promising to come back a few hours later on his way home to Long Island. When he didn't show up, Gram went outside looking for Uncle Ralph to see if he'd seen or heard from Pat.

Uncle Ralph had his own café right next door to Gram's building, so she knew she'd find him there. But as she was walking out the front door of the dungeon, Uncle Ralph was rushing in, frantic. He ushered Gram back inside and told her the news: Uncle Pat was dead.

"No!" Gram yelled, collapsing into her recliner in the living room. "Not my Pasquale!"

Dad came in from the bedroom. He'd been asleep, but the crying and loud voices woke him up.

"What's happened?" he asked Ralph. *"Cosa succede?"* he asked Gram.

"He's dead," Ralph told him, "our brother's dead!"

Pat had gone back to the office after visiting Gram, and soon after had a heart attack while he was on the phone. A co-worker found him dead in his office minutes later and called Uncle Lou right away, who rushed over and administered last rites.

As soon as we got the news in Jersey, Mom, my sisters, and I drove over. When we arrived at the dungeon, Gram was sitting in her recliner clutching her rosary beads, sobbing and praying, with Uncle Lou and Uncle Ralph on either side of her.

I went up to Gram, thinking, *What could I possibly say to make her feel better? No words exist that can do that.* So I leaned down and hugged her. Gram had no words, either. She looked up at me and lifted her hand to touch my cheek. When she looked into my eyes a deep moan came out from her gut that was so primal in anguish, it cut right through me.

I wandered around the apartment hugging aunts and cousins —family had started to show up—in search of my parents. I finally found them in Dad's bedroom, but I stopped frozen at the door without going in. The door was open maybe two inches, and through that small space, I watched a scene I'd never witnessed before and never saw again.

Dad sat on the edge of the bed, hunched over, sobbing. My mother's arm was around him, and she was trying to comfort him like he was a child. I had never seen my father show emotion like that before, and it shocked me. He'd never made me feel very protected or safe in my life, but at least his tough demeanor was one of the few constants I had. Seeing him fall apart like this made me feel like everything was shot to hell.

I backed away from the door and joined the others in the living room. Everyone was talking about Uncle Pat and what a kind, happy, wonderful man he was. But I wondered if they were also secretly asking the same question I was: *Uncle Pat lived a gay lifestyle—does this mean he now goes to hell?* And once again, I worried that *I* was going to hell. My uncle's death slapped that terrifying possibility right back into my face again. I also had another new worry to add to it: *I dropped the olive oil—does that mean I killed him?* I slumped into the chair, all the energy drained out of me.

A few minutes later, my parents came out of the bedroom. Dad had composed himself so that no one else would witness him crying like a little boy. He whispered a few words to Uncle Lou and motioned for us all to gather together. Lou stood by Gram's recliner, like it was a pulpit, and led the family in a prayer.

My REVIVED WORRY ABOUT BEING GAY, going to hell, and killing Uncle Pat was followed by a reluctant act of penance.

Come September, I was informed that I'd be going to Catholic school for eighth grade. Yolanda had suggested the idea to my mother, thinking that a smaller, more intimate school might be good for me.

I argued and debated with them heatedly. I'd finally reached a good place in my other school. I had made a lot of friends and no one bothered me anymore about being different. It had been a difficult, uphill battle. Now they wanted to send me to a strange new school to start all over again? Besides that, I was also hesitant to go to a Catholic school because of my growing confusion about the religion. And to top it off, I'd have to wear a uniform every day at this new school—a *skirt*. Oh my God, are you kidding me? A skirt? Every *day!* Did they know me *at all?*

I started eighth grade at Immaculate Conception and, sure enough, had to wear one of those blue and white plaid skirts with a vest and nondescript, uncomfortable shoes. I was still dealing with my clothing obsession, so initially I was worried that I might "reject" the uniform. But when I first tried it on, I was relieved to discover that it was "safe." It was like the little voice in my mind had no choice but to accept the uniform, so it kept its mouth shut for once. Even though I hated wearing skirts, the uniform was a surprising relief in that I didn't have to agonize every morning over what I was going to wear.

When I got home from school each day, though, it was the same shit. I'd stand in front of my closet wondering what to change into. I was getting tired of arguing with the contents in my closet. It was bad enough I was *in* the closet, never mind arguing with it.

I took my "safe" school uniform as a good sign and decided to be as positive as I could about my new school. After all the troubles I'd had in the past, I wanted to fit in and was determined not to backslide into depression or fistfighting. I was going to be good and follow all the rules.

Luckily, I was developing a new weapon in my arsenal of social interaction.

I was a bit of a jokester at home, but no one outside the family knew I had a sly, quirky sense of humor until the day I said something incredibly sarcastic and brilliant in class and made everyone laugh, even the nuns. As with sports, I began to use my humor to make friends and gain acceptance, and that was the goods to me.

By the end of the second week at school, I had firmly established myself as the class clown, knowing how to work the room and how far I could go without getting in hot water with the nuns. I had already been unconsciously reading people's individual energies by then; now I was able to sense the vibrational awareness of an entire group. Like any good stand-up comedian, I could read the audience. Those nuns were a tough crowd, but my classmates were easy marks.

It felt good to fit in, and I didn't want to rock the boat. So in an effort to simplify my life, I decided to do everything possible to hide my attraction to girls. It didn't stop me from liking them—in fact, there was one classmate whom I immediately had a crush on. So to distract myself (and others), I jumped headfirst into the weird, hetero-dating world at Immaculate.

In the middle of English class one month into the school year, my new friend Stephanie leaned over and cupped her hand around my ear when the nun wasn't looking. "Paul really likes you," she whispered.

I looked over at Paul, who sat two desks to the right of me. His face was sprinkled with freckles, and he was copying down the lesson from the blackboard.

"He thinks you're funny."

Well, I guess that was as good a reason as any for a 14-year-old girl to get married.

Because at Immaculate, you didn't date a boy—you "married" him in a faux sacramental ceremony in the schoolyard. It was a time-honored tradition at the school that if a boy wanted to ask you out, you had to go through a whole elaborate ritual as if you were his bride. It was a serious undertaking, not to be entered into lightly. Much like grown-ups getting married in the Church, we had rules—for example, we couldn't even hold hands at school without getting married first.

A few days later, I allowed myself to be baptized into the world of boy dating. Even though I knew it was a farce, I had to go through with it as part of my trying-to-fit-in regimen. When

Stephanie gave me a conspiratorial nod in class, I knew that today was to be My Big Day.

After class was over, my giggling bridesmaids led me through the yard to the footpath behind the soccer goalposts, where we met with Paul, my husband-to-be, and his groomsmen. Both the bride and groom wore school uniforms, and one of the girls plucked dandelions from the grass and handed me a bouquet. Then, another girl walked me down the aisle to present me to Paul, who was waiting five feet away.

One of the boys acted as master of ceremony and mumbled a few words.

"Do you take this girl . . . "

"I do."

"Do you take this boy . . . "

"Yeah."

And then he pronounced us going steady, and it was time for the Big Kiss—my first. The idea of kissing a boy felt wrong, but again, there was no getting out of it. I was a nervous wreck and didn't know what to do—and neither, it seemed, did Paul. He stood there, hands shoved in his pockets, so I took charge. I leaned over, he puckered up, and we exchanged a peck on the lips that lasted a millisecond.

Everybody clapped, and I was now officially Paul's girlfriend—which basically meant we walked down the hall together between classes and had a few more stolen pecks by the lockers. But, alas, Paul and I soon had a troubled union. As sad as it was, he and I had a few good weeks together and then we drifted apart. And the day came when I told him to meet me by the soccer posts, the recent site of our beautiful wedding.

"I don't want to go out with you anymore," I told him.

He shrugged, then nodded, and we both decided to remain good friends.

If only divorce in the Catholic Church was this easy.

No sooner was I back on the market than another boy proposed. His name was Steve Levy, and he was funny like me. We rode bikes and played Wiffle ball at recess—this time, I married for like.

And I did the next time, too. By the end of the school year, I'd had more husbands than Eva and Zsa Zsa Gabor combined. At least it had given me a chance to hone my kissing skills. Yet no matter how many times I kissed a boy, it was no use—I just didn't feel anything. Meanwhile, my feelings for girls refused to go away. Whenever we played spin the bottle in someone's basement, I always hoped my bottle would point to one of the girls in the circle.

My religious waywardness didn't make me feel guilty enough to go back to confession or communion. But that year I did take part in a major sacrament of the Catholic Church—my confirmation. The purpose of getting confirmed is to "make your bond with the Church *more perfect*," the priest told me. Oh, if he only knew how far from perfect my bond had become.

Getting confirmed was a formal occasion, so I had to wear a dress and heels and a white graduation-type gown, with my confirmation name, Marie, embroidered in red letters down the front. Dad didn't come, but I didn't expect him to. He didn't attend occasions in my life. At least I didn't have to worry ahead of time about him not showing up at my wedding— I already assumed I'd never have one.

With my mother and my sisters watching from a front pew, I walked down the aisle of the church with the others, bathed in clouds of incense wafting from the metal thurible. I knew what I was supposed to feel on such an occasion. I was supposed to feel like I was becoming closer to the Church and to God, a union of spirit.

Instead, I felt . . . nothing. Zip. My biggest concern at that moment was not falling off my patent-leather high-heeled shoes.

I saw the faces in the pews looking up at me with expectation, and I knew that this was supposed to be my big moment where I became overcome with emotion and infused with the Holy Spirit. The truth was, I didn't feel emotionally connected to any of it, and I was going through the motions. I believed in God, that I knew— that part felt right to me and made sense. But the rest of the details involving my belief were murky. The God I yearned for was loving and all-forgiving. The God I heard the priest talk about in church was vengeful and going to toss me in a pit of hell. I wanted the loving one Who was going to accept me as He had made me.

The only day out of that whole year at Immaculate when I felt like I wasn't pretending to be someone else was when we had "dress-up" day. That's the day we did a uniform switch and the boys put on our skirts, and we dressed up in their pants, white button-down shirts, ties, and vests. A group of us girls changed in the bathroom and stood in front of the mirror, laughing at our reflections.

I lingered a bit longer, not able to tear my eyes away. I recognized that girl in the mirror; it was the real me. And she didn't want to be buried anymore; she wanted to live.

ENTER GABRIELLA ON THE SCENE. I met her through a friend on the block, and we'd been hanging out, throwing the football around. She was a jock, like me, and I sensed we had even more in common than that.

One day the following summer when I was 15, we were playing catch in my backyard when my mother shouted out the window that she was going to the store for an hour.

"Okay, Mom!" I yelled back.

We heard the car pull out of the driveway. Gabriella had the ball in her hand, but she didn't throw it—she just stood there, looking at me. All thoughts of church, God, and hell vanished from my mind. Without saying a word, we both went through the back screen door and down to the basement. Once we got there, we stood face-to-face, hearts pumping. In one desperate glance, we both realized that we were in the same confusing boat.

We hugged tightly, and I awkwardly leaned down and kissed her neck three times and she did the same to me. And that was it. We heard a noise, jumped, and ran upstairs and went back to playing catch in the yard. The whole romantic encounter lasted about one minute, and not one word passed between us.

Our few chaste kisses had left me both exhilarated and confused as ever.

As innocent as our brief basement moment had been, I knew what Gabriella and I had done was considered deviant in the eyes of the Catholic Church and my family. At the same time, unlike kissing Paul or any of those other boys I married at Immaculate, it felt natural, normal, and exhilarating to be with a feminine energy.

How could something so wrong feel so absolutely right?

PART II
OUT OF THE SHADOWS

CHAPTER 7

PAPA, DON'T PREACH

There's nothing like sitting in church to make a girl contemplate sin.

Mom had convinced me to go to Mass with her one Sunday—I hadn't gone since the Gabriella incident less than a year earlier—and we slipped into the back pew so that she could do some heavy-duty praying and I could do some heavy-duty thinking.

As it turned out, the priest, Father Kelly, was delivering a rousing sermon on Sodom and Gomorrah, which was obviously appropriate. He was getting passionate about the sins of the flesh and judgment and God's wrath . . . and the more passionate he got, the more frustrated I got. For years I had tried to fight my natural feelings and inclinations, to no avail. Now as I sat there listening to the priest, I wondered if he really did speak for God.

If I was born gay, then that's the way God had made me. The Church told me that if I was attracted to another woman, this meant I could never get married and was therefore called to a life of chastity. But why would a good and loving God make me in a way that sentenced me to either a life of loneliness—which would be hell on Earth—or an afterlife in hell itself? It didn't make sense. Why would God punish His children for being and living as He made them?

God is about love and forgiveness; those were the basic teachings of Jesus. But his words were passed along orally for decades before being written down, then translated, and then copied. Centuries later, a group of men sat together over many, many years and interpreted his words to make up the doctrines of the Catholic Church. I thought, *I know I'm simplifying it, but the point is . . . do I trust these men who made the decisions? I don't know. I don't even trust my own father. But I do trust Jesus, yes. And I wonder if his words had been twisted into a regime of control, fear, manipulation, politics, guilt, and punishment. Hmm. Sounds a lot like home to me.*

I glanced up at a crucifix of Jesus, bleeding and suffering on the cross, and pondered this until I felt my mother flinch next to me. I looked over to find Father Kelly zeroing in on us.

"We must root out the sins of a certain family in the neighborhood," his voice boomed, as he fixed his gaze on my mother and me.

The entire congregation turned and looked at us, too.

"We have members of our congregation here in this very room today who are committing crimes, who are corrupt! We must root out these undesirables from the community lest their sin spread among us!"

I looked at my mother, whose face was crimson with embarrassment, and I gave her one of my "What the fuck is going on?" expressions.

Was the priest talking about us? Did he know what I had done with Gabriella? Was he talking about Dad's mental illness? We'd known this elderly priest for nearly a decade and had been attending

Mass at this church for 15 years; it's where I walked down the aisle in my virginal white satin-and-organza dress and veil for my first communion. So I was shocked to be singled out like this for no apparent reason.

My mother nudged me and rose, and I followed her lead as she hurried from the pew and out the church door as everyone stared. Her head was held high, but I could see that her heart was broken. I kept my head down as I trailed behind her. What the hell had just happened?

On the drive home, I asked her what the priest had meant, but she was so shaken up that she didn't want to talk. I stayed up all night worrying and wondering. I knew there was something going on that I didn't know about. And I had a feeling that something was about to explode.

I WAS IN A STATE OF COMPLETE EXHAUSTION and confusion when I stumbled into school the next day. I was now a 16-year-old tenth grader at Northern Valley Regional High School at Old Tappan following my year "doing time" at Immaculate. After that year, I told my mother in no uncertain terms that I wasn't going back, and I'd started at Northern the following year.

After my terrible night, I was in no mood to hear that Tina, a popular girl from a nearby school—famous for her acid-washed jeans and over-gelled hair—was spreading rumors about my family. She was playing hooky from her own school that day to visit a friend at Northern Valley, and my best friend had heard her big mouth from down the hall.

"Tina's talkin' shit again," Madison told me during chemistry class. "She's going around the whole school calling you— get this—a Mafia princess!"

Madison and I were like two mismatched peas in a pod when we stood next to each other. I was a short pipsqueak with an unruly mop of dark, layered hair; while Madison was tall and twice my size in width, like a football player, with close-cropped golden curls. We'd known each other since grammar school and were loyal comrades no matter the fight. She was in the schoolyard the day of the infamous Josh Gold incident; she knew what I was capable of.

Madison continued, breathlessly, "Tina's telling everybody that your family is . . . connected."

Tina had been insulting my family behind my back all year, but I'd always ignored her because she was an idiot. But this was not a good time to mess with me, especially as I stood there holding a sizzling test tube over a flaming Bunsen burner. I didn't consider if Tina was speaking the truth or not. I couldn't think at all. As I stared into the hot flame in front of me, all I could see was red. Like that time with Josh, something inside of me snapped. Maybe, I later imagined, it was Dad's paranoid schizophrenia finally kicking in and taking over.

"Where is she?" I asked Madison.

"She always goes into the bathroom with her friends."

I hatched my plan in seconds.

"Okay. I'm going to follow them into the bathroom, and you're going to stay outside and keep watch. Don't let anybody in," I instructed. "I need to straighten her out. I've had enough of this shit."

My voice had a chilling finality to it that I'd heard in my father's voice many times before, and it made me shiver. We waited outside the bathroom door until only Tina and her friends were inside. I went in, positioning myself against the sink, arms crossed.

Tina's two friends came out from the stalls first, armed with lip gloss and making their way to the mirror.

"Get out," I said, glaring at them. "Now."

They scurried out without a word, so quick to betray their leader.

A minute later I heard a flush and Tina cracked open the stall door an inch, her eyes darting around as she searched for her minions.

"They're gone," I told her.

Tina opened the door wider and made a move to slip by me.

"Let me ask you something, Tina," I said, stepping in her way. "How many fucking times do you have to talk about me and my family?"

She rubbed her sweaty palms across her acid-washed jeans.

"I mean, who the hell do you think you are?!"

"I . . . I . . . "

She never got a chance to answer. I didn't let her. And for the first and last time in my life, I forgot the lesson Mrs. Gold had so lovingly taught me a few years earlier, that violence solved nothing.

As soon as the poor girl opened her mouth to speak, I grabbed a chunk of her stiff tresses. In one swift move, I wrapped her hair around my hand and yanked her head toward the sink, slamming it hard against the porcelain. I heard a crack, like the sound when my bat hit the ball perfectly, and a second later I saw blood everywhere. Exactly where it was spouting from, I wasn't sure. Did I break her nose?

Tina fell to the floor in a heap and whimpered. I almost felt sorry for her. Almost. She didn't fight back, and she didn't say anything—I think she was in shock.

"Don't ever . . . *ever* . . . let me hear you talk about my family again," I said, giving her a last kick in the ribs as she lay crumpled on the floor. I had a split-second flashback of my father's shiny shoe stomping on a man's head, but shoved it back into my subconscious. I left Tina on the floor and joined Madison in the hall. I was in and out in all of five minutes.

"Let's go!"

I must admit, beating up Tina felt great—that same adrenaline I had post-Josh. In my mind, I was certain that she deserved it, as Josh did at the time, and that defending the family honor was the right thing to do. Years later, of course, the memory appalls and haunts me. It didn't occur to me at the time that, like the Josh Gold incident, I was venting my own pent-up, personal anguish. Thanks to Tina's stupid mouth, she just happened to be my punching bag that day.

Madison and I walked toward our lockers as if nothing had happened. Ten minutes later an ashen-faced teacher collared us and steered us toward the principal's office, where a bloodied and teary-eyed Tina lay in the fetal position on a couch. The middle of her face was starting to puff out and turn the color of my mother's lilacs.

"Wow! What happened to you?" I asked, feigning shock.

"Holy moly!" Madison gasped, playing along.

The principal wasn't buying our act.

"Miss Gigante, did you hit this girl?"

"Me? Nah. Madison, did you see anything?"

"Nooo . . . "

"Me neither."

After a stern talking-to, one I'm sure Tina would have enjoyed witnessing had she not been in such agony, the principal told Madison and me that he'd be punishing us severely and contacting our parents immediately about "this most upsetting incident." Then he ordered us to get out of his office and march our sorry, delinquent asses home.

But home wasn't where I went.

Instead, I hopped on my bike and gripped the handlebars. I had blood on my hands—Tina's blood. Suddenly, I was overwhelmed by doubt. What had I done? I had told myself that Tina was a liar and she had to go down. But a creeping, sick knowing now boiled up from my gut until it formed actual words that I said aloud: "What if she's not lying?"

I started pedaling, knowing exactly where I needed to go.

I HAD STAYED IGNORANT ABOUT MY FATHER for years because I'd been told to. And at some point, I got weary of asking questions and not getting answers, so I had stopped asking them. With all this secrecy about Dad, and the way his friends treated him—with the reverence of a king—it had occurred to me that maybe he was in charge of something shady. Yet I had left well enough alone and pushed it out of my mind. I couldn't push it anymore. I needed answers; I wanted to know who my father was.

I sped through the windy streets with a purpose, pedaling toward the only person I hoped would give me an honest, clear, direct answer. I couldn't go to my sisters or my mother. Yolanda had been my only source of information so far, but I knew this time that she and Roseanne would not be able to help me. I skidded into the driveway of a close family friend, whom I will call Alessandra, and parked my bike. She didn't know it yet, but Alessandra was to become my version of Watergate's Deep Throat.

I burst into her house, flushed and out of breath.

"What happened to you?" she asked, startled. She eyed my T-shirt, speckled with Tina's blood.

"I'm hearing all this shit at school about my father," I said, talking at a rapid-fire pace, "and I need to know the truth. No one in my family will tell me. Will *you* tell me? Please?"

Alessandra sighed, then motioned for me to take a seat on the couch. I waited as she left the room, then came back with a wet towel. She sat down across from me and gently helped me clean the blood off my hands. "What do you want to know, Rita?" she asked.

"Well, what exactly does my dad do?"

She looked at me slightly baffled. "You don't know?"

Was I in the fucking *Twilight Zone?* "I don't know what? Is he sick, is he not sick—what?" My head was pounding.

"Yes, he's sick—physically," Alessandra said, choosing her words carefully. "He has a heart problem; you know that. But . . . "

Her voice trailed off. I stared at her, blankly.

"But what?"

"Just a minute," she said. She got up and made sure the front door was locked, then sat down in front of me again, this time taking my hands in hers. I braced myself.

"What do you know?"

"Only what my sisters tell me or what I see," I replied. "I know he's important. I know he's got people working for him and they're somehow afraid of him. But what he does exactly, I don't know."

"You don't know who he is or how far his hand reaches?"

"What? Oh for God's sake . . . just . . . "

"All right." She slid her chair closer and lowered her voice. "Rita, you know how there are five families in organized crime in New York?"

"No."

I sat there, dazed, as she explained the five clans of the Mafia—Lucchese, Genovese, Gambino, Bonanno, and Colombo.

"From what I've been told, your father is the boss of the Genovese crime family."

My jaw dropped. "The boss?"

"And that's not all."

God, there's more?

"He's not just the head of the family," she continued. "He might be the head of the commission."

"What does that mean?"

"The head of the commission is the boss of *all five* families. It means he'd have power over the entire organization. If anyone wants to do anything big, they'd need your father's permission."

I felt dizzy and leaned back into the couch. Neither of us spoke for a few minutes. Alessandra watched me for a reaction, but I was motionless and mute.

Could it be that my father was the most powerful Mafia boss in the country? It sounded ridiculous, and yet it made perfect sense. In that instant, little fragments of my life that never added up suddenly snapped into place like pieces of a puzzle. *So that's why Dad doesn't live with us. So that's why all those men come to the apartment. So that's why some kids weren't allowed to come to my house to play. So that's why Mom didn't tell Dad about the molesting crossing guard. So that's why the radio is on all the time, to muffle their voices. That's why the scribbled notes, the back doors, the whispers, the fear and admiration in people's eyes.*

"Rita, you are never to repeat these words to anyone—ever. You understand?"

I nodded.

"If anyone asks, you say he's sick. Like always."

I nodded again, still mute.

I was a pro at following that instruction, having perfected it over the last 16 years. The only difference now was that I knew the whole truth—or so I thought. There was one last piece of the puzzle still missing.

"But how does he do all this when he's so sick? His delusions, his schizophrenia?"

Alessandra sighed, and looked at me with sympathy.

"Rita, he's been faking the mental illness all these years."

I BARELY REMEMBER RIDING HOME. Alessandra offered to put my bike in her trunk and drive me, but I needed to feel the air on my face. I weaved through the streets aimlessly, barely looking at the road in front of me, lost in thought. The whole day had been surreal, and my brain was flooded with horror. What do people in the Mafia do? In the movies, they were organized criminals who laundered and extorted money and ran illegal gambling and drug rings. Could my own father be involved in all that? But they did a lot worse than that, too.

I stopped my bike on a corner, paralyzed by one thought: *Oh, God. Does my father kill people?*

I felt nauseated, and dropped my head onto my handlebars to stare at the black asphalt below me for a minute. To me, it made no difference whether a person killed by his own hand or told others to do it. Either way, they were responsible. If my father killed people, how was I supposed to still love him? At that moment, I hated him. He was my father, my blood. My mind reeled. *How could he do this?*

I made it home somehow, and my mother was waiting for me at the kitchen table with a sad, resigned look on her face. I assumed that she'd heard about my beating up Tina in the bathroom that day and I was about to get in trouble big time, but that wasn't it.

"Now that you know about your father, you can't tell anyone," Mom said. I don't know how she found out about my informant, but I was glad she did. I didn't have the energy to fake like my world hadn't just completely turned inside out that day.

She actually seemed a bit relieved that the secret was out. It must have been difficult keeping it from me all those years. Now that I was privy to this big family secret, I too was part of the secret-keeping club.

"It's our business, it has to do with our family, and no one outside the family needs to know," she told me.

I took a deep breath. I'd heard it all before, and I was drained. I'd had a rough day, and once again the moral of the story was about protecting Dad. My mother didn't have any explanation, apology, or comfort for me—it was all about him. Honestly, I was getting tired of protecting him. Did it occur to either of them that I, their child, needed protecting, too?

I went to sleep that night feeling like I'd just jumped out of an airplane, then realized I'd forgotten my parachute. I was falling fast and had no idea where or how or if I'd land on the spinning Earth below. In one day, I'd smashed a girl's head in until her blood was on my hands and discovered that my father was a Mafia boss whose own hands were likely covered in blood.

As far as crimes and punishments for my father and myself, I wasn't sure how either of us would fare. And I wondered whose crimes were worse, the sins of the father or the sins of the daughter? I held out hope that mine weren't too bad, and his were all a bad mistake.

But I had yet to learn of my father's other sins.

CHAPTER 8

SEX, TRUTH, LIES, AND VIDEOTAPE

My father, I soon came to learn, was a brilliant actor. And after I became privy to two of his big secrets—that he was a Mafia boss who pretended he had paranoid schizophrenia—it wasn't long before I was swept into his dramatic world. I was given a new supporting role to play: that of his reluctant but devoted co-star.

In the dark dungeon on Sunday afternoons, the scene would now start like this: Dad would be sitting at the dining-room table, silently drinking coffee, and I'd be lying on that creaky old couch 20 feet away in the living room, watching football. He would have barely said a word to me all day, but then I'd suddenly be summoned for an all-important task.

"Rita," he'd whisper, "walk with me."

I'd nod and get up. I knew he wasn't asking me to go for a leisurely stroll with him through the park. When my father ordered me to walk with him, it meant that he had to go to the café to do some business or play cards, and he needed to put on a good show during the one-block walk to get there.

Even though I'd found out the truth about Dad, we never talked about it. I'm not even sure if he knew that I understood he was pretending to be ill so he could use it as a defense if he ever went to court.

I was amazed to see the lengths he would go to, delivering an Oscar-worthy performance for any FBI agents who might be lurking outside the apartment and watching his every move from their dark, nondescript sedans. Dad knew he was under surveillance and that law-enforcement agents were videotaping and photographing him, looking for evidence to nab him at something. So he took his role as a disheveled, deranged outpatient seriously, and with the commitment of a professional thespian. His meticulous mental and physical preparation to get into character would have put Sir Laurence Olivier to shame.

Take the wardrobe, for instance. Dad's home "uniform" of casual slacks and a shirt, which was later revised to underwear and a T-shirt, had now morphed into an updated version that worked both in the apartment and on the street: a pair of powder blue pajamas with navy trim, and a dark robe.

After he'd inform me about our impending walk, he'd put on his pajamas, slide his feet into his slippers, and top off the ensemble with his worn-out, black velour bathrobe from the Golden Nugget casino in Las Vegas.

Before leaving the apartment, Dad would run his fingers through his hair and muss it up a little, check his unshaven face, and pull the hood of his robe over the newsboy cap on his head. Sometimes he'd tie the robe with a belt, sometimes he wouldn't—that part he'd ad-lib. Then, as we walked from Gram's front door down the long hallway to the front of the apartment building, I'd see the rest of his transformation take place. Dad's head would drop so low that half his face was covered by the hood. He'd stoop his body over and let his arms fall heavy and limp at his sides, and then he'd start shuffling his feet. Before my eyes, my powerful, in-charge dad had become a fragile, senile old man.

"Take my arm here—make like you're holding me," he'd say, before we went out the door, onto the world's stage.

As I slowly led him along Sullivan Street, my father would stay silent unless he needed to mumble a few more orders, like "Hold me closer to you" or "Walk slower." I never said a word; I just listened carefully and did what he told me to do. I didn't have any definitive lines in this play, anyway. I had to keep alert in case he wanted to improvise.

Sometimes as we walked, he'd teeter as if he couldn't hold himself up and was about to tip over. That's when I'd take his cue and pretend to catch him. Other times, he'd abruptly stop and point and start mumbling gibberish. If he thought for sure that he was being taped or filmed by the feds, he'd really lay it on thick and stop in front of a parking meter and stare at it for a long time, silent, wide-eyed. And then . . .

"We're going for a walk, parking meter," he'd say to it. "Wanna come?"

It took all my restraint to keep from laughing when he did that.

We looked strange, even to New Yorkers, who are used to seeing freaks talk to parking meters. Still, everybody and their mother would watch us from the restaurants and on the stoops because we were such an odd pair: Dad, practically drooling; and me, half his size, holding him up defiantly.

I mostly kept my head down to avoid the stares. *Fuck you all! Yeah, this is my life and it is what it is and mind your own business!* As we walked and stopped, walked and stopped, I'd feel a combination of embarrassment, protectiveness, and anger, depending on what kind of day I was having. Every so often I looked at Dad hobbling along and, even though I knew he was putting on an act, my heart believed him a little bit. I'd be overcome with a fierce feeling of family loyalty and want to shield him from the world.

Now that's fucked up.

All of these conflicting feelings—in my world, it was never just one simple feeling—would culminate into a big, fat lump in my throat of: *Oh God, this is bullshit. I don't want to be involved in this crap! What's he doing? What am I doing?*

But there was no way out of it for me; I was in it until the end. I could never tell him, "No, Dad, I don't really feel like going. Can you go by yourself?"

The amazing thing about my father's sense of himself was that even though he looked like an unkempt Alzheimer's patient as we walked, he still gave off that feeling that if he snapped his fingers at you, you had to jump. For those who recognized him, it was like seeing a local celebrity. People in the neighborhood knew who he was way before I did, thanks to word of mouth. They'd look at Dad with a mixture of fear, awe, and excitement. Those were the very rare moments around my father where I felt a sense of protection. *Wow, this is cool! Nobody's ever gonna bother me when I'm with Dad.*

I NEVER USED MY FATHER'S NAME TO GET POWER, but as word spread around school about who he was, I became untouchable. I quickly discovered that I had protection and power by association, and learned that membership in "the family" had its privileges. I barely got in trouble over my bathroom brawl with Tina—not at home or by Tina's parents. I could have killed her, but all I got was a week's detention after school.

One week after I smashed her skull against the sink, I was putting books in my locker after school when Tina came flying down the hallway toward me. She was all smiles, even with a bandage stretched across her nose (ah, so that's where the blood had come from!).

"Rita! I was hoping we could put last week behind us and be friends."

To what did I owe this complete turnaround? I imagine that when she got home and told her parents who had beat up on her, they too let her in on my family secret. And everyone was afraid to do a thing about it.

As far as I know, Mom never told Dad about my Tina fight, and that's too bad. He probably would have been proud to hear the story of his daughter dropping some blabber-mouthed bitch onto a cold bathroom floor to defend the family honor.

Then there was the day I was walking down the hall and got shoved by Gino, a big gorilla of a guy. He was known to pump steroids and hit his girlfriend, and he purposely bulldozed into me because he was the kind of guy who picked a fight with anyone, even a girl.

"Hello?! It would be nice if you said 'Excuse me'!" I said to him.

"Fuck you!" said Gino.

"Fuck me? Fuck *me?!*"

"Hey, take it easy, Gino," squeaked Pauly, Gino's little sidekick.

By three o'clock that afternoon, Gino was frantically looking for me. After our hallway tussle, Pauly (whose family was also connected, I learned) had pulled him aside and given him the goods. Madison had seen it all unfold by the lockers.

"Are you fucking nuts?" he'd asked Gino. "Do you know who that girl is?"

"Just some lezzie bitch. Why?"

"That's Chin's daughter!"

All the blood had drained out of Gino's steroid-flushed face. As the magnitude of his blunder soaked into his thick skull, I was pulling out of the school parking lot in my sister's car. A minute later I heard honking and saw Gino and Pauly chasing after me in Gino's pimped-out purple Camaro.

"Wait! Wait! Roll down your window! Please!" Gino yelled out, beeping his horn and pulling up next to me.

I stopped and rolled down my window, but kept my engine running. "What do you want?"

Gino was stuttering. I couldn't figure out if it was a steroid thing or if he was that scared. "I-I j-j-just wanna apologize. I had n-n-no idea who you w-w-were. I didn't know!"

"Who am I?" I couldn't help torturing him a bit.

"You . . . you're . . . "

"I'm nobody."

"I know you're the daughter of . . . "

I wasn't ever supposed to admit it, of course. Above all, protect the family. But at least I could have a little fun with it. So I said, "You're out of your fucking mind. You don't know what you're saying."

"Just . . . please forgive me, okay? It will never happen again."

Gino was practically begging for his life. I was chuckling on the inside, but I said to him very seriously, "Look, I don't know what you're talking about, but it's forgotten. Leave it alone."

"So you won't—?"

"Just leave it alone." And I drove off, gunning the engine.

AT SOME POINT IN THE WHOLE PAJAMA GAME, the local tabloids began giving Dad funny nicknames like "The Oddfather" or "Daffy Don"—a play on a nickname the same tabloids used for another alleged crime boss, John Gotti. They called him "Dapper Don," and they compared the images of the two: Gotti's expensive suits and flashy jewelry against my father's ratty robe, jammies, and mussed-up hair.

At home, even Gram Crackers became part of Dad's make-believe world. Gram didn't like what my father did for a living and looked down upon it. This is a woman who came from an educated family. She herself wanted to be a pharmacist, like her father back in Italy. But since she was a mother, she protected her son no matter what.

When doctors would come to the dungeon for a visit to see how "crazy" Dad really was, we'd all get prepped. My grand-mother knew what to say in case she was asked any questions. So while she hated doing it, she went the whole nine yards for her son. If we were in the dungeon and Gram thought my father was talking too lucidly or too loudly, for example, she'd shut him up with: "Vincheeennsszzzeee! *Prendi mediciiiina!* Get the medicine!"

That the dungeon might be bugged solved one of the many mysteries of my father's behavior the first 16 years of my life. Dad's signature whisper, his low mumbles, the passing of the notes with his crew—I finally understood the reason why. I also realized that I'd never even seen or heard my father talk on the phone before.

I'd gotten used to oddities like that and, to me, they were normal. Whatever "normal" was, my so-called life up to that point was nowhere near it. And now it was going loop-the-fucking-loop. I had these new suspicions to face about my father—and although it had been many months since I'd found out the truth, I still didn't know how to process everything.

I was well aware of Dad's temper and his flaws, but I also saw his gentle side. This was the man who rubbed my back until I fell asleep, the man who grabbed my mother and hugged and kissed her in the kitchen. This was a man who helped the old and poor people on our street and who prayed the rosary by the religious shrine in his bedroom.

I imagined Saint Rita on my father's wall, and Gram going to church dutifully every morning in her chunky shoes and black widow's dress. I imagined him proposing to my mother in that very church. I thought of the thousands of Hail Marys he must have said in his nearly 60 years on this earth. This was a completely conflicted man, and none of it made sense to me.

So I ended up visiting my secret "informant" several times that year to ask more questions. I wanted to know how my father might have gotten mixed up in this world. Little by little, I pieced it together.

"He was young and interested in boxing, and older people 'in the street' took him under their wing and helped him," Alessandra explained. "But at the same time, they also saw him as a good prospect."

They wanted to groom him, she said, so they offered him good money to start as a driver and work his way up. Apparently it was a common practice in the boxing world then, and some walked away while some did not.

"He wanted to help his family, since they didn't have a lot, and he watched his mother and father work so hard," Alessandra continued. "Times were tough, and they were desperate. So he made a choice. And once he was involved, he couldn't step away."

I wondered if he was tortured by his choice. I wondered if Gram protected him so much because she knew he did it to help the family. As the proverb goes, the road to hell is paved with good intentions. If I was having a hard time dealing with the truth about my father, I wondered if he himself agonized about it every day of his life. It must have taken him a lot of rationalizing and living in denial to convince himself that he was doing the right thing, and he obviously got better and better at it as time went on.

"If a soldier is fighting a war and he kills someone, what makes that killing okay?" I remember my father saying once. "Just because the government or the President says it's right, does that make it moral? We think it does because the government says so. That's organized crime, right there! The government can do whatever they want and get away with it. So how is my organization any different from the government? And what makes any of them right? If they were getting a piece of my business, maybe they'd leave me alone."

My father had a way of convincing himself—and others. When he wanted to, he could take you over to his side with logic, charm, and passion. And when you love someone, you twist your brain up in knots and do somersaults to make yourself believe that person isn't doing something wrong.

I saw the rest of my family do their best to rationalize Dad's actions, but I assumed they'd had a long time to get used to it. It was new to me—and there was a part of me that loved him, and a part of me that really hated him. I kept them separate in my heart, for sorting out later, and almost yearned for the days when I knew nothing. But what was better: to stay ignorant and happy but in a limited way; or to seek the truth, no matter how difficult or scandalous the road may be?

I chose to seek.

THEY SAY THAT WHEN A STUDENT IS READY, the teacher appears. I was more than ready for a different kind of knowledge and truth when I walked into Mr. Kahn's 11th-grade English class. At age 17, even with all my reading-comprehension tutoring with Mrs. Russo, I'd never read a book from cover to cover. My preferred reading up to that point had been the long columns in medical encyclopedias describing illnesses from which I was sure I suffered. That was until Mr. Kahn introduced our class of rambunctious teenagers to the poetic beauty and tragedy of F. Scott Fitzgerald's tale of thwarted love and broken dreams, *The Great Gatsby*.

What did I have in common with rich, white-bread, high-society Long Islanders and their pretty mansions? Nothing. But one day in class, the magic happened. Mr. Kahn talked about the novel with so much passion that he got us all riled up—especially me. He asked us about the characters and what we thought they felt, as well as why we thought they did what they did and what their actions meant. And even though I had nothing in common on the surface with these characters, I sat in the classroom that winter listening to Mr. Kahn explaining their plight and I understood their pain. I related to it, and it made me feel less alone.

For the first time in my life, I couldn't wait to get home to read. It wasn't so much an escape from my world (though it was some of that) as it was a continued exploration into other people and new worlds. I kept a dictionary by my side when I read and looked up every word I didn't understand, so my vocabulary flourished. After Gatsby, I was reading three novels a week—devouring them like I was starving, finding stories that helped me understand other people and, therefore, myself.

At home on the bookshelf in the den, I came across some of my mother's paperbacks by a writer named Marilyn Harris. She wrote a series of books set in 1800s England about the Eden family that spanned generations. Even though I seemingly had even less in common with the Edens than I did Fitzgerald's spoiled, bored Jay Gatsby and Daisy Buchanan, I shared an inner truth this time: two of the characters were gay and ostracized by their friends, family, and community.

In one scene that was seared into my memory forever, a young woman stands in front of the entire town for a brutal whipping because she refuses to live her life their way. As I read that scene,

I felt the sting of every bloody lash inflicted upon her. I was amazed by the power of the printed word, but more than that, that these characters were living their lives honestly despite the consequences. I wanted to do that, too.

My introduction to these bold characters who fought to live true, independent lives set the stage seamlessly for my first girl-friend. I met Angela at a friend's party, and I'll never forget my first image of her: She was wearing an orange halter top and paisley bell bottoms, and when she leaned over, her long hair swung forward to show a tattoo that she had on the back of her neck—a pair of angel wings. Part loner, part rebel, part mother of the earth, this was the kind of girl who didn't give a rat's ass what people thought of her.

Angela was Greek and went to a nearby school, and after the bell rang we'd meet up and hang out in her basement. We'd blare Duran Duran and Madonna and sing and dance for hours, until her mother called us up for dinner—a spread of tzadziki, lamb, and moussaka. There wouldn't be a pasta in sight, and my taste buds were in culture shock. Angela's parents owned a restaurant in Queens, so their fridge was spanakopita-ed to the brink.

Once again, I watched in wonder as a family sat down for supper together every night with a father who not only ate with them, but also talked and listened. I absorbed their tight-knit togetherness like a sponge soaking up water.

Angela and I would talk for hours on the phone each night about everything—school, sports, movies, music—everything but boys. Angela had dated one boy in class the year before, but she never mentioned him. I had no idea if she was straight or gay; I wasn't even thinking like that. I was attracted to her, but more than that I just loved hanging out with her. I figured that we'd be great buddies, and that was as far as it would go.

Yet I felt a subtle shift happen a few months into our friendship —a new flirtatiousness, a deeper sense of intimacy. One night after dinner at my house, we were listening to the Bee Gees, with me sprawled across the floor in the living room and Angela curled up on the couch a few feet away. We were both giddy from an hour of dancing around, and the energy in the 15 feet between us was palpable. I was silent, lying on my back and staring at the ceiling, letting the lyrics of "How Deep Is Your Love?" wash over me.

That's when Angela said softly, almost matter-of-factly, "It's okay if you want to lie on top of me."

It felt like the most natural next step in the world. My mother was upstairs watching television, and I could hear the opening theme song of *Dynasty,* so I knew there was no chance she'd be popping downstairs for at least an hour.

"All right."

I got up and walked over to the couch, then lay down and wrapped my arms around her, putting my head on her chest. She hugged me tightly.

When we looked into each other's eyes and kissed for the first time, it was one of the most intense moments of my life— we shared a deep soul connection, and that made for an electric chemistry together. We got up and slow danced to the rest of the song, humming along to the part about knowing the door to the other person's soul.

After that night, Angela and I became a secret item. In front of our families and friends, we acted appropriately and didn't get touchy-feely. When we were alone, though, we were in love. I allowed it all to happen, pushing away thoughts of what my parents or the Church would think. I don't know if either of our families knew what was going on behind closed doors, but if they did, they pretended not to.

And even if they had known, that wouldn't have stopped me. My mind-set was in fuck-you mode for my family: *Dad is doing all his shit and you tell me what my morals should be? Not gonna happen anymore.* Now I wanted to do what I wanted and experience what I needed, and to hell with them.

ANGELA KNEW WHAT MY FATHER DID FOR A LIVING. I had told her early on because I didn't want any secrets between us. I felt she had a right to know, even though it meant ignoring the family omertà.

And I had a feeling that the time would come where I'd bring her home to meet Dad.

Meeting my father came out of necessity. I was now 17 and giving Mom a hard time about going to the city on weekends, saying that I wanted to stay in Jersey to be with my friends (meaning, my girlfriend). It was unheard of to bring a friend over for Sunday-night dinner at the dungeon, so when I proposed it, it caused quite the uproar. It just wasn't done. But since it was the only way Dad could have his treasured quality time with me, I got the green light.

When Sunday night came, I was nervous. It was weird enough having Angela's lovely, light energy in the dark dungeon, but to then see her and my father in the same field of vision was beyond wild.

"Dad, this is my friend Angela," I introduced her. Mom had made sure Dad was wearing actual clothes for dinner that night: a white shirt, black slacks, and a black Member's Only jacket.

"Nice to meet you, Mr. Gigante," she said, and kissed him on the cheek. I was shitting bricks.

Dad was wary at first because she was Greek. Mom had tried to "warn" him ahead of time to soften the blow a bit that I was bringing someone home who—gasp!—wasn't Italian. My parents were so provincial, it was as if they had no idea there were non-Italians in the world. If they did know, it didn't occur to them that we should mingle. Had Angela been black, forget it. I could hear Dad now: "You bring a 'moulinyan' into my house? Are you nuts?"

Dad was as racist as Archie Bunker, I hate to say, and I'd hear him put down African-American and Latino people, or anyone who was a different religion. It was as if he was afraid of anything different. "They're not our kind," he'd say, "stay away from them. I don't trust them."

Before I was born, Dad and Uncle Ralph had a dog named Bullets who would patrol the three-block radius by Gram's apartment. Bullets loved my father and would sit by his side at the café like he was Dad's sidekick. He was never trained, but Bullets always knew exactly what Dad wanted him to do. He knew, somehow, that Dad didn't like black people and that it was his job to keep them off Sullivan Street.

Really, no black man—or woman, for that matter—could walk that block, and it was a known thing to everybody. If you didn't know it, you found out pretty quickly because in minutes, Bullets would have found you and chased you down. However racist that was, the people in the neighborhood in the early '60s considered Bullets their collective guard dog and didn't mind his politically incorrect methods. But the police minded, and whenever they'd get wind of the dog hounding the minorities, they'd come looking for him. When my mother used to tell me about Bullets, it cracked me up. The cops would go to the café to look for the *dog*, and leave my father and the others alone!

If Dad got word that the police were looking for Bullets, he'd say, "Go, Bullets!" And the dog would tear out of the front door of the café like a criminal on the lam, run down the street and into a neighbor's apartment to hide. Bullets would stick his head out the window and watch the flurry of activity on the street below with the cops. He'd wait there safely, patiently until he heard my father whistle from below that the coast was clear.

Twenty years later, my father still felt uncomfortable with anyone who wasn't exactly like us. But Angela was so endearing that she charmed my noncommunicative, distant father—by the end of the night, she was playfully calling him "Dad" and helping Mom do the dishes. I watched her chitchat with Mom and Gram and laughed to myself. *She's a daughter after their own hearts, unlike me.*

On the phone late into the night, Angela and I wondered what our families and our churches—she was Greek Orthodox—would say if they found out about us. In our eyes, we were a modern-day Romeo and Juliet. (Or, more accurately, Juliet and Juliet.)

"Do you think what we're doing is really a sin?" she'd ask.

"I don't know. The priest says so, but—"

"So does that mean we're going to hell?"

"God is the one Who decides that sort of thing, not priests."

"I don't understand. We love each other."

I didn't understand it, either. But there was one thing I was sure of: That warm spring night when we had our first kiss and slow danced in my mother's living room changed my life. Right or wrong, it sealed my future. It was a moment of truth that felt so right that I knew for sure I'd never be with a man. And once you feel something so powerfully and know it so completely, there is no way to ever go back in time and un-know it.

FOR THE PRESENT, I HAD TO KEEP PRETENDING I was something I was not. And I had to deal with my father pretending he was fucking nuts. Once in a while, Dad would check himself into a mental ward for a few weeks. If he was the consummate actor, then the behavioral-health facility in Harrison, New Jersey, was his Broadway stage.

At first glance, the place was beautiful. Outside, the grounds were huge and lush and the brick building stood majestically in the center. On a warm day, patients sat in small white gazebos outside with their families and bought frozen yogurts from a little café like it was a country club.

Once you got inside, though, it was like a scene out of *One Flew Over the Cuckoo's Nest.* Dad would always have a private room on the third floor, where they put the sickest and most violent patients. As soon as we'd get off the elevator, I'd dread the walk down the ghastly white corridor to get to him. Mom and I would hold on to each other and the goodies we'd brought for Dad— baked chicken cutlets, salad, apple pie, and cookies. We'd do our best to avoid the other patients, but it was like winding our way through a haunted house at the amusement park. Dozens of patients roamed the halls in catatonic, zombie-like states, staring at us with desperate eyes, or they'd be frantic and reach out to grab at us.

After a while, I got to know their faces and even their names. So I knew that the old man shouting "Fuck, fuck . . . fuck you!" was Mr. Johnston. Generally, after such an outburst, an orderly dressed in white would soothingly say, "Now, Mr. Johnston, you leave these nice people alone," and lead him away. I often wondered what was wrong with Mr. Johnston and the other patients

—they obviously were grappling with real mental-health issues, unlike Dad's pseudo ones.

My father's room was tiny and bare. I was always surprised that he never had security at his door and that we could walk in, no problem. There was barely security in the lobby, for that matter. Once we reached his room and shut the door behind us, I'd breathe a sigh of relief—but not for long.

He'd be lying in bed or sitting in a chair waiting for us in his pajamas and robe, and the next ordeal was watching him pretend to be ill in league with the rest of the patients. Dad took the more catatonic, zombie-like approach rather than the climbing-the-walls option. As for me, just the five-minute walk down the hallway would tap me out. I'd pick up on the feelings and pain of all the patients and by the time I got to Dad's room, I'd conk out for an hour.

When the nurses came in with his 4 P.M. meds, they'd hand Dad a little paper cup of pills and a Styrofoam cup of juice to get them down with.

"Thank you," Dad would say to the nurses, who would stand next to him impatiently until he swallowed the colorful array of anti-psychotic, mood-stabilizing, antidepressant drugs. He'd throw his head back and gulp—a tad too dramatically, I thought, but it convinced the nurses. They'd rush out of the room with their medicine cart to continue their rounds, and never checked to see if Dad had actually swallowed them. After they left the room, he'd spit the pills—which he'd hidden under his tongue—out of his mouth and into a Kleenex.

While my matter-of-fact grandmother knew my father was faking it, my mother kept herself in a comfortable state of on-and-off semi-denial. I couldn't tell what she knew or believed. I did know that she loved him despite everything and played along with whatever he wanted her to do. But there was a part of her brain and heart that wanted and needed to believe the best in her husband, that he could never lie, steal, or hurt a soul. Besides, she was Catholic with five kids—where was she gonna go?

"I think he hurt his head when he was a boxer, that's what happened," she'd say on the ride home. "This must be what the doctors see."

Well, if Dad did have anything wrong with him, it sure didn't put a dent in his job. From the third floor of the loony bin, he apparently still managed to get his orders out using go-betweens.

"It doesn't seem to affect his ability to work," I'd tell Mom. But my words, as usual, fell on deaf ears.

I hated the visits to the hospital for so many obvious reasons. But what bothered me the most was seeing actual sick people in anguish and knowing that my father was making a mockery of them. It was enough to make *me* sick—and it did. When we'd get home, I'd pass out and sleep for hours. Maybe, like Mom, I didn't want to deal with the reality and looked for ways not to.

IRONICALLY, WHILE DAD WAS THE ONE IN THE MENTAL HOSPITAL surrounded by people in straitjackets, I was the one who finally went to see a headshrinker.

I had thought about seeing a therapist before, but always pushed the idea out of my mind. How could I trust a stranger? I didn't even trust my own family. How could I trust that the person would keep my secrets? Yet I ultimately had no other choice but to try—as Dad got deeper into his act, I grew more desperate for sanity.

I finally decided to see Dr. Stein, although when I first walked into her office, I had no idea what I was going to say or how she was going to help me. I was committing a big family sin just by being there. How many more sins could one woman commit?

"Just talk about yourself, Rita," my mother pleaded, when I told her that I'd made an appointment with a therapist. I'm sure I was the first in the family to do such an outrageous thing. My father would've been livid had he known.

"You don't have to tell anybody anything about the family," Mom cautioned me. She was afraid for me, for all of us. My father's world frightened her, and rightly so.

"No, Ma, don't worry. I'm going to talk about myself and my anxieties."

It didn't occur to my family that my anxieties were at all linked to them. They all thought it was just me being a weak, overly sensitive kid.

As soon as I sank into the leather couch in Dr. Stein's office and she shut the door behind me, the secrets wanted to spill out. But first, I had to make sure it was safe to pull the plug. I eyed all the degrees framed on her wall and began nervously.

"What I'm about to tell you, you can't tell anyone," I said to her.

"No, no, of course not. What you say in here is strictly between us."

"Are you sure?"

"I'm sure."

"Are you *positive?*"

"Yes."

"What if you had to go into a courtroom and swear to tell the whole truth, would you tell then?"

"No."

"Do you tell your friends or your family what goes on in here?"

"No."

"Do you keep a diary, do you write it down?"

"Well, I do keep notes on my patients . . . "

"Can anyone read them?"

"No."

"Because if anyone knew what I was about to tell you, we'd both be in deep, deep shit."

Dr. Stein was a very prim and proper, no-nonsense woman with pulled-back hair and an honest, straightforward gaze. I didn't scare her one bit. She took my interrogation in stride and explained about doctor-patient confidentiality. She was bound to the same kind of secrecy I'd known my whole life, and once I understood that, I breathed a sigh of relief and was free to speak. I told her I was sick about the life I was leading and that I came to her to talk about my family and the anxiety, depression, frustration, and anger I'd always felt around them.

"Yes, we can do that," she said, nodding. "We can work on releasing your anger."

"I've been sick my entire life, and I think it's from my emotions."

"We can certainly sort that out for you, find the root—"

"And I'm gay," I broke in. "I know this for sure, and I'm tired of pretending I'm not. I'm tired of thinking that I'm going to go to hell. "

That didn't faze her. "Yes, of course. I've had many patients who are gay. You can feel comfortable talking about that with me."

"I don't want to be sick anymore. I don't want to live in fear anymore. I don't want to lie anymore. I don't want to keep secrets anymore."

"I understand."

"I feel trapped. I don't want to play their game anymore. But I don't know how to get out."

My voice trembled a bit, and Dr. Stein handed me a tissue. There was no way I was going to cry, though. I still had to get the words out to tell her the big one, and she could tell it was coming.

"And my father is . . . "

The prim and proper doctor's eyes widened as I revealed the family secrets, but she kept her cool.

"Well," she said, after clearing her throat and giving me a comforting smile, "I see we've got a lot of work to do. We better get started."

WHEN I WALKED OUT OF DR. STEIN'S OFFICE THAT DAY, I felt as though I had a hundred-pound weight lifted from my shoulders. Just the mere fact that I could *speak out loud* about everything to someone was such a relief in itself. After only my first session, I felt hope—hope that I was finally taking a first step on the long road to finding and saving myself.

But not before I had to endure one last humiliation: the high-school prom.

When I told my mother that I had no desire to go, it was like I had slapped her in the face. "Are you kidding? You *have* to go!" she said. "This is something you can't miss!"

The wheels were in motion immediately to find me a date. I couldn't tell her or my sisters that I wanted Angela to be my date, naturally. But once I saw how they were hell-bent on setting me up with a romantic suitor, I took matters into my own hands and arranged to go with a second cousin. At least with relatives, there'd be no funny business, and we could get the whole thing over with without any complications.

First, however, there was the matter of the dress. I'd as soon have gone in my jeans and T-shirt, but my mother said, "I'm going to get a dress made for you."

"Ma, I don't want it!"

"You gotta! You gotta wear a dress to your prom!"

The next week, she insisted on calling up an Italian seamstress she knew who was a friend of Gram's, and the dress was conceived.

"Rita, look . . . here's a picture of the dress I'll ask her to make for you," Mom said excitedly, holding up a page she'd torn from a fashion magazine. It was a photo of a white, frilly mass of fabric. I might as well have put on my damn communion dress. Ah, fongool.

"Isn't it beautiful?!"

My mother was in heaven setting all this up for me, so I let her. I knew it would probably be the last time she'd ever get me to do anything so girly ever again—and maybe the last time she'd get to pretend I was like all the other girls—so I let her have it. She bought swaths of fabric and dragged me to fittings. I stood on top of a wooden crate in a stuffy little room as the Italian seamstress, Anna, folded, pinned, and draped me.

Mom and Anna oohed and ahhed and told me how beautiful I looked. When I spun around and saw myself in the fitting-room mirror, I nearly fell off the crate. I looked like I was going to a costume party as a loaf of Wonder bread.

The day of the prom, I felt like an idiot in the dress and wanted to kill everybody for making me wear it. My date and my friends had already arrived at my house and waited for me in the living room as I descended the stairs, resplendent in my poufy Cinderella dress. I tried hard not to trip, clutching onto the banister for support.

The prom was exactly as I suspected—boring and stupid and a waste of time. The country club was decorated with flowers that looked like they'd flown off my dress and attached themselves to the dance-hall walls. We drank Cokes and made small talk with our friends, but when "Stairway to Heaven" came on over the speakers, my cousin and I sat it out.

WHEN I GOT HOME THAT NIGHT, my mother was waiting up in the kitchen, eager to hear about what a magical evening I had at my prom in my special dress.

"I had a great time, Ma, it was very nice. I'm really tired, though, so I'm going to bed."

I couldn't wait to get that dress she loved off me.

As I stood in front of the mirror, unzipping it and pulling it off my skin, I felt sick about the night I'd just had. It was a night of total forgery, symbolizing everything that was wrong with my life.

I hung up the wilting dress in my closet and looked at it. It was my version of my father's Golden Nugget bathrobe; it was my costume to pretend to be something I wasn't.

The difference between my father and me was, I didn't want to pretend anymore. I closed the closet door. My play was over, and I had put away my costume forever. It was time to tell my parents who I really was.

CHAPTER 9

JUST WHEN YOU THOUGHT YOU WERE OUT

In Italian, the word *gigante* literally means "giant." I've seen it in other languages to mean "a giant, legendary manlike creature of great size and strength."

As I look back, I realize that was my father. To everybody around him—his family, his crew, his enemies, and the FBI guys who tried in vain to catch him—that's what he was becoming. He was the head, the giant, of the "organization."

So when someone like the flashy, hotheaded member of the Gambino family, John Gotti—or anyone else of similar rank—misbehaved, he had my father to answer to.

It was December 1985 and Paul "Big Paul" Castellano, the presumed boss of the Gambino family, was facing life in prison on racketeering charges and had named his bodyguard, Tommy Bilotti, as his new underboss. Castellano, a very well-loved, respected, and admired man in the organization, had information that members of Gotti's crew were involved in drug dealing— a *disgrazia*, a disgrace and a forbidden act of disfavor in the family —and he was intent on disbanding Gotti's crew as a result. That never happened.

Instead, Gotti hatched a daring and defiant plot and enlisted his closest and most trustworthy associates to gun down Castellano and Bilotti in front of Sparks Steak House in midtown Manhattan. Gotti and his fellow crew member Sammy "The Bull" Gravano watched the murder from their car parked up the block and across the avenue. It was reported that they even drove by the scene of the hits immediately following so that they would have firsthand verification of the plot's success. In mob circles, what Gotti did was a travesty of justice. Yet two weeks later, he was reportedly named the new boss of the Gambino crime family.

My father couldn't stand John Gotti; the two men couldn't be more different. While they both embraced the power of their positions, Gotti blatantly broke the rules while my father, it seemed, lived by a certain criminal code of honor.

"If you stick to the rules, you have peace in the families," he used to say.

One scene that was described to me particularly shows the difference between the two men. Since Dad didn't want anything to do with Gotti, they didn't cross paths too often in person. They did come face-to-face at sit-downs, though, where representatives of the five families would get together to discuss business.

On this occasion, Gotti was bubbling over with excitement when he greeted my father. "Hey, guess what? I made my son! He's a 'made man'!"

My father looked at him sadly. "I'm really sorry to hear that," he said. "That's a shame."

Gotti was shocked at Dad's reaction.

To be a "made man" meant that you were sworn in to be a part of the organization—forever. And while my father may have trapped himself, he never wished the same fate upon his children.

"This is my life; it isn't yours," he used to say. "When I die, it ends. Nobody else is going to be involved in this shit. This ends with me."

Yet he knew he had no way out. "Not unless I'm in jail, or in a box," he'd say. "And even in jail, you're not really out."

This may have been the only thing that Gotti and my father saw eye to eye on: that they were in it until death did them part.

I myself didn't pay any attention to the Gotti-Castellano drama playing out in the newspapers and tried to stay as ignorant about it as possible. Looking back now, I see how the terrible wheels of fate were being put in motion. Gotti had allegedly killed a top crime boss without asking permission, and at some point he was going to have to answer for that.

I HAD MY OWN PROBLEMS TO WORRY ABOUT. While Dad was getting more embroiled in his world, I was adrift in mine.

I'd graduated from high school and had no idea what I was going to do with my life. Had someone bothered to ask me, I would have said I wanted to be a dancer. When I put on a record and danced around the living room, it was the only time I felt true freedom. I loved to move to music, something I inherited from my music-loving mother. But following a dream like that was never an option for me. My father didn't approve of his children going into the entertainment business—my sister Ro had once been approached to be a model and he went nuts—so even to imagine it was self-defeating.

Instead, I worked a string of boring, nine-to-five odd jobs, keeping myself busy doing anything I could find: I made sandwiches in a deli, I cleaned fish in a fish market, I was a cashier at the local hardware store. When I got bored and lost interest, which was always too easy for me to do, I moved on to the next one. The jobs were meaningless to me, but I was glad to be busy and making money so that I didn't have to ask my parents for everything for the first time in my life.

More worrisome than my career, which was going nowhere, was my love life, which was going downhill. A few months after prom night, Angela and I broke up. Sneaking around and pretending that we weren't a couple was making both of us crazy. And our phone conversations alone in our respective rooms in the still of the night grew more serious as time went on.

"I don't know if I can do this anymore," she said one night. "I feel such pressure."

I was stretched out in my bed, gazing out at the moon. I had that familiar feeling that I used to have looking out of Mom's window at the weeping willow. Angela was scared, but I was Catholic (albeit a lapsed one)—I had a lot more experience with guilt and fear than she did, so I was used to the anguish of our predicament.

Even though I understood and respected her pain, I knew for myself that organized religion and family could or would no longer stop how I felt or who I was. I wanted to be true to myself and I wanted to feel close to God, but I couldn't figure out how to match those two deep desires with the rules of the Catholic Church. I was slowly coming to the conclusion that perhaps I'd have to give up being an "official" Catholic—I clearly did not fit into their setup.

They did not want me the way I was, but I wasn't sure I wanted them the way they were, either. Some of the rules of the religion made no sense to me and only made me feel bad about myself. I also had a strong feeling that giving up being a traditional Catholic didn't mean there was no God, or that I had to give up on God—not at all. But Angela's truths may have been different from mine. And I knew that we each had to follow our own feelings.

"Okay, we'll end it," I told her, sadly. "Let's be friends then."

For the rest of the night I lay awake, heartbroken. And then out of hurt or maybe out of need, I immediately jumped right into a new romance. Suzanne was like the anti-Angela: tall, long blonde hair, flirty . . . and married with two children. We worked together at my current job-of-the-month, and I was her very first girlfriend—she'd only been with men before me. We dated in secret, while I continued to date young men out in the open. Yes, I wanted to live true to myself. But that didn't mean I was ready for my parents to know about it—one thing at a time.

"Rita, you bring home the most beautiful men," Mom said to me one day. "But then you never keep them!"

I did meet gorgeous guys, and they often fell hard for me. As soon as they wanted to go past kissing, though, I'd put the kibosh on the fake romance. I'd make up some excuse that I was Catholic and not that kind of girl (if they only knew just how much!). I couldn't bear to lead them on, anyway. I felt like too much of a fraud.

My father never really took much notice of whom I was or wasn't dating—until Carlo showed up. I met Carlo at a friend's graduation party that year. He was dark, handsome, street tough, Italian, Catholic, and connected. Sound familiar? But unlike Dad, he could talk up a storm. We dated for a while, and then I gave him the "Let's be friends" talk and we became great buddies. Had I been straight, Carlo would have been the kind of guy my father would have liked me to marry and pop out a zillion kids with. Except for one tiny detail: Carlo worked for Dad's nemesis, John Gotti. I didn't know all the details of his involvement; I only knew that ours was a forbidden friendship.

In the Mafia world, it's not as though the five New York crime families were one big happy bunch that got together at picnics and played softball and drank lemonade. The mob wives and daughters didn't hang out together and go shopping at the mall like you see on current reality-TV shows. It was explicitly understood that you were not supposed to cross family lines in any way except for the men, who had to get together and discuss business once in a while. But the women and kids in the extended families were to be kept separate at all costs.

"It's what you call 'bad business,'" my father used to say.

Besides seeing each other at the occasional sit-down to discuss disputes and work through family problems, Dad had nothing to do with the other crime bosses. Carlo told me that there was no mingling, socializing, or dinner dates. Did Dad like these men? Although he was vocal about his feelings toward Gotti, a question or concern like that wouldn't even cross his mind—they were not his friends, they were business associates. I don't know if my father even had real "friends."

If Dad had to get a message to another family boss, Carlo explained, he'd whisper something to one of his crew—most likely an underboss or a consigliere—and the message would get passed down the food chain until it reached whomever it was supposed to reach. If Dad did want a rare one-on-one meeting with one of them, you can bet no one would know about it—not even the driver of his car. It would have to be clandestine and in the middle of the night at some deserted warehouse or other obscure and unexpected location God knows where. Not that he was afraid he'd be someone's target. The others respected and feared my father and would have known he was untouchable. It was a rule that you never go after another made member's family, and you never, ever, *ever* go after the big boss.

WHEN MY FATHER FOUND OUT THAT CARLO and I were friends, he tried to put a stop to it pronto. Carlo was at John Gotti's hangout in Queens —a dumpy room behind a nondescript storefront—when one of Dad's crew showed up at the door.

"I need to see Carlo," one of the Doms of the day said to whomever answered the knock.

My friend came to the door. "I got a message for you from him," Dom said, pointing to his chin. "He says, 'Stay away from my daughter. You can't be friends and you can't see each other. Nothing.'" Dom turned around and left, without waiting for a reply.

Carlo showed up at my house soon after and told me what happened. We both looked at each other . . . and laughed hysterically. We laughed so hard we doubled over.

"Whatever!" I said, sputtering out the word.

The whole thing was so overdramatic and ludicrous—what movie did my father think we were in? Carlo and I refused to take my father seriously, and our friendship grew even closer. We had a strong bond because we understood each other's worlds. We were like two people who find themselves at a party and discover that they come from the same hometown—we spoke the same language and understood the same unspoken rituals.

Carlo would come to my house for the weekend and sleep over on the couch, and we'd watch reruns of *I Dream of Jeannie* and *M*A*S*H* all day like bums. We'd swim until Mom called us in to dinner, and the three of us would eat and laugh together. Dad never knew because he was never there! And Mom loved Carlo, so she didn't tell my father about our forbidden friendship. I'm sure that secretly she was hoping that Carlo and I would fall in love and have a fairy-tale happy ending. Because in the big picture, me marrying a boy in the mob would *still* have been better than me being gay, I suppose. It was the lesser of two evils to my family— and at least it was a known one.

Anyway, Dad needn't have worried about Carlo and me. It wasn't as though we sat around all day exchanging underworld secrets. Maybe if we *had*, I would have known that Gotti had committed the most unforgivable sin you could in that world. Maybe I would have foreseen that my father would have been slightly distracted, trying to figure out how to exact retribution on Gotti. And that now wasn't the best of times for me to come out of the closet.

But I didn't know any of that. So for me, it was now or never.

It had been ten months since my high-school prom, when I'd hung up that horrid costume at the end of the night and vowed to tell my parents the truth.

I opened up my closet and saw it still hanging where I left it, abandoned. When I looked at it all I saw was a straitjacket, a symbol of the sickness and lies around me. I shut my closet door and marched over to my parents' bedroom. Dad was visiting for the weekend, and I could hear the two of them talking, so it seemed like good timing.

I moved quickly before I had a chance to change my mind. What I was about to do would either kill me or make me stronger —I wasn't sure which, but it was time to find out. My body and soul had taken a beating because I held so many secrets—this one in particular—and I hoped that revealing it would help me get healthy physically and emotionally. I had continued to see Dr. Stein and she had been very helpful, rooting for me to be honest with my parents. It would free me, she had said.

Both of my parents were sitting on the bed when I got to their door. Mom had just finished praying the rosary and was stringing up her white beads on the bedpost. I knocked lightly on the door-frame, and when they looked up, I went in. My palms were so wet, I rubbed them against my jeans and they left soggy handprints.

"Mom, Dad, I have something important to tell you."

They looked at me and waited. I stood there, not knowing what to do next. I could feel the telltale signs of an oncoming panic attack creep up. My legs started shaking, and the anxiety traveled to my stomach, then inched its way to my throat, bring-ing pangs of nausea with it.

Forget it. This is the worst idea in the world. Are you crazy? You can still save yourself! You can leave the room right now and not tell them anything. Run! Run!

"What is it, Ri? You can tell us," my mother said, looking at my shaking body with alarm. "Whatever it is, we won't get upset."

I had practiced the words hundreds of times in my head, and now I was at the plate, bases were loaded, and I was choking at bat.

God, help me.

How ironic that I was praying for help to a God Who I'm told would condemn me. But I felt that God was the only one Who could help me find courage when I was about to go into the ring with my father. I took a deep breath and blurted it out.

"I like women. I'm gay."

Silence.

Stone cold, black-hole, eardrum-shattering silence.

Two seconds after the words flew out of my mouth, I wanted to leap into the air, snatch them with my wet hands, and shove them back down my throat. Because my father's reaction was much worse than I had anticipated. I had fully expected him to flip out and yell and maybe send me to the nunnery that night. That's the reaction I was prepared for. What I didn't expect was to hear a voice come out of my father's mouth that I had never heard before.

He was calm—*too* calm—and sickly, sweetly nice. He sounded like the dad on *Leave It to Beaver* who wore cardigans and smoked a pipe and talked things out logically with Wally and the Beav.

"You're going through a phase," he said, in a soothing tone, but his face was as red as if he were holding back an inferno. "Most kids your age go through this. Don't worry about it."

"Yes, that's right," my mother jumped in. I could see that she was stunned and was going along with whatever Dad was saying, thinking he knew best. I knew what response they needed out of me. If I didn't immediately take back what I said, I was dead.

"Yeah, you're right, it's only a phase," I told them, nodding my head. I felt numb as I went to leave the room.

"Oh, and by the way," Dad called out to me when I got to the door. His voice was still calm but his undertone made me tremble. "You're not allowed to see any of your girlfriends anymore."

And in that moment, I knew I was finished as far as my father was concerned. I knew it would be impossible for me to ever, ever have this conversation with him again and that he would never accept me the way I was. He didn't want to know the truth or he couldn't handle it—or both.

So on that beautiful spring evening, I came out and I jumped right back in.

I went back to my bedroom in a daze and dove under the blankets and pulled my knees up to my chest, wrapping my arms around myself.

As I rocked back and forth in my bed, my numbness opened up to sadness, disappointment, frustration, and rage. I was sad that I would have to continue living a fake life to keep the family peace. I was frustrated and disappointed that my own flesh and blood was so ignorant that they had no understanding and compassion for me and could not see beyond their rigid, closed world. And I was angry with myself for being weak and giving in to them.

I rocked back and forth for hours. *I'm trapped.*

CHAPTER 10

THE FAMILY BUSINESS

I spent the next few weeks in bed, curled up into myself. I couldn't eat, I didn't want to move, and I didn't want to talk to anybody.

All I did was sleep and try to escape my world. I felt like an animal locked in a cage with no hope of ever getting out. My mother brought me meals on a tray, but I wouldn't touch them. I had no will to eat because, at that moment, I had no will to live. What for? I'd rather be dead than live in a world that would not accept the true me. Is this how things were going to be for the rest of my life? Sick and trapped . . . it would never end.

I slid in and out of consciousness, vaguely aware of the shadowy figures of my mother and sisters hovering above me. Their words were fuzzy, like a staticky radio station in need of tuning, but I could make out one of them saying, "If she doesn't eat soon, we'll have to take her to the hospital."

All I could do was stare at the wall.

"Rita, please eat something!" Mom begged me.

Eventually, the panic in her voice made me worry for *her*, so I tried to eat. Solid food made me throw up, so I tried applesauce and that worked. Then I tried some of the baby food that one of my sisters pulled from her diaper bag and fed me with a spoon. That worked, too.

"She's lost so much weight; she's so pale. What in the world is wrong with her?"

"Does anyone know the name of that doctor she's seeing?"

Instead of calling Dr. Stein, Mom and Dad decided to give me some pills on their own. Dad was visiting Jersey after two weeks of this, and the next thing I knew, both my parents were looming above me, handing me pills—Ativan, Valium, and a third anti-anxiety pill that they found in Mom's medicine chest.

"This will relax you, Ri," Mom said.

"You'll be okay, Rita," Dad said.

But I was far from okay. A few hours later, my parents' home-made drug cocktail started to take effect. I sprung up in bed.

I could hear a loud thumping from the stairwell—it was an angry mob running to my room. I yelled, "Mom! People are coming up the stairs to get me!" But as soon as she got to my door, they disappeared. I kept hearing it, over and over, like a loop in a horror film.

"Try to sleep, Ri . . . you'll feel better."

"Don't let them get me, Mom!" My mother lay in bed next to me for the next few hours as my hallucinations continued until I fell asleep.

The next day, I sank my skeletal frame into Dr. Stein's soft couch. I had barely eaten in two weeks and was down to 98 pounds.

"What happened, Rita?"

"I tried to tell them. But it's no use. They can't accept me. I'm tired. I'm so weary."

"What does it matter what everyone else thinks?"

"Why can't they understand? I need them to love me even if I'm gay."

"You're an adult. You've got to live your life the way you need to live it. It doesn't matter if they don't understand. You don't need anyone's approval to follow what is true in your heart."

"They're worried for me. They think I'm going to burn in hell."

"You can't live life for them," she pointed out. "Listen to your own feelings, Rita. Your feelings are valid."

After my appointment, I felt a surge of hunger—I was suddenly starving. It had something to do with what Dr. Stein had said, and a feeling of surrender.

In Catholicism, they say that when you are in pain or have troubles, you can "give it to Jesus" and let him deal with it and make it right. Talking to Dr. Stein sometimes felt a little like being in the confessional at church—or, at least, how I imagined it felt when the system worked as it was supposed to and the bad feelings inside you were gone with a few Hail Marys. I left her office that day with a big weight lifted off my shoulders and walked into the bright sunlight toward my car.

My feelings are valid. Wow.

I knew exactly where I needed to go to celebrate this revelation. I craved salt, sugar, and grease desperately, so I steered my white Oldsmobile Calais with the blue ragtop roof—a graduation present from my parents—to the nearest McDonald's drive-through. I ordered two large fries and a vanilla milkshake, pulled into the parking lot, and downed it all in two minutes. Then I drove in a little circle back to the drive-through window and ordered more of the same. This time, I dipped the salty fries into the shake and stuffed them into my mouth, ecstatic as my throat opened up to greet them. An hour later, I sat at Mom's dinner table, and she fed me the works. An hour after that, I was sitting on the toilet bent over with a case of the runs so bad, my ass was on fire.

I didn't care. I was hungry and wanted to eat, and that meant I wanted to live.

A MONTH AFTER I DROPPED THE "YEP, I'M GAY" BOMB in my parents' laps, my father allegedly dropped a real bomb in John Gotti's. Or so he tried.

On April 13, 1986, a bomb exploded in Gambino underboss Frank DeCicco's car, killing him instantly. It was front-page news, and the word was that the bomb was meant for John Gotti. For whatever reason, Gotti had canceled going to a meeting with DeCicco that day, and that had saved his life.

As always, I had no idea what was going on. I heard rumors that Dad was involved somehow, that he may have ordered the hit to avenge the unapproved Castellano murder. My family was shocked and appalled by the accusation.

"Don't they know he's sick?" I'd hear my mother say. "Are they kidding?"

If my father was involved, no one in the family was saying it— not to the public, not to other family members, definitely not to me, and maybe not even to themselves. First, everyone was being extra careful about being bugged at Gram's and maybe even in Jersey, so anything you didn't want the cops to hear, you didn't say. Second, even though it still may have been conjecture as to what my father was up to, it was still hard to swallow. So when possible, we turned our heads and didn't look at it.

Even in therapy, in that safe little room with Dr. Stein far away from everybody, I couldn't admit out loud to her the darkest thing I thought about my father. Part of me still wanted to protect the family. Another part of me just couldn't say the words about my own flesh and blood.

"Do you know if your father was ever involved in the killing of anyone?"

"I have no idea."

"But do you feel like he has? Does that worry or upset you?"

I paused. "I have no idea."

At the time of Gotti's botched murder attempt, I was still recovering from my own botched coming-out attempt and its emotional and physical aftermath. The "Teflon Don" may have been lucky enough to have missed the bomb meant for him, but my life had exploded.

I continued to fortify myself with visits to Mickey D's and to Dr. Stein's office (which were conveniently located a two-minute drive from each other), as the tabloids trumpeted my father's alleged involvement with the bombing attempt, and the family name was splashed across the newspaper headlines. I was doing temp work in an office at the time and had tried to keep a low profile because of the newspapers, but people were starting to link me with the Gigante on the front page. Soon enough, a co-worker I had become friends with pulled me aside and told me that Helen, the mousy, bug-eyed, no-lipped office busybody, was telling everyone at work that my father was "a cold-blooded killer."

Three years after the Tina incident, I now knew the truth about Dad. But that didn't mean I was now fine with other people talking about it. The protective gene, never too far from the surface, kicked in and I followed Helen into the stairwell that afternoon.

"Excuse me!" I called out to her. She was a few stairs below me and froze.

"I hear you're talking nonsense about my family." My voice echoed against the whitewashed cavern.

Helen stared at me for a few seconds. "Well, it's true, isn't it?" she shot back. "That's who you are!"

"I think you need to mind your own fucking business. How *dare* you," I said, starting to move toward her, step by step. "I'd appreciate it if you kept your fucking mouth shut."

She slowly backed away, frightened, and I backed down. This time, I remembered my lesson from Mrs. Gold and kept my hands in my pockets. But as Helen scurried away, I yelled one more warning: "And get your stories straight before you talk about people!"

Yet how did I expect other people to get their stories straight if I didn't even have my own straight? I had no idea if Dad was involved with the Gotti incident or not.

After a session with Dr. Stein, which I chased with two large fries, I needed more answers. This time I went to Carlo. He was the first person inside that world whom I could trust to give me some information and tell me the truth. We trusted each other.

He was coming over for the weekend, and I knew I'd have a chance to ask him then. As soon as he arrived, I pulled him into a room out of earshot of my mother and asked him point blank. We were close enough friends that I could do that.

"Carlo," I asked, "did my father have anything to do with this Gotti situation?"

He looked me straight in the eye and didn't hesitate. "Yes."

I'm sure I looked horrified.

"But Gotti broke the rules, and now he has to pay with his life. That's how it goes."

"My father has that kind of power?"

"Of course he does."

"He's . . . *capable* of it?"

"He's the boss. He has to be."

I was still taken aback by the idea that my father would be such a force in that world, and that a few muffled orders from him while playing cards at the café could mean someone's life. It was an unforgiving world he lived in, with no space for confession, penance, or redemption.

Yet it wasn't the first time a hit hadn't worked out for Dad, from what I've heard. In the early days, when he was trying to move up in the organization, he wanted to show his loyalty to then crime boss Vito Genovese by completing an important job. Vito had helped my dad get a boxing license in 1944 when Dad was 16 years old, too young to fight legally in New York. Dad had become Vito's driver after that and little by little, moved up in the ranks.

In 1957, ten years before I was born, Vito allegedly asked my father to do a hit on fellow mobster Frank Costello. In Costello's Manhattan apartment lobby, it was reputed that Dad pulled out a .38-caliber handgun, but made one fatal mistake.

"This is for you, Frank!" he reportedly yelled out, before pulling the trigger.

Who knows why Dad might have done that. Maybe it was a sign of bravado. Maybe he was nervous. Maybe he just didn't want to kill a guy. Either way, this taunt made Costello turn his head, and that saved his life. Costello staggered to the ground, bleeding, but the gunshot only grazed his fedora, giving him a superficial wound across the skull.

So Gotti was the second alleged murder attempt Dad had failed at and Costello was the first. But Dad didn't seem too concerned that first time. Entering court for his trial for attempted murder, a reporter asked him if he gave himself up because he was afraid.

"Nah, are you kiddin'?" Dad answered, scoffing.

Seems Dad didn't have anything to worry about. In court, according to newspaper reports, Costello wouldn't identify his attempted assassin.

"Tell us the truth—who shot you?" he was asked on the stand.

"I'll ask you who shot me," Costello replied. "I don't know. I saw no one at all."

Dad was found not guilty, and when the trial was over he reportedly walked up to Costello in the courtroom, stuck his hand out to Frank, and said, "thanks, Frank." And Frank shook my father's hand.

But two years later, Dad was convicted of heroin trafficking with Vito Genovese and was sentenced to seven years in jail, getting paroled in five. That's when my brothers and sisters thought he was in the Army.

Now I asked Carlo, "Is he going to try to kill Gotti again?"

"No, he's not going to try that again," he assured me. "The FBI is on his back, so he can't."

WHILE THE FBI WAS SUPPOSEDLY WATCHING DAD, he was definitely watching me. The feds were trying to catch him red-handed, and he was trying to catch me. As far as I was concerned, he was to be feared way more than the law.

Ever since that day of my non-coming-out party in my parents' bedroom, I had to sneak around even more when I dated.

But Dad was suspicious, and started adding new dialogue to our age-old script together.

"So, what friends are you seeing?" he'd ask, as soon as I'd arrive at Gram's for a weekend visit. And each time, I lied straight to his face. I saw no other way. He couldn't handle the truth, and I wasn't going to stop, so what else was I going to do? He'd pump me for information and ask the same questions over and over again, trying to make me slip up. I had to have my stories meticulously straight in my mind.

"Where'd you go? What'd you do? What time?" He was an interrogator by nature, my father. And he did the same with my sisters. "Who's Rita seeing? Did you meet them? Did she bring a girl home? Is she dating any boys?"

By summer, I had broken up with Suzanne and was now secretly dating Tracy. She was calm, genuine, and compassionate. Like Suzanne, she wasn't gay before I met her. In most of my experiences I was to have with women, only one would end up being actually gay from the start, which is funny to me. But I was the kind of person where so-called gender didn't matter, just the love you felt. I didn't put labels on people that way—gay or straight, good or bad.

What did worry me was that Tracy was the second married woman I was having a relationship with. Even though I was gay and going to hell, I still had my morals. I knew you weren't supposed to be with someone who was married; it wasn't ethical.

Keeping my relationships with Suzanne and Tracy on the down low proved even trickier than what I'd gone through with Angela. Not only were we all covering up the fact that we were gay (temporarily gay, in their cases), but they had to keep the affairs from their husbands. We couldn't go to my home or theirs, so we'd meet where we could. If an opportunity arose where I had the house to myself, which was rare, we'd leap at the chance to hang out there.

That summer of 1986, when I was 19 years old, Mom went into the hospital for a hysterectomy. Since she'd be there to recuperate for a few days, I invited Tracy to come over one night to watch movies. It was heaven to be by ourselves, hanging out in a safe, private place with nothing and no one to worry about. We were flipping the channels on TV and about to make popcorn when the phone rang.

It was Roseanne. "Tell your friend to leave," she ordered. "We're coming over to talk to you."

The "we" in question was Ro; my brother Sal; and his wife, Janet. I found out later that Sal called up Roseanne because he needed to pick up something from Mom's house and wanted to get a set of keys from Ro.

"Rita's home," she told him. "You don't need keys."

"Is she alone?"

"I don't know. I think she might have a friend over."

That put Sal over the edge. He immediately had thoughts of his sister performing God only knows what sinful acts with another woman, so he raced over to Ro's with Janet in tow.

Once they arrived, Roseanne and her husband, Jimmy, tried to calm Sal down—but he was enraged beyond reason.

Ro had only a minute to telephone and warn me before they left.

"Shit, you better get outta here," I told Tracy. "Trouble is on the way."

Within five minutes, Tracy was screeching out of the driveway as Sal, Janet, and Ro were furiously pulling in. A minute later, the three of them bounded into the kitchen and stood there, staring at me in disgust.

"What the fuck did I do now?" I asked.

"What are you doing in Mom's house," Sal asked, seething, "with *that woman*?"

Uh-oh.

"Nothing! We were watching a movie."

Sal looked like an animal ready to pounce. He could get angry just like our father. "How could you disrespect Mom and her home?"

Roseanne was standing next to Sal, getting nervous watching him. Janet was in the corner, quiet. Yet after a few more reprimands from Sal, I'd had enough.

"Are you finished?" I asked him, "because *I* am."

I went to the kitchen door to leave, but my sister jumped up and pushed the door closed. "You're not going anywhere," she said.

I looked at all three of them—Roseanne blocking my way, Janet in the corner, and Sal puffed up and maniacal with his crazy eyes. What I said next just popped out.

"This. Family. Sucks!"

Everything happened fast after that, but I remember it in slow motion.

Whoooosh! The back of my brother's hand slammed against my neck and the force of his hit lifted me midair for a second, then I dropped to the floor in a crumpled, stunned heap, hitting my head on the kitchen table on the way down. He grabbed my shirt to drag me across the floor and ripped it. Holding my head up off the floor in front of him with one hand, he cocked the other fist back to punch me in the face.

I was bruised and bleeding and limp like a battered rag doll. Sal was yelling at me, frothing at the mouth, but I had no idea what he was saying. Then, for a split second, my brother and I made eye contact.

Holy shit, I'm gonna die now, I thought. *Here we go.*

"Please don't kill me, Sal! I'm sorry . . . please, please . . . " I begged him, as my bowels exploded into my pants. I was scared shitless. Literally.

"Sal, stop it! Get off of her!" Roseanne was screaming. Janet was in the corner mumbling something, who knows what. Ro jumped on top of me to shield me from Sal's oncoming blow. He tried to get at me but our sister was protecting me, so he turned and punched the kitchen door, smashing a hole straight through it.

After that, everything was silent.

I was numb, like I was out of my body. Ro tried to help me up.

"I need to change and take a shower," I mumbled. My body trembled uncontrollably as I crawled on my hands and knees up

My great-grandpa Pasquale, Gram Crackers's father, in Santa Lucia, Naples. He committed suicide using poison after threats by the Black Hand.

Grandma Yolanda and Grandma Rose at my parents' wedding in 1950. They lived one block from each other their entire lives.

My parents feeding each other cake at their engagement party not long after Dad proposed during Sunday Mass in church.

Mom and Dad having their first wedding dance—one of the few times Dad ever danced in public.

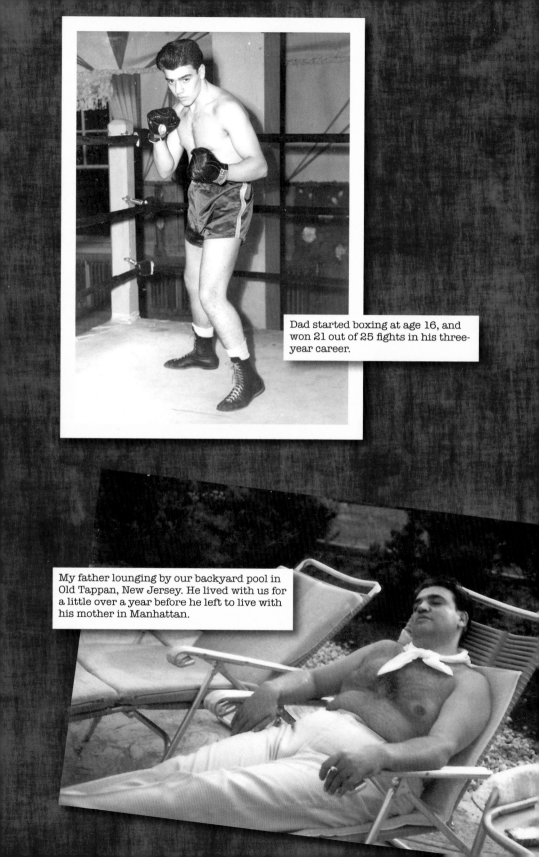

Dad started boxing at age 16, and won 21 out of 25 fights in his three-year career.

My father lounging by our backyard pool in Old Tappan, New Jersey. He lived with us for a little over a year before he left to live with his mother in Manhattan.

Mom and Dad at a family function; they were always a beautiful, striking couple together.

Dad holding me at my first birthday party in Jersey. He left home a few months later.

At age two, horsing around with our dog Spike.

Here I am in kindergarten, where I spent most days crying and wanting to go home. The official anxiety attacks began soon after.

Having fun by the backyard pool with Spike. Mom and Gram fed me too well—I was a chubby kid.

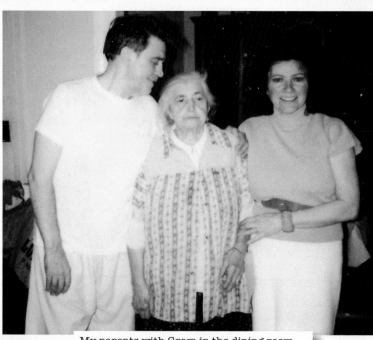

My parents with Gram in the dining room of the dungeon. Gram called Dad "Chinzee" as a kid, which inspired his later street nickname, Chin.

Mom, Gram Crackers, and Dad in his infamous black robe at their apartment on LaGuardia. Dad went on house arrest soon after this photo was taken.

My gorgeous mother with her siblings: From bottom left—Aunt Chubby, Uncle Emmie, and Mom; from top left—Aunt Sally, Aunt Josie, and Aunt Carmella.

My favorite uncle, Pat, on one of his travels. He was gay, but the family rarely talked about it.

Sweet and innocent-looking at my first communion, three years before my bully phase when I beat up Josh Gold.

My school photo around age 12, with my Farrah Fawcett-Majors hair—this was around the time I met her.

Getting confirmed at age 14, but I had already begun questioning the teachings of the Church by then.

Dad didn't come to my confirmation in Jersey, but we all celebrated at Joe's Restaurant afterward in the city.

The only day at my Catholic school where I felt like myself—the day the students switched clothes and I donned the boys' uniform.

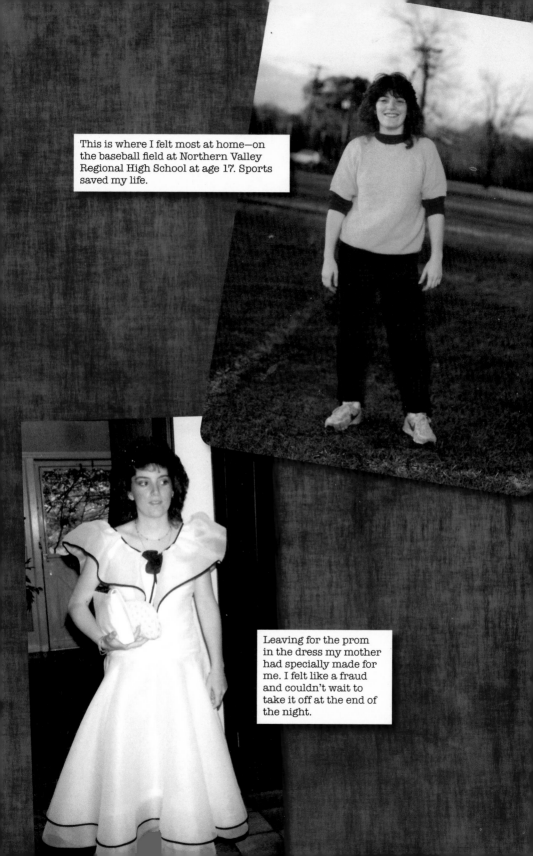

This is where I felt most at home—on the baseball field at Northern Valley Regional High School at age 17. Sports saved my life.

Leaving for the prom in the dress my mother had specially made for me. I felt like a fraud and couldn't wait to take it off at the end of the night.

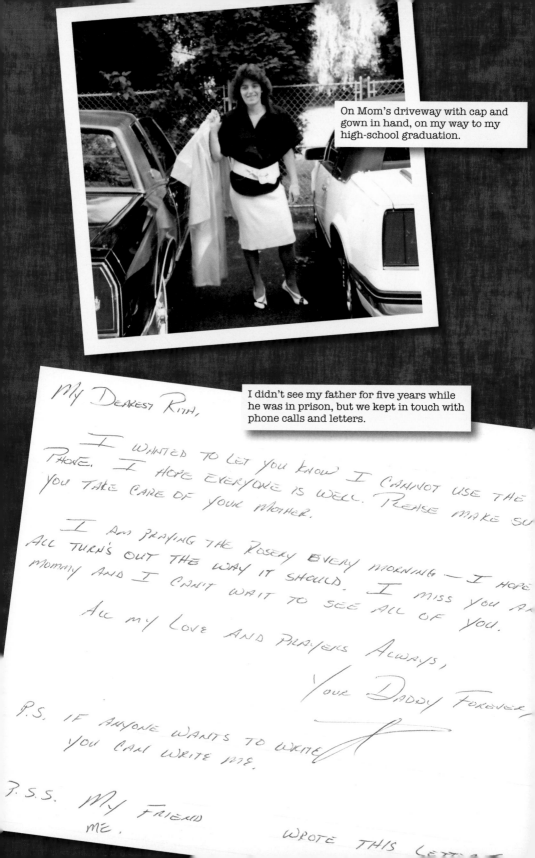

On Mom's driveway with cap and gown in hand, on my way to my high-school graduation.

I didn't see my father for five years while he was in prison, but we kept in touch with phone calls and letters.

My Dearest Ruth,

I wanted to let you know I cannot use the phone. I hope everyone is well. Please make su you take care of your mother.

I am praying the rosery every morning — I hope all turn's out the way it should. I miss you an mommy and I can't wait to see all of you.

All my love and prayers always,

Your Daddy Forever,

P.S. If anyone wants to write me you can write me.

P.S.S. My friend wrote this lette me.

Here I am in my early 30s with Mom—
and my new liberating haircut, symbolic
of my life out of the closet.

Standing in front of Dad's old,
boarded-up café. It was empty for
years until 2011, when someone
bought it and turned it into an
organic tea shop.

© Andrew K. Stauffer, akstauffer.com

Saying a prayer with the Collective Healing Network before we perform a group healing. From left, Debbie Abatta, Barbara Antanies, Bobbie Sterchele, me, Dr. Jennifer Mattiello Egan, Peggy Tierney, and RoseMarie Cappiello (who communicated with Dad within hours of his passing).

On vacation in 2010 on the Jersey shore with Bobbie and her son, Joe.

Me and Mom at my niece's wedding in October 2011. Mom is my biggest supporter today in my work and in my personal life.

With the love of my life, Bobbie, at our fifth anniversary dinner in March 2012—the night I proposed.

the stairs to the bathroom. I took a shower and got dressed, throwing my jeans and underwear into the trash. I couldn't speak. The only way to survive what had just happened to me was to cut off all senses and emotions.

Someone decided we needed to go to Yolanda's house, so I silently and obediently got in Sal's car. No one said a word until we got onto Yo's street, and that's when Sal, now calm, blurted out a question: "Why are you interested in women?"

"Why are *you* interested in women?"

He thought about it for a second. "I like their long hair and their nails," he said. "I like their legs . . . "

"Yeah? Me, too."

Yo opened her front door and found the four of us standing on her welcome mat, looking lost. Then she took one look at my neck—Sal had left a five-finger imprint on me from that backhanded slap.

"What the fuck happened?!" she yelled. Thank God for Yo. She was my second mother, and I was her first baby.

She ushered us into her kitchen as Sal and Ro tried to explain, and that's when Janet finally decided to chime in. "That's nothing," she said, smugly. "She's lucky she didn't get worse."

Yolanda threw her a look: *Don't even go there.* Yo could also give Dad's famous look. It was a good talent to have.

She examined my head and neck, and her hands were comforting. She looked into my sad eyes, and I thought I was going to dissolve into a puddle of tears. I'm sure Yo would have been crying, too, except she was too busy yelling at the others like a mother lion defending her young.

"What the fuck business is it of yours who she spends time with and what she does?!" she yelled at Sal. "Look at this, you hit her head bad. She might have a concussion! We've got to take her to the hospital."

"But how are we gonna explain it to the doctor?" Roseanne asked.

We ultimately decided that we wouldn't go to the hospital, but Yolanda wasn't going to let Sal get off so easy. "You are going to tell Dad what you did," she told him, with the authority of the eldest child.

Sal shuffled his feet.

"If you don't tell him, *I* will."

"But she shouldn't have been . . . "

"Take your insanity elsewhere," she cut him off. "She's not the crazy one here."

FOR THE REST OF THE NIGHT, I WAS IN A FOG. Yolanda drove me home and helped me into bed, and I telephoned Tracy to explain what had happened. I called in sick at work for the next couple of days to let my bruises and swelling go down and my head stop pounding.

Mom came home from the hospital a few days later, time enough for the black and purple bruises on my neck to fade a little. We had all decided we weren't going to tell her what had gone down so that she wouldn't worry during her own recovery from surgery. But there were some things I couldn't hide or repair. One was the big hole in the kitchen door. The other was the damage left inside of my heart.

The next week, I sat at the kitchen with Mom, Yo, and Ro staring at that gaping, angry hole in the door. Mom had asked us about it, and my sisters and I were trying to come up with a plausible story. As they mumbled excuses, I felt a hot surge inside of me, like a volcano wanting to erupt.

"Roseanne," I said to her, grabbing her by the wrist. "Open the front door . . . quickly!"

She jumped from her seat, startled, as I ran to the now-open front door and tore out of the house.

I ran across our front yard, down the street, and as far and fast as my bare feet would take me. I wanted to run however long and however far it would take for me to get away from that house, from this family.

CHAPTER 11

KILL, PRAY, LOVE

My grandmother had a little table in her dining room on which she'd placed a figurine of the Blessed Mother and surrounded it with bottles of holy water. This is where Gram would pray her rosary every morning.

Dad, of course, did his praying in his bedroom. I'd see him do it sometimes, when he'd left his door open a little. Was he praying for forgiveness? Was he praying to not get caught? Was he praying that God would help him change his ways and be a better man?

Sometimes when I caught sight of him, his face seemed so unlike the man I knew. His eyes were shut and his brow was furrowed. As he mouthed the holy words I could see a desperate struggle churning inside of him, just as it did inside of me. Before I was born, Dad used to regularly pray the rosary with Mom and my brothers and sisters. Because his eyes were shut, he never saw my brothers and sisters making fun of him when he'd make the same mistake every time:

"Hail Mary, full of grace, the Lord is with thee; blessed art thou *ammungissst . . .*"

At Gram's, Dad and I were both surrounded by dozens of reminders to give up our respective sinful ways—organized crime and disordered lust—and repent. Wherever you looked, rosary beads dangled from bedposts or were strewn across tables. The holy water was always within reach in case you had a need to dip your finger in and cross yourself. Depending on what time of year it was, Gram's pocketbook and drawers might be stuffed with plastic medallions with pictures of saints engraved on them, or palm leaves if it was Easter time. The dungeon often took on the atmosphere of a mini-chapel . . . yet another of the many confusing contradictions in my world.

AFTER SAL BACKHANDED ME IN THE KITCHEN, Yolanda made him confess to Dad what he had done. He went over to see Dad the next day and told him the story—well, half the story. "I slapped her," he told Dad, "because she said our family 'sucked.'"

Sal never mentioned Tracy. I wonder if he felt a bit guilty about what he had done, and worried Dad would do a lot worse to me had he known.

"Then you did right," Dad said. "She deserved it."

As I've said, Dad followed an old-fashioned code of ethics that was fair and just according to his world—much like the character Marlon Brando played in *The Godfather.*

For the record, my father was mildly amused by that movie. (He really preferred *The Good, the Bad, and the Ugly* with Clint Eastwood.) But he was a fan of Brando—he'd often been compared to him in looks, especially after *On the Waterfront* came out. When he saw the scene in *The Godfather* when the movie producer discovers a bloody horse's head in his bed, Dad pointed to the TV.

"I remember when that actually happened!" he told a family member. He never said to whom it happened or any more details, but just knowing that severed racehorse heads appeared in the world of my father was detailed and troubling enough.

Dad's emotions were immune to that ruthless world, but I guess Sal's were not. Within days after knocking me around the kitchen, he telephoned and then showed up at the house to apologize. "Rita, please, forgive me," he said, over and over, as he stood in the hallway at Mom's house, unsure of what else to say or how to explain his actions. "You don't know how sorry I am. And I didn't know how right you were. This family does suck."

His speech was heartfelt and I could see remorse in his eyes, but I still didn't trust him. Yet I could hear myself say, "Yes, I forgive you, Sal." The words were there, but my body and heart didn't believe them. I wanted to, but I wasn't ready. Still, I wanted to relieve Sal from his own anguish about what he'd done.

I never told my therapist about the Sal incident or anyone else for that matter, for the same reason I never went to a doctor to get my head, neck, or ribs checked. I didn't want to get my brother into trouble. But a few weeks after the incident, I did finally tell my mother. We were in her room folding clothes and she noticed the fading bruises on my neck.

"Ri, what happened to you here?" she asked, pointing to the pale purple marks.

I burst into tears and told her about that night, repeating what Dad had said to Sal afterward: "She deserved it." Mom sat down on the bed and shook her head, both angry and sad. But like the crossing-guard incident, I don't think she ever said anything to Sal or my father about it. At least now I understood why not—she felt powerless.

After my failed coming out to Mom and Dad when I was 19, I hoped that they had forgotten about it. But word of my "I like women" speech had reached my siblings quickly, and they took it seriously. My sisters told me they had suspected all along.

"When you went to the prom, you looked so outta place in that dress. Like a fish out of water," Ro told me. We were discussing my "I like women" predicament and what I should do about it.

"Why don't you get married to appease Mom and Dad," Yo suggested, "and you can live the life you want on the side, in secret? That way, you will keep peace in the family."

Wasn't that what I'd already been doing? Dating men as my cover, and dating women in secret? Before that, I had tried to convince myself that my true feelings were bad and wrong, and I tried to shove them down and pretend they didn't exist. But all that had done was make me sick, physically and emotionally.

"It still wouldn't be living the truth," I told them, sadly. "And besides, I couldn't do that to someone else. My morals aren't like that. I couldn't say to a guy, 'Hey, I'm gay . . . but I need to get married for the sake of my family and to keep up appearances in the community and to fool God. But it's not what I really want. I'm going to live the life I really want in secret.' That wouldn't be fair. And what man would agree to that?"

Ro and Yo shook their heads. They didn't know what the right answer was for me, and neither did I. At least now I could talk openly about it with my sisters—that was some relief. My head was still down low, but I was slowly crawling out of hiding.

MY ROMANCE WITH TRACY HAD FIZZLED, and I was now dating Debbie. I met her when I joined a local softball team. Like Suzanne and Tracy, she was also married and straight. How could I resist?

Dr. Stein had her reasons why not. "You're playing it safe, Rita. By dating married women, you don't have to commit to anything. You don't have to put anything out into the open. You're able to keep hiding your true self. What are you so afraid of?"

"Everything, Dr. Stein. Losing my identity, hurting my family, going to hell. You know, the usual."

I tried to funnel my post-Sal, post-coming-out frustration into my part-time job-of-the month, shucking oysters and cleaning shrimp at a fish shop. Three times a week for eight hours a day, I'd dunk my hands into icy buckets of water, scoop up handfuls of fish, and drop them on the cutting board in front of me. Armed with a white smock and heavy chef's knife, I'd rip off the translucent shrimp shells and snap off their tails, then pry open the oysters and clean out the crap. The methodical nature of the work somehow soothed me. But as I did with all my odd jobs, I got tired of that one, too.

On one of my weekends at the dungeon soon after, I complained to Mom that I was tired of my these jobs and was ready for work that was more fulfilling. Dad was sitting a few feet away and, surprisingly, joined the conversation.

"Rita, I have a friend who's in the balloon business. How would you like to learn that kind of work?"

That was the most I had heard out of Dad in months. And for him to offer to help me in some sort of career, that was big.

"What would I have to do?"

"There's a banquet hall in the Bronx, and my friend Carmine will hire you to take care of all their parties. It would be good for you."

"Yeah, sure, Dad. I'd like to try that."

The next week, I hung up my fish apron for good and started apprenticing with my dad's friend. In the months that followed, I threw myself into the balloon trade—learning the best place to buy them, where to find the cheapest helium tanks, how to twist the balloons into funny little shapes for kids' parties and wedding arrangements. I was enjoying myself, and for the first time, I was proud of myself for following through on a serious, full-time job.

I found a used van and made a sign with a snappy moniker— Ballooney Tunes Entertainment, an ode to my love of cartoons and all the years I'd spent eating my lunch in front of the TV with Bugs as my best friend.

My father's attention, minimal as it was, gave me a glimmer of hope for our father-daughter relationship. We were very alike, but I don't know if he saw it. When I looked at his carefully placed menagerie of icons next to his bed, I could see myself painstakingly choosing what I had to wear or eat or how many times I had to walk through a doorway to feel "right." I had inherited his obsessive-compulsive gene and was still battling it at the age of 22. Dad was still battling it in his early 60s.

Every night before he went to sleep and every morning before he got out of bed, Dad checked that his religious icons were carefully positioned on the nightstand. If he ever saw that anything had shifted out of place during the night, he'd panic. And if he ever thought someone had accidentally—or worse, on purpose—moved them, he'd go ballistic. My sisters and I were the ones who got blamed if something was knocked out of place because we were the only ones except for Mom and Gram who were ever in his room.

Dad was so nervous about strangers coming into the apartment and planting bugs or eavesdropping on conversations that he wouldn't allow a cleaning lady to come in. Besides, it was our duty as daughters to do the domestic chores that needed to be done. What else were daughters for?

Once a week, my sisters and I would go over to Gram's and vacuum, dust, and scrub the apartment. When we were done, Dad would pull out cash from his pocket and hand over a few twenties to each of us, always giving Yolanda the most. Ro got less than Yo, and I got less than Ro. Why? I have no idea. Gram would watch him and pull me aside later and slip me an extra $10.

"Shhh, don't say anything!"

"Thanks, Gram!"

She'd always slip Roseanne an extra $20 and tell her the same thing.

I'd usually be the one in charge of dusting Dad's bedroom, and that included my namesake, Saint Rita, on the wall and Dad's beloved icons by his bedside. Even though I knew how he felt about them, I couldn't resist messing with them—and him. So I'd move the icon of Jesus to the right, then move the holy water to the left a few inches. Sometimes I'd hide a medallion in a drawer for added dramatic effect. Later, my sisters and I would be hanging out in the kitchen, and we'd hear Dad roar from the bedroom.

"Who moved my shit?!"

"Whaaat?" I'd yell out back to him, trying not to laugh. Roseanne would shoot me a pissed off look, as in: *Don't tell me . . .*

Dad would only swear when he was really, really angry—otherwise, he never did it in front of family or women. It was one of the qualities Mom adored about him when they first fell in love. Well, this was one of those times when he swore.

"What is it, Dad?" I'd call out. "What's wrong?"

He'd show up in the kitchen, fuming. "All my stuff on the table, all my religious stuff. Who moved them?"

"Roseanne did it," I deadpanned.

"What? I did not!"

"Roseanne, did you move my shit?!" Roseanne was usually the one he accused when something was wrong.

"I didn't touch anything!" Ro would say, exasperated.

"Well it wasn't *me*," I'd say.

Dad would spend a few minutes interrogating us until I burst out laughing.

"*Cosa succede?*" Gram would ask, rushing to the kitchen to see what the fuss was all about.

"Go fix it," Dad would order me.

Honestly, I think I'd tease Dad in this way to connect with him. When I'd return to the kitchen, I had to deal with Roseanne.

"I'm going to fucking kill you," she'd say, but she'd also be laughing.

"If we can't laugh," I'd tell her, "we're gonna have to hang ourselves in here."

I WAS ALWAYS YEARNING TO MAKE DAD LAUGH, to get some sort of human reaction out of him. Sometimes if I could see he was in a good mood, I'd pop an Elvis cassette in the tape player and start dancing around the living room.

"How about a little bit of the King, huh? C'mon, Dad! Let's see you move!"

Dad would smile, then get up from his chair and start moving around in his boxer shorts to "Jailhouse Rock." He wouldn't dance, exactly. Even with his impressive boxing past, the man was stiff and had no rhythm, so he'd shrug his shoulders and sway from side to side. He was such an awful dancer that when he and Mom used to go to the Copacabana when they were young, he'd tell his buddies to dance with her.

Once Dad was up, shrugging his shoulders to Elvis, Mom would join in and the two of them would cut a rug.

"Look at him go!" I'd yell out, egging him on.

Dad would sing along, too, barely carrying a tune or even knowing the lyrics. It was awesome to see him enjoying himself, and I think he even surprised himself. After a few songs, though, he'd sit down and motion for me to turn off the music. In those few moments, he was so "normal" I treasured it. But I don't think he was very comfortable being that way.

Dad was funny, but without meaning to be. When I was 19, he had surgery to get a pacemaker put in his chest, and his fear surrounding the pacemaker and what evil it could do to him was an endless supply of laughs for us. For instance, the doctor had told him not to go near the microwave or else it would mess up his heartbeat. Dad was afraid that meant he'd get a heart attack— so he'd stand in the kitchen in his underwear, put a dish of food in the microwave, press the START button, and then spin around like the Tasmanian Devil and tear across the kitchen, racing into the living room, so that the radiation waves wouldn't reach him. He'd stand at the other end of the apartment until the "ready" beep sounded and he was safe.

He was very aware of his heart. There was a time when Dad weighed well over 300 pounds—but when his doctors told him that his weight would be dangerous to his already damaged heart, he began to obsessively watch what he ate and to exercise diligently. You wouldn't see him jogging around the Central Park Reservoir, though. Like everything else, he got his exercise on the inside.

Every day, Dad had a set regimen he followed. First, he'd drag his stationary bike in front of the television and pedal for 45 minutes, doing bicep curls at the same time. Then he'd get off and follow a diagram of special calisthenics that his doctor had given him.

"Look at this paper," he'd say to me. "Three sets, ten reps, five-pound weights. This is good. You should do this."

"Dad, I do this already. I know how to do all of this."

"Yeah? That's good. Keep doing it."

Dad didn't indulge in any luxuries in his life. He didn't wear expensive clothes or jewelry. Other than their honeymoon in Florida, he and Mom never went on another trip together. He was a powerful man who must have made a lot of money at one time, but he lived like a pauper and never wanted to or had time to spend it. He never went away on vacations because his allegiance went to his family members (and the family) before himself, so he stuck close to home to make sure everything ran smoothly.

He didn't care for expensive things, anyway. For him, it was never about the money—it was about the power.

One thing he did splurge on was massages. Twice a week for 90 minutes, Dad called in the specialist—Joey the Rubber (pronounced, *ruh-buh*), but we called him "the Rubber" or just "Rubber." Joey was a sweet, polite, middle-aged man whom my father paid to come in and beat him up. He wasn't officially a massage therapist—we had no idea what his real job was or where Dad found him—but what he did certainly worked for my father. Dad had his own portable massage table, which he kept folded up against the wall in the bedroom. Rubber's job was to beat my dad's muscles into submission.

Dad would stretch out on the table, and Joey would pull and punch and knead and slap him around like pizza dough. I couldn't believe my eyes. That my father would let someone throw him around like that was unheard of. *Nobody* touched my father. I thought that he was going to get up any minute and pummel sweet Joey with his fists. Yet he'd stretch Dad's legs over his head and twist him around, chop him up with his hands, and dig his elbow into him. When they were done, Dad would hand Rubber cash, and he'd kiss my dad on the cheek and thank him.

"Sit, eat!" Gram would say to Rubber. She saw how hard he worked.

Rubber always came with his little doctor's kit—even though he wasn't a doctor, or even a nurse. But he played one in our living room. He'd take out a contraption that measured blood pressure and oxygen in the blood, and after he was done checking all of Dad's vital statistics, he'd do the rest of us.

My father's blood pressure was always healthy and low— unless there was a problem at work. Not long after the Gotti bomb incident and reports that Dad might have been involved, the newspapers were shouting new revelations in their headlines: Gotti had been tipped off by the feds about the bomb in his car, and that's why he wasn't there that day.

If this information was true and Dad was disturbed by it, he didn't show it. He was his usual moody self, nothing more, nothing less, the next time I visited. Maybe he was calm because he always believed Gotti would get his in the end.

"He'll be his own demise," my father used to say. "And he'll take everyone down with him."

DAD EXPECTED AND GOT LOYALTY FROM BOTH HIS FAMILIES—at home and on the street. But it's a funny, tricky thing this family loyalty. How does one define it?

I had been working my ass off at my balloon business all year, but the promise of work from Dad's friend Carmine at the banquet hall was not coming through. I did a party here and there in the beginning, and then the phone stopped ringing, which was very odd: When someone promised my father something, they did it. When someone owed my father a favor, they surely paid it. Or, as we all knew, there were consequences.

As I waited for work from Dad's friend, I set up a few parties in the neighborhood on my own and tried to promote myself as best I could. For local children's birthday parties, I had bought a *Sesame Street* Elmo and a *101 Dalmatians* costume to wear while twisting up the balloons into animal shapes. But I still wasn't getting enough work.

"Hey, Dad, what's going on?" I asked him at my next visit. "They haven't called me for any parties or anything."

He looked annoyed. "Go to the banquet hall and find out what's going on," he ordered me.

I hopped in the car and went straight to see Carmine. When I got there, he didn't look too surprised to see me—or worried.

"We've been a little slow lately," he explained, "but we've got New Year's Eve coming. We're gonna give you New Year's Eve."

"Okay, so things should pick up after that, then?"

"Yeah. Things will pick up. We'll call you."

We kissed good-bye and all was fixed. It didn't occur to me to wonder why, in the beginning of December when the holidays were in full swing, business over at the banquet hall would be slow.

True to his word, Carmine used me for their New Year's Eve party. I decorated the catering hall with black and gold balloon centerpieces on the table, and set up hundreds of balloons to fall from the ceiling with streamers at the stroke of midnight. A week after the party, I went to Carmine's office to get paid. The party had been a success, and I walked into the office excited and proud of myself.

"I hope business will pick up next year and you'll be seeing a lot more of me," I told Joyce, one of the office secretaries. She had become my friend as I was learning the ropes, and we'd had a few impromptu sandwiches together. She knew how hard I had worked to do well . . . and now, she looked utterly distressed.

"Joyce, what's the matter?"

She silently motioned for me to meet her outside for her cigarette break. I followed her out the front door and around the corner. It was freezing outside, and her hands shook as she leaned against the cold bricks and lit her menthol cigarette.

"Rita, I have to tell you something," she said, "but you have to promise, promise, *promise* you won't say anything to anybody that you heard this from me."

"I promise."

"I mean, I could be dead or something if anyone knew I told you this."

"My God, Joyce. What is it? I won't tell anybody!"

She looked around to see if anyone was watching, then took a long drag and exhaled.

"You won't be getting any parties from this place. You won't be getting any work from this place at all."

I froze. What the fuck? I tried to stay calm to hear the rest of it.

"How come?"

"Because he doesn't want you to get any work."

"Who doesn't want me to get work?"

"*He* doesn't."

"Joyce. Who's 'he'?"

She paused, as if she was unsure if she really wanted to continue this conversation. "Your father," she finally said. "He told my boss to make sure you didn't get any steady work from us."

I leaned my head against the bricks and fixed my stare on the glowing end of her cigarette. I felt like a punctured, deflated balloon sputtering and spiraling down onto the cold pavement. I didn't doubt her words for a second—they rang clear and true as a bell to me.

"Oh," I said.

I thanked Joyce for her honesty and the risk she took telling me, and rushed across the parking lot to get to my car. I sat in the driver's seat for a few minutes after putting my key in the ignition and tried to keep my cool. Okay, *breathe.* . . . Why? Why? *Why* would my father not want me to get work?

I started driving, although I wasn't sure where I was driving to. I wanted to go to my father to confront him, but I couldn't betray Joyce's confidence. So I just drove, for about an hour, winding through the streets of Jersey until I came up with an answer: *He doesn't want me to succeed.*

I was now a young woman of 23 who had been drifting from meaningless job to meaningless job, refusing to do as my sisters had done: find a boy, get married, get pregnant—in that specific, sanctified order. Dad's so-called help for my career was another ruse of his, this one to keep me in a holding position until I played the game his way. I was heartbroken. Any trust I had in my father—and it was scant already—was now completely shattered.

I drove home and found Mom in her room, lying down with a headache and a bag of ice on her head. I did my best to hide my mood and gave her a speech I'd concocted and practiced in the car.

"Ma, I'm quitting this balloon idea. Business is slow, and I'm losing interest. I'm also tired of haggling with people over every penny."

"But I thought you were enjoying yourself! Are you sure?"

"Yeah. It's become a pain in the ass."

"Well, you better tell your father before he hears it from some-one else."

The next day I went to see Dad and repeated my fake story. I was nervous I wasn't going to sound convincing but apparently, I was pretty good at pretending.

Dad, on the other hand, couldn't fake interest in me for one minute. He barely reacted. "Okay," he said, and went about his business.

Within the week, I had sold all my costumes to a kids' store and my van to a cousin. I shut Ballooney Tunes Entertainment down and never told a soul what Joyce in the office had told me. I never confronted my father for fear of what might happen to her.

But there was no way I would forget what he had done— and now, more than ever, I wanted to completely cut myself off from him.

CHAPTER 12

CRIME AND PUNISHMENT

Instead of cutting myself off from my father, I cut myself off completely from the world.

The aftermath of Dad's betrayal threw me into a tailspin. This time, in addition to the inability to eat, I was trembling and had night sweats so bad that my mother had no idea how to help me.

I went to doctors who could find nothing wrong with me, so I waited it out. I lay in bed thinking about how my anxiety was going to make my body so sick that I would die. Then I worried about my family and what horrible things would befall them on the way to their own impending demise. My body ached so bad that even though doctors could find nothing wrong with me, I obsessed with the idea that I had a fatal disease they couldn't see and was facing imminent death.

I was still seeing Dr. Stein, so I told her the balloon story. "They betrayed me," I said.

"Rita, you can't trust your father in the way that you want to, and you know it. You will only be disappointed. You have to figure out a way to love your family but protect and love yourself first. Trust yourself. Put up healthy boundaries so they can't hurt you."

After my session, I drove to the nearest fast-food Chinese place. Like my McDonald's gorging before, I wanted sugar, I wanted salt, and I wanted them mixed together in a greasy kind of a way. I broke my fast this time with egg rolls, fried rice, and sweet-and-sour balls drenched with that sickly sweet neon pink sauce. I inhaled it from the little cardboard take-out cartons sitting in the front seat of my car in the parking lot, like an addict on a secret bender, hiding from her sponsor.

By the time I got home, my stomach was preparing for a mutiny. I went to my mother's bedroom, turned on the TV, and resumed my fetal position. I could feel the bile and pink sauce boil up from my stomach and bubble its way to my throat. This time, the food did nothing to temper my anxiety.

Mom came into the room and sat on the edge of the bed, looking at me sadly. I was racked with pain, physically and emotionally, and could barely open my eyes. Of the dozens upon dozens of anxiety attacks I'd had so far in my angst-ridden life, this one was about to win the award for most brutal.

As I was gasping for breath, Mom said, "Rita, do you want me to tell you something that will make you feel better?"

"Yeah, Ma, please."

"So that you'll know you're not the only person who has problems?"

"Yeah," I croaked. "Tell me." I was clutching my stomach with one hand and my throat with the other. *Hurry up and tell me something good, Ma! I'm about to die here!*

"All right, listen," she said, with a dramatic sigh. "You know how Mr. So-and-So down the street has another woman?"

Oh, God. She wasn't about to tell me that she and Mr. So-and-So . . . ?

"Yeah, Ma. I heard that. I heard that he lived with another woman and has that other family."

"Well, Ri, your father . . . he has the same thing."

I caught my breath.

"What do you mean?"

"Your father has another woman. He has a whole other family, with children. And it's been going on for 30 years."

I couldn't believe my ears. "What?" I made her repeat it.

"Ma, what are you saying? This can't be true. When did this happen?"

I tried to sit up in bed. I didn't want to believe what my mother was telling me. Mom explained a little of the history and details about the woman and her kids, and then dropped another bomb: "And the other woman's name is Olympia."

"What? Are you saying she has the same name as you? How is that possible? Only you and Olympia Dukakis have that name!"

"Well, believe it."

"I never thought Dad was the type of man to do this. Who else knows?"

"Just you and Yolanda."

"Do those other kids . . . do they know about us?"

"Yes. So you see, Rita? Things can always be worse."

Worse? How much fucking worse could things get? And furthermore, how is this supposed to make me feel better? That drug cocktail Mom and Dad fed me a few months earlier was starting to look really appealing about now.

Suddenly, so much about my mother made sense and fell into place. Her anxiety throughout my childhood and the bottle of pink pills in the bathroom, the happy moods turning blue on a dime, and those afternoons crying in the den after school. My poor mom.

I couldn't cry; I could only sit up in shock and try to keep breathing. At least the news had jolted the anxiety out of me and given me a much preferable numbness. I went to my own room exhausted and distraught, and fell asleep immediately—a welcome escape from the news I'd just heard. It would take days before I could process all of this, and there was only one other person I could talk to about it.

I went over to Yolanda's to get the full story.

"I've known for 12 years," she said. "Mom told me, but I was sworn to secrecy."

Yo found out on Mother's Day when she was 26 years old and had gone to take a card and flowers to Mom. When she got there, she found my mother sitting in the den holding a letter, crying.

"Ma, what happened? Did someone die?"

Mom wordlessly handed her the note. It was an anonymous typed letter, just two sentences, like a ransom note:

> Your husband is having a relationship with another woman.
> They have three children together.

And now I looked at Yo with new respect and understanding as well. Now I understood why she was so helpful to Mom and me, why she became a second mother to me and tried to explain Mom's mysterious "illness" with compassion and understanding for so many years. She knew of Mom's heartbreak all along. At the same time, she was also Dad's confidante and the only person to whom he told his private agony over the situation. She was in the middle of this whole mess and in the middle of the two of them.

The story of my father and his double life with another family would be doled out to me bit by bit, on a need-to-know basis, over time. Mom and Yo were my storytellers, and it amounted to quite the soap opera.

IT ALL STARTED MORE THAN A DECADE BEFORE I WAS BORN, when Dad was introduced to the woman by a family friend. He didn't have any intentions to cheat on Mom, but in his business it was expected and even encouraged. If you didn't do it, you weren't a team player.

Dad's affair had started as something temporary, and he kept it secret for a while—until he was arrested for the first time in 1957 and charged with attempted murder after he allegedly shot at Frank Costello, nicknamed the "Prime Minister" (of the underworld).

While he was in court on trial, my eagle-eyed grandmother noticed a short, plain, dark-haired woman sitting in the gallery every day watching the proceedings. She also noticed her son looking over at the woman from time to time. My grandmother was no fool and recognized the situation immediately.

At the end of one day in court, Gram approached the woman and didn't mince her words. "You stay away from him!" she said angrily. "He has four children!"

My grandfather and his brother saw the altercation, and when she went back over to them, they told her, "This is none of your business!"

Gram shut up but was furious because of what her son was doing—she had brought him up better than that.

It wasn't long until my mother found out anyway. After a day at court a few weeks later, Mom left the courtroom and stepped onto the elevator, and was quickly followed by the other woman. In the elevator, the woman gave my mother the once-over from head to toe during the ride down, whispering something to the friend she was with. Instinctively, Mom understood who and what this woman was . . . and as the elevator plummeted from the tenth floor to the ground, so did my mother's heart and her future.

While Dad was away in jail in the late '50s Mom didn't say a word to him about what she knew. But once he got home from jail, she confronted him and told him she wanted a divorce.

"What do you mean? We can't divorce!"

In a Catholic marriage, there was no divorce. It was like being part of the mob—or a guest at the Hotel California—you could never leave. The only way out was death.

"Then I want an annulment."

Dad cried and begged and promised to stop seeing the other Olympia, and my mother believed him. He may have even gone to confession over it—but he never did stop seeing her. Instead, he set her up in an apartment and had three children with her. Lucia was two years older than I was, Vincent was six months younger than I, and Carmella was two years younger than I.

"Dad didn't mean to have kids with her," Yo told me, "but after several years, the woman insisted on it, so . . ."

When my mother became pregnant with me, ten years after she had found out about the affair, she didn't know that my father was still seeing his mistress and they already had one child together. When Mom told my father she was pregnant with me, his reaction was one that she would never forgive.

"I want you to have an abortion," he told her.

He might as well have spit on God. It was the first time in her life that my mother ever used the F-word, and it shocked my father beyond the pale. "You can go fuck yourself!" she yelled at him. "There is no way I am aborting this baby!"

Dad raised his right arm and slapped Mom across the cheek. A piece of her tooth broke off and went flying through the air. It was the only time he ever hit her.

Seven months later—amid the drama, heartache, and duplicity of a mob man living two lives—I was born. Dad was in the process of shipping us to New Jersey so that he could keep the families in separate states, juggling the two. It's no wonder that my Gram named me after the Saint of the Impossible. That I even got into this world was a miracle.

AFTER YO AND MOM TOLD ME THE DISTURBING details about the other woman, they also told me, as usual, to keep it a secret. Sal, Andrew, and Ro didn't know yet about my father's other life— but they found out soon enough. A few weeks after Mom broke the news to me, the scandal hit the local newspapers.

My father immediately called an emergency damage control meeting with us five kids at Mom's. We all sat in the living room, waiting nervously for Dad to show up. The others had seen the news in the papers by now, and we all wondered what he was going to say to us. Did he gather us together so he could apologize?

Dad arrived, seeming more irritated than apologetic, as if we were inconveniencing him somehow. He paced back and forth across the living room and blurted out his brief speech in one minute. "I want you kids to understand, I didn't do anything to *you*," he said. "I did it to your mother. And I don't wanna hear another word about it. Nobody should have an issue with this."

He didn't even mention the other woman or her children, or that he was sorry. The meeting was now adjourned, and the floor was not open for questions or comments from the gallery. Dad had said his piece and went into the kitchen to have a cup of coffee with Mom. He left us all there stunned and continued on as if nothing out of the ordinary had just happened. But our whole world changed in that one moment.

We were all still reeling from the news that Dad had been living his double life when a few weeks later Yo got a phone call from my Uncle Lou.

"Your father's been arrested. He's in a rat-infested cell in Brooklyn."

The feds had broken down my father's door early that morning. He was asleep and Gram had gone to church, so when no one answered the door, they broke it down using a battering ram. That woke Dad up.

My father was told that he was being charged with racketeering and murder, among other crimes, and then they handcuffed him and took him outside in his pajamas and robe. He went quietly, but I'm sure he talked to a parking meter or two on the way to the cop car, just for the record. They took him to a holding cell in Brooklyn for a few days until we could post bail. My siblings put up their houses for collateral to get him out.

That day, though, Gram was in an absolute panic. "What about my boy's health? He can't go to jail with his bad heart!"

Mom was equally scared, but trusted that God would help the family through this. "Everybody, we've got to pray. Pray the rosary. Pray that those people leave your father alone and that he won't stay in jail."

I prayed the rosary with Mom in her bedroom and then, for the first time in months I went to church. As I walked in, I eyed the confession box to my left. If Dad was sitting in a tiny, rat-infested jail cell, I wondered if my going into the tiny confession box would be of help to him.

So for the last time in my life, I went to confession. Maybe I thought I could get absolution for Dad's sins. Maybe I was looking for a miracle for all of us and wanted to check one last time if miracles resided here.

"Bless me, Father, for I have sinned. I missed church for a lot of months. I swore ten times today. I thought angry thoughts about my dad . . . "

Oh, who was I kidding? I had no intention of telling the truth to this priest. It was a half-assed confession because I just didn't believe in it anymore.

What I really wanted to say was, "Bless me, Father, for I have sinned. I hate my dad because maybe he's a murderer and he's cheating on us and now he's in jail. But I'm not honest, either! I'm gay, and I want to be brave enough to come out. Can you help me with that one? Oh, yeah, I'm also dating a married woman. But I do feel bad about that. We're breaking commandments left and right over here, Padre . . . how many Hail Marys will it take?"

Of course I couldn't say any of those things; he wouldn't have understood. So how could the priest be the one to dole out the punishment for the crime? I couldn't help absolve my father's sins for him anyway—he'd have to work on that himself. As for me, I already knew in my heart that my being gay and loving someone was not something to be punished for. I needed to talk to God about this directly so that we could figure out together how I was to live, and what was to happen to my soul later.

I abandoned the confession box and went to the front of the church and slipped into a pew—*ahh,* that felt better.

I sat there and prayed for an hour. And as I did, I knew that Mom was praying at home, Gram was praying on Sullivan Street, and my father was probably praying in his shithole of a cell in Brooklyn.

What good it would do, I wasn't sure. But we all prayed anyway—for forgiveness, for understanding, for divine help, and for freedom.

PART III

INTO THE LIGHT

CHAPTER 13

CAPTIVITY
AND FREEDOM

I woke up at 2:30 A.M. and couldn't breathe. What else was new?

It was the winter of 1990, and for days I'd been in one of my depressive states. This one was even worse than usual, if that's possible. I had a feeling that it was going to lead to something big and explosive, but I wasn't sure what. I was groggy, because I'd barely slept or eaten in days, but I also felt a powerful and clear force directing me.

"Mom. Mom!" I shook her awake in her bed. "Take me to the city. I need to go. I need to see him. Take me to him."

Mom didn't ask me any questions. She knew exactly who "him" was, and she could see that whatever my reasons were, I was desperate. She got up, we bundled ourselves in heavy winter coats and hats, and then we made the familiar drive to the city that we'd done for decades.

This time it was in the middle of the night, and the sights outside Mom's car window as we made our way across the George Washington Bridge and down through the city were different, ominous—the streets lit up by neon signs were nearly deserted, the sidewalks were silent, and I shivered from the freezing cold.

My father and grandmother were now living in an apartment on LaGuardia Place, a few blocks away from the old dungeon on Sullivan. It had been Uncle Pat's apartment and was bigger and brighter, with more windows and alabaster walls. And because it was on the seventh floor, the drapes didn't have to be closed all the time for fear of people peering in. It was no dungeon, and I welcomed the new light.

We slipped our way across the icy sidewalk and took the elevator up to the apartment door, where we were surprised to find Dad standing in the doorway, greeting us in his robe, slippers, and pajamas—the usual uniform. Since we'd gotten him out on bail months earlier, he'd been on house arrest. He couldn't sleep either and had been pacing the floors already when Mom called to tell Gram we were on our way.

It was always funny to see my father wearing pajamas in the middle of the night, at the same time the rest of the world wore them. To me, they were his "work clothes" or his "day clothes," and I half-expected to find him wearing a suit and tie at 4 A.M., as if his world was a topsy-turvy one of opposites where night was day and day was night and all the rules were broken.

As soon as I saw him, I threw my arms around his waist and buried my face into his chest. Hugging him tightly, I burst into tears. Dad didn't know what else to do but hug me back, and then Mom joined in. In one tangled mass, the three of us moved to the couch in the living room, where I lay down and rested my head on my father's lap and my legs on my mother's.

As I cried, Dad began stroking my hair with his hand, like he used to do when I was a kid. I moved in and out of awareness and could hear bits of my parents' conversation.

"What is wrong with her, Hon?" Mom asked.

"I don't know."

"I don't know what to do, Hon. This keeps happening. How can we help her?"

As I lay there hearing my parents' disjointed voices in the background, I realized that they *couldn't* help me. Yes, they loved me, but they were not emotionally equipped to help me. Dad had three families he was responsible for—"the" family, the one containing my mother and siblings, and the one uptown. Mom was worn down by more than 30 years of Dad's deception and lies, trying to keep her family together despite them, and the threat that her husband would be put away. If they didn't feel safe in their own lives, how could they make *me* feel safe?

In that moment, the force that drove me to my father before dawn that morning drove another message, loud and clear, into my mind: *Nobody is ever going to help me but me. If I don't do this myself, I'm never going to get better. I'm tired of playing the victim. It's time I take responsibility for myself.*

I didn't know exactly what that meant or what action I would take, but it was a feeling of both surrender and victory that felt incredibly empowering.

THE VERY NEXT DAY, I FELT THE SHIFT BEGIN. I went into a long, deep sleep when I got home after my emergency trip to Dad's, and when I woke up, my stomach opened up and I ate voraciously. It took me days to gather my strength again, but when I did it was a new kind of strength that had to do with getting clear. After so much confusion in my life, I wanted clarity.

My family was currently dealing with the aftermath of my father's arrest and the shocking revelation that he had a whole other family. As Mom and Yo had known for years, I soon found out that so did much of our extended family. Now that the truth was out to the entire world, it was humiliating for my mother. She kept close to home and family instead of visiting friends, and stopped going to church. She didn't feel comfortable going alone, and none of us wanted to go, either.

"I don't want people to judge me, to judge our family," she said one Sunday morning.

I finally realized why Mom never came to any of my softball games by herself all those years ago—she didn't know what to say or how to deal with the other mothers who already knew about Dad, and was worried about them judging us. These days, she was even more sensitive about what people might be thinking and saying behind her back—and I, in turn, was overly sensitive to her.

Mom and I had been symbiotically attached to each other since the day I was born. I used to absorb her feelings even as a toddler, and her mysterious depression used to make *me* depressed. Now that I knew the origin of her pain, I had a whole new set of feelings to process, and they mainly involved anger.

I was angry with my father for what he had done. Adding to that, I was angry with my mother for taking his shit for so long, for giving up her voice and self-respect. And I was angry that she wasn't angrier, so I took it upon myself to be angry for *both* of us. It was a lot of work, being angry on someone else's behalf for more than three decades of shit done to them. As if I didn't have my own stuff!

Soon enough, though, Mom started to let her own anger surface. Now that we all knew, at least she didn't have to hide her emotions from us anymore.

Some days, the two households became like war zones, and my siblings and I were called upon to be go-betweens and carrier pigeons to transfer messages to and from Jersey and Manhattan. Something would upset Mom about the whole other-woman situation and she'd blow a fuse.

"Fuck him! You go tell your father I'm not going to visit him anymore! He's not going to see me! I'm sick and tired of this!" It had been more than two decades since Mom first used the F-word and since then, she had become quite adept at it. There had been a lot of things to say *fuck* about.

Sometimes she'd write him a letter and say, "Take this to your father!"

I'd refuse. "Ma, I don't want to get involved."

Even though I'd been taking orders from my father my whole life, he didn't dare ask me to send any messages for him. He knew how close I was to my mother and that I wasn't about to do his bidding when it came to her.

"Your mother's nuts!" he'd bark at me. "You go back there and tell her . . . " and then he'd see my resistant face.

"Tell your mother that I love and miss her. And to please come and see me."

During Dad's house arrest, he wasn't allowed to come to Jersey and visit. So if Mom wanted to punish him and stage a boycott, it was all in her power. But the longest she ever lasted in staying away from him was three weeks. By then, she'd give in and rush over to LaGuardia with his freshly ironed shirts and favorite cookies, and they'd be hugging in the kitchen again.

Seeing how close and affectionate they were with each other, I couldn't wrap my head around the fact that my father had another woman and kids ten minutes and ten stops north on the Lexington local number 6 train. The older I got and the more I found out, the less I knew about my dad. And it's not like I started off with much to begin with.

With my new quest for clarity, I had a lot of questions that I needed answered. As always, I went to Yo first. Since my father rarely trusted anyone, Yolanda was probably the only person he was able to talk to about the other woman, so he told her things no child should have to know.

"He loves Mom," she explained to me, when I cornered her for an interrogation one afternoon when our mother was out. "But he told me he loves *her*, too, and their kids—a lot."

Yo explained that Dad had started off with a mistress, which was usual for the men in his line of work. He never intended for it to be a serious relationship, but she got pregnant and he got pulled into it. "He loves both of them; they both love him; he won't leave either one; neither of them will leave him," my sister said, shaking her head.

"But if he loves Mom," I asked, "what does he see in this other woman? Why is he with her?"

"She gives him things Mom doesn't. She doesn't back down from him like Mom does," she said. "She's a challenge. Mom is very compassionate and forgiving, and more old-fashioned, like, 'Whatever you say, Hon, you know best.' This one stands up to him and asks for what she wants and tells him what to do. She's more like Gram—she speaks her mind and isn't submissive. Dad needs that, too. He needs both of them."

Apparently, about two months after Dad asked Mom to abort me, his mistress found out she was pregnant with their second child. Meanwhile, our tiny place on Sullivan was too cramped for our still-growing family. Mom wanted more space and asked my father to move us into a brownstone in the city. He knew he had to keep the two women and two families separate, so when I was six months old, he moved us out to Jersey, and at some point moved the other family into a brownstone on Manhattan's Upper East Side. Dad then spent most of his time either at Gram's or uptown with occasional weekend trips to Jersey.

In surveillance reports made by the FBI, agents noted that many nights during the week, my father would be driven after midnight from Gram's—his official home address—to the other family uptown, where he would spend the night.

"He was in their lives more," Yo told me. "He treated them differently than he treated us. He gave them more of himself."

But while the other woman may have been more outspoken about what she wanted for herself and her kids, there was one sacred vow that remained in our family.

"Dad never wanted to divorce Mom," said Yo. "Instead, he lived two lives with two families."

IN THE MONTHS FOLLOWING DAD'S ARREST, I tried to talk to Mom about who my father was and why he made the choices he did. But it was difficult to get clear answers from her because she kept herself in her on-and-off state of denial for her own emotional survival, I guess. At the same time, I don't think she knew the answers herself. I suspect she never confronted him directly with her own questions—and even if she had, he never would have given her adequate answers.

Nevertheless, I drilled her for all she knew. Even if she couldn't give me answers, the fact that I was finally asking questions was a big deal on its own.

One evening when my mother was cooking dinner, I sat down at the kitchen table and let loose. "Mom, why did he do this?" I asked her, as she stirred a big pot of red sauce. "Why did he make this whole other family?"

Mom sighed and didn't look up from the pot. I could almost hear her thoughts: *If I haven't asked myself that same question a thousand times.* Aloud, she said, "He made a mistake, Rita. And then there were the children . . . he didn't want to desert them."

To her credit, my mother never harbored any ill will toward my half-siblings. "I don't blame those kids," she always said. "They didn't ask for this."

"When did you find out about Dad's business?"

"At first, I didn't know anything, and it wasn't my business to ask. I didn't realize until later how deeply he was involved."

"But, Ma. After all this, after everything, why did you stay with him? Why did you allow him to treat you this way? When you found out about that other woman? I don't understand!"

"He said he'd stop seeing her, and I believed him."

Did she really? I'm not sure. But what was she going to do at the time: Threaten to take the family away from him? Threaten to tell his children that their father had been seeing another woman for years? She could never be so cruel as to emotionally blackmail him that way. And even though she had asked him for a divorce when she'd first found out about the other woman, they both knew it would never happen. They loved each other, and neither of them wanted to get a divorce.

So my parents stayed married, and my mother was able to maintain her starry-eyed image of my father whenever she could, which was about 90 percent of the time. She'd see him as the sweet, 12-year-old kid who kissed her in the park, before he got in with the rough street crowd and made choices that would send his life toward a downward spiral.

"He was a gentle, kind, and respectful young man," she'd say, reminiscing about their early courting years. "He was a good boy."

"But how am *I* supposed to feel about him?"

"He's your father—you have to love him."

"Well, if that's the only reason to love him, that's not good enough. Just because he donated his sperm to me? Why should I forgive him?"

"Because he's your father," she said, over and over. "I loved him no matter what. I forgave him for whatever he did. Don't forget that he does a lot of good things for people, too. He helps a lot of people."

She was using the same logic I tried on myself after I found out who Dad really was when I was 16. It had worked for me a little then, but it was lacking for me now. I did love my father, but I didn't like the choices he made with his family and with his work.

Once in a while, in a weak moment, Mom would sadly admit her struggle with her husband's being in love with another woman. It was usually during one of their long-distance tiffs, and I'd find her sitting in the kitchen. "I wish he would have just left me alone," she'd quietly say.

I FOUND OUT THAT YOLANDA AND GRAM had been seeing the other family off and on for years and now Roseanne and my brothers, at my father's request, were doing the same. In solidarity with my mother, I refused to meet Dad's other family. I was told my whole life to stick by my mother and I intended to do so.

My family talked of loyalty, but did they really know what it meant? What I saw in them was a conditional loyalty, same as the conditional love. Then again, if I wanted to receive unconditional love, did that mean I had to show it by forgiving my father and embracing his new family? Right now, I felt my mother needed me more.

I'm not sure exactly when my grandmother had found out about Dad's other kids. In the first place, she was troubled that my father was in "the life." This was a true disappointment to her because of the long line of respected pharmacists and doctors in her family, as well as the fact that the Mafia-like Black Hand was responsible for her dear father's death when she was a girl. So when she found out that Dad was cheating on my mother—that was another blow to her. Then, when she found out he had children with another woman, she upped her rosary count.

According to my sisters, she read Dad the riot act, scolding that he had "created a big problem." She wasn't about to applaud his actions that went against everything she believed and everything she had taught him. She was heartbroken because she felt he had taken us away from her, moving us far away to Jersey just because of this other family. I'm sure that if my dad had his way, he would have wanted all of us to live in one big, happy home.

When Gram chastised him, he'd try at first to keep her quiet. "I'm the boss in this house!" he'd tell her.

She would sit up in her chair, shoot him a look (I think Gram *invented* "the look") across the dining-room table, and set him straight. "You think you're the boss of this house?" she'd ask, pointing her finger toward the hallway. "You're the boss of the *toilet*, that's what you're the boss of!"

I think that Dad knew she was right. When it came to matters of the home, he wasn't a very good boss at that.

My sisters said that it took our grandmother a long time to accept these other children. She felt, just as I did, that to meet them was to be disloyal to my mother and us. But those children were also her blood. So she finally relented and opened up her home and her heart to them as best she could.

"But she would not accept their mother," my sisters said.

Gram loved her son no matter what. Mom loved her husband no matter what. And everyone was telling me to love my father no matter what. Yet they didn't realize that their logic contained a fatal flaw: if I was expected to love my father no matter what . . . why, then, would he not do the same for me?

DAD'S HOUSE ARREST WAS TO BE INDEFINITE, until the trial. Assuming there would be a trial, that is. The next several months, stretching into years, would consist of various doctors coming in and out of Dad's apartment like a rotating conveyer belt of medical men, evaluating him in order to report back to the court on whether he was mentally fit to stand trial or not. Dad's goal, of course, was to never seem fit enough. And he did a good job convincing the doctors.

"He manifests organic brain damage by his inability to, for example, subtract 7 from 100," one of his longtime doctors reported, according to *The New York Times*. "His memory is impaired. He sometimes is very confused and doesn't know where he is or the time of day, the year. His recall is very poor. If you would give him two or three objects to recall, he would have difficulty doing it immediately after you tell him and certainly after a period of three or four minutes."

At home, Dad had to wear a bulky device that sat on a black cuff around his ankle and had to report whenever he wanted to go farther than a certain radius from the apartment, which basically included visits to the other family uptown and doctor appointments. He wasn't allowed to come to Jersey, that was too far. But he was still able to go to the café and play cards with his crew and keep up his bathrobe walks around the West Village.

The new regimen didn't exactly cramp his style—it's not like he was usually out at dinners at Lutèce and hitting the nightclubs. Except for the discomfort of the ankle bracelet, which rubbed at his skin and "hurt like hell," his house arrest didn't feel so physical to him as it did mental. He suspected he was on his way to becoming a truly caged man.

I, on the other hand, was on my way to becoming a free woman. I was now dating Jessie, whom I'd met at a party during my balloon-business fiasco. Unlike all the women I'd dated before, Jessie was single—but more important, she was "out" to her family and friends. After my last relationship with a married woman, I'd made a vow to myself not to do that again. Jessie was a disc jockey and she was the first gay woman I'd known who was living openly and honestly, which relieved and inspired me beyond words. Indeed, it inspired me to action.

Unlike Dad, I was now really, truly done with living a double life. And unlike Mom, I didn't want to live in denial anymore.

So one afternoon as she and I were doing dishes, I decided it was time—*I have to do this now.* I brushed away memories of the first time I'd tried this and embraced the second coming (out), as it were.

"Ma, I have to talk to you about something."

She turned off the water and looked at me, concerned.

"I can't do this pretending anymore. I told you a few years ago, and I'm telling you again. I can't hold it in anymore. I'm dating a woman, and I want you to meet her. This is going to be my life, Ma. Like it or not, I like women. So you are going to have to accept me as I am because I'm not living a lie anymore."

She took a deep breath, and I could see from her expression that what I said was no surprise to her. As if she had already known, but hadn't wanted to face it. "I understand, honey," she said, now sitting down at the table and wiping her hands. "You can't help it; this is the way you were born. But . . . " she trailed off, looking distressed.

"What?"

"Ri, I'm afraid of how people will treat you. You know how your father and uncles talk about gay people. And I want to make sure you're . . . safe. I'm worried for you."

"Safe?"

"I'm afraid for your soul."

Oh, yeah. *That.* I was still working on that one. Unbeknownst to me, Mom had been working on it for me, too. Ever since my coming-out-interruptus when I was 19, she'd been praying for my soul every day.

"I've been asking God to change your inappropriate ways so you can meet a man, get married, and have children," she confessed to me now. I was both hurt and touched by this: hurt that she hadn't been accepting of me all those years, but touched that she was trying to help me the only way she knew how. She felt deep in her heart that my soul was going to suffer for this.

"I know, Ma. I know. But I can't believe that God would make me like this and then punish me. I can't believe that! It doesn't feel right. And I have to do this—this is who I am. I can't survive one more day pretending."

She nodded and gave me a hug. I could see that she was struggling with all of this, so I didn't tell her that I was still waiting details from God on the whole heaven thing. But for now, it felt right and healthy and liberating, so I had to go with that or else die.

"Honey, we're not going to tell your father about this."

"No way, Ma. No way."

I wished I could have been honest with my father, too, but my mother and I both knew that he wouldn't be able to handle it. We both knew that, at least for the time being, he was incapable of accepting and loving me no matter what.

MY RELATIONSHIP WITH JESSIE YIELDED two of the most important and freeing moments of my life. The first was truly coming out to my mother. The second was forging a new relationship with God.

Like me, Jessie was a lapsed Catholic, and a sporadic churchgoer who had been disappointed and confused by the Church's teachings on homosexuality and how it related to her authentic self. We were both living in a gap between our true selves and this "one, true religion," seeking a connection with a God Who would accept us.

Jessie had found a local church where the priest performed the laying on of hands, or what I'd heard some Catholics call the "slaying of the spirit," for small groups of people each month. I remembered reading in the Bible that the apostles laid hands on new believers. Jesus was one of the great faith healers of our time, and many Christians believe that some people today can perform this spirit slaying and that it will cure you of whatever ails you. I'd seen it when flipping channels on TV and passing one of those evangelist shows where the well-coiffed and tanned Southern preachers would yell out "You have been healed!" and touch a person's forehead, and then he or she would collapse.

Hell, I was game. I had so many things ailing me my whole life, I was willing to try anything. So Jessie and I arrived at the church one summer night a little nervous, not certain what to expect.

A group of 25 people sat in a semicircle at the back of the church, and we began a prep session of prayer and singing, and a discussion about what would happen during the laying on of hands, which we would do the following night with the priest. The goal of the religious ritual, we were told by an organizer, was to invoke the Holy Spirit. And in the presence of the Holy Spirit, he promised, some healing would be done.

We'd already been praying for about 45 minutes with our eyes shut and had 15 more to go. Someone near me started speaking in tongues, which startled me, as it sounded like gibberish. A wave of heat swept through the room.

I peeked open one eye to see if someone else was fiddling with the radiator, and that's when something colorful and luminous across the room caught my eye.

I looked up at the large window and I saw him. Or should I say, I saw *him*. That face was unmistakable, like all the paintings and movies I'd seen in Catholic churches my whole life: baby blue eyes; flowing, dark blonde tresses; a serene, all-knowing expression.

"Oh. My. God. Jessie!" I whispered to her, interrupting her prayer. "Look up, *look up!*"

It was a gigantic, fantastic image of Jesus Christ, from the shoulders up, which took up the entire window. He was looking right into my eyes and didn't say a word, but sent the most peaceful energy like a laser beam of love right at me.

Jessie gasped. "Holy shit!"

We were both stunned and could barely speak. All we could do was nudge the people next to us, who then opened their eyes. Only six others could see him, and I don't know why. We were all bewildered; no one could explain it.

When the session was over everyone went outside, but I didn't want to leave the room. I couldn't! I sat in my chair, afraid to move, then rubbed my eyes and stared at the image for another 15 minutes. Finally, I went outside to check on Jessie, who was talking with the others, but after 30 minutes, I couldn't take it anymore. I had to go back inside and see if he was still there.

He was, so Jessie and I sat there for another 30 minutes. I didn't want to tear myself away; I would have slept in the church all night if I could. I already knew that the feeling of peace I was experiencing would change my life profoundly.

After I left the church that night, I felt opened up to Jesus and Mary and the Holy Spirit in a way I'd never been before. The next day when I woke up, I felt light as a snowflake. There was some-thing missing that normally pulled me down: fear. I could feel a chunk of that albatross that I'd been carrying around my neck loosen and lift up away from me.

The next night when we returned for the actual laying on of hands by the priest, I immediately checked to see if the Lord was in the spot I had left him in, but Jesus had left the building. We went deep into prayer and singing to invoke the Holy Spirit, and when it was time for the big show, we all lined up in front of the priest.

One by one, I saw him touch people on the forehead and watched them drop. When it was my turn, I didn't "go down" as they say, and was a little disappointed—especially in light of my new relationship with Jesus.

"It often doesn't happen for first-timers," the priest explained. "You may be a little nervous about surrendering or letting go."

I didn't let it worry me, though. I knew I had reached a new, higher level of spirituality than I'd ever known before. It was something I'd always felt was there, but had never been able to express because of my family and their faith. The feeling was be-yond any "organized" religious structure I had been taught. It was bigger and more inclusive—most important, it was inclusive of *me*.

Jessie and I went back to the same church a few months later, hoping that this time we'd "go down" like the others during the laying-on-of-hands part. I was also hoping to see my new friend, Jesus, again, and get another injection of the peace.

This time when the priest reached me in line, and he began to pray and lightly touched my forehead with the tip of his finger, I felt a surge of heat rush through me. My knees got weak, and I fell to the floor. But it wasn't like a faint or like when someone slugs you and you're knocked out. It was gentle and buoyant, like a leaf falling from a tree in slow motion.

Two other people stood behind me and gently lowered me to the ground. Once I got there, I didn't want to move. The peace this second time was so great, I nearly cried. I was in complete bliss—a state of perfect grace. I lay on the floor for a few minutes, reveling in the joy. When I finally sat up several minutes later, I saw other people on the floor crying or laughing or in a woozy peaceful place like me.

Similar to that force I'd felt months earlier, when I woke my mother up in the middle of the night and whispered "Take me to him," I felt a pull to go to the front of the church.

Take me to him, I heard, in my mind.

I don't know why I had the strong urge to do it, but I knelt down by the altar and prayed. It had been months since I had prayed like that, and even longer since I had been in a church. Then I talked to God in whispers: *Thank You; thank You; thank You, God.*

It was an ultimate moment of grace.

In that moment, I realized that God was perfect. And in that perfection, He or She created me as perfect, too. Even though the Church or my father on Earth didn't accept me as I was, I knew that my Father in heaven did.

I also knew for sure, for the first time in my life and deep through the core of my being and the infinity of my heart, that my soul was in good hands—my soul was safe.

CHAPTER 14

LIVE AND LET GO

I was speeding down the Joe DiMaggio Highway in my black-on-black Eldorado at 85 miles per hour, hitting every bump and pothole. As I cruised along, I loudly sang my own made-up lyrics to my favorite Earth, Wind, and Fire tune, "Fantasy":

Yeah, yeah, yeah . . . I'm so damn free . . . and you can bet your sweet fuckin' ass I'm on my way . . .

I'd just finished a day of massage classes at the Swedish Institute in Manhattan. Although my hands tingled and ached, it was a good hurt.

Since that day in church several months earlier when I'd knelt by the altar and made peace with God, the serenity I felt had stayed with me and helped me move forward in my life. I realized that day that God was with me and was on my side, even if man-made religions and the mortals in charge of them were not. In so many ways, it was a moment of rebirth for myself, spiritually, emotionally, mentally, and physically.

Once I knew my soul was safe—that I was indeed worth "saving"—I began to save myself. To do so, I began the journey of letting go of past hurts and beliefs, one by one, and making room for something else in my life I'd never fully tried before . . . namely, living.

I began my new path by restructuring my body, which had held on to so much sickness my entire life, into a strong machine that would propel me forward, much like my speeding Eldorado. Once I took the responsibility of making myself healthy and stopped expecting others to do it, I began exploring all possibilities.

I saw that conventional medicine, like organized religion, had limited my thinking. Now I felt free to think for myself and realized that conventional doctors had dosed me with antibiotics, antianxiety pills, and painkillers for 20 years—yet they still couldn't fix me. I began investigating holistic methods to heal myself, and my search led me to a whole new team of experts who spoke an entirely new language. Chiropractors, herbalists, and healers taught me that my illnesses were not caused by some unseen germ or genetic defect or satanic force, but by my own emotions and thoughts.

All along, I had thought that my body was betraying me and was my jailor—but really, it was the other way around. I had been holding it hostage with my unspoken, buried pain and unexpressed, true desires.

I learned that the mind-body connection is so immediate that each of them sends messages back and forth like two people communicating on walkie-talkies. And the effect they have on each other is so great that any negative emotion can affect the body, and vice versa. As philosopher René Descartes famously wrote: *Cogito, ergo sum* ("I think, therefore I am").

Dr. Stein recommended two books for me to read: *The Boy Who Couldn't Stop Washing* by Judith L. Rapoport, and *The Highly Sensitive Person* by Elaine N. Aron. Both of these helped me understand my actions better and made me realize I wasn't crazy. My fixations on peanut butter and clothes and walking in and out of doors until it felt right had a name: obsessive-compulsive disorder.

As I worked on my mental and emotional life to heal my body, I also worked on my body to heal my emotional life.

It had been a few years since I played softball on the town league, and while I'd continued to stay in good shape for the most part, I wanted to get stronger and leaner. I set up sessions three days a week with a personal trainer and soon saw my body change and become solid and muscular. I also discovered that my body and emotions were extra sensitive to sugar, which zonked my energy and immune system. So I began eating organic, cutting out all sweets, and diligently measuring and weighing my food to get the proper balance of nutrients, carbohydrates, and protein needed to slowly rebuild every cell in my body from square one.

Once I knew that I could trust my body, and it knew it could trust me to take care of it, I felt secure enough to ask myself a question I'd never asked before:

What do I want to do with my life?

The notion that I, the youngest daughter in an old-fashioned Italian-Catholic family, would have a real career was never an option presented to me nor encouraged. My father's balloon-business betrayal was an example of the lack of seriousness he'd given to the subject. And I don't think I'd ever given it serious thought, either, because buried deep inside my inner quagmire of death days, self-destruction, and discouragement, I suspect I didn't think that I'd *survive* to adulthood.

But now that I had—and now that I intended to thrive— I sought out my destiny.

After seeing how significantly my body had changed with exercise and healthy eating, I took a course on physical training and learned to help others work on their bodies. That led to a job working in a little gym at a chiropractor's office, where I noticed a team of massage therapists come and go. Their patients would arrive stressed out and bent over, and leave relaxed and happy. That was enough to intrigue me to sign up for my current classes at the

Swedish Institute. I felt I was on the right road toward my destiny, which had something to do with helping people.

BUT FIRST, I STILL HAD MORE HEALING of my own to do. And the next step in my progress was signaled by the return of the Messiah. I was at home one day getting ready to go out with Jessie as she waited for me downstairs, talking with Mom. I'd introduced the two of them a few months earlier and, thankfully, they'd hit it off great. Mom hugged and kissed her like any good friend and later said to me, "She seems like a really nice girl, Ri"—even surprising herself, I think.

I could hear Mom and Jessie chatting away happily as I headed into the bathroom. As I sat down on the toilet, I prayed to the Blessed Mother about a flight I was going take the next day. Mom, Yo's family, and I were going to see Yo's son play in a college-football game—and even though it was only a short flight, I was a nervous wreck.

The last time I'd been on a plane was when Jessie surprised me with a trip to the Bahamas for my birthday the previous year. She had told me we were driving to Atlantic City, but we ended up—surprise!—at the airport. I was so emotionally unprepared that I went into a panic attack.

You might say I was my own cartoon version of an in-flight horror flick. I ripped off the stale blue case from the airplane pillow, threw up in it, then ran down the aisle dragging my dripping pillowcase until I reached the bathroom. Inside, my bowels exploded with what looked like mutilated Shredded Wheat and felt like S.O.S soap pads coming out of my ass (God knows what I had eaten that day). My temperature shot up, and I leaned my head against the wall to steady myself, I'm not sure for how long, until a flight attendant knocked on the door to check on me.

I flung open the door—and, with everyone watching, pried open a giant vat of ice in the galley area, ripped my shirt off, and threw the top half of my body into the mountain of ice. After I had cooled down, I emerged from the ice to find rows of male passengers in the back staring at me.

"You seein' something you haven't seen before?" I asked them. And then I spent the rest of the flight sitting in the back with the sympathetic stewardesses.

So I was understandably nervous about trying this plane business a third time. The thought of being trapped in an oversized tube of aluminum and steel and shooting through the air 30,000 feet above the solid ground made me panic. I prayed to Mary to ease the way.

Please, Blessed Mother, protect us. I'm petrified of getting on the plane tomorrow. Please let the plane ride go smoothly . . .

Something to the left of me caught my eye. There, on the glass door of the shower, I saw an image of Mary holding her baby, Jesus. I'm glad I was already on the toilet, or I would have peed my pants. (I'm surprised I didn't fall off.) They were three feet in front of me, a translucent mother-and-son mural two feet high and two feet wide, made of shimmering light. I felt the same things I had that day I saw Jesus for the first time in the church window—peace, serenity, and love. It lasted a few minutes, then disappeared.

I tore out of the bathroom, pulling my pants up, and yelled out to Mom and Jessie as I ran down the stairs, "You are not going to *believe* what just happened!"

"What? What happened?" they both asked.

"I just saw Mary and Jesus."

"What do you mean you just saw Mary and Jesus?" my mother asked. I had told her about my first church sighting—but after all, that was a church.

"Mary and Jesus just appeared on the glass door in the bathroom." I turned to Jessie. "Remember how we saw Jesus in the window? It was like that."

"Oh my God, really?"

"Yup!" I said, with a grin. "Everything is going to be fine on the flight tomorrow!"

Not only did I take it as a sign that my plane ride would be smooth the next day (which it was), I also saw the return of Jesus as a confirmation that I was moving in the right direction, in the right way.

The next day when I returned home safely, I raced to the bathroom to see if mother and son were still there on the shower door. They weren't. But as they say, God is everywhere, and in the smallest of details. I took a shower that night, and as I rinsed the shampoo out of my hair, through my half-squeezed eyes and steam I saw him again. On one of the brown tiles high up on the wall, his face stared down at me, full of love.

Why he was choosing to come to me in the bathroom, God knows. Is this what people meant by a "close, personal relationship" with the Savior? Perhaps I was taking that concept a little too far. But the image on the tile did not go away for months; every time I took a shower and looked up, there he was. I was so curious as to how long my very personal one-on-one time with Jesus would last, that I think my showers that year doubled in length and quantity.

MY SIGHTINGS OF JESUS IN THE BATHROOM were almost a good enough reason for me to stay at my mother's house, just in case he'd come back. But I knew that one of many steps toward my healing was to move out on my own.

It had been tough enough telling my mom at age 12 that I was moving out of her bedroom. The notion that I'd want to move out of the house would be startling, especially since as the youngest daughter I'd been groomed by Dad to live with Mom forever. But it was time for me to address the separation anxiety that had suffocated me ever since my crying days in kindergarten, when I was afraid to be away from home for five minutes. I had to cut the umbilical cord.

Jessie and I pooled our money together and bought her father's ranch-style house only a 30-minute drive from my mother. It really was more of a symbolic gesture for me rather than a move of the heart, I must admit. Mom still lived only five minutes from where I worked at the chiropractor's office, so I went over every day for lunch and then after work, too. And even though Jessie and I had shared our recent Jesus experiences together, our relationship had been as up and down as my car rides along the Joe D highway, so I wasn't sure how long we were going to last. Still, the move out was a little leap toward freedom.

Mom wasn't so happy about it; she had her own separation anxieties to deal with and never liked to be alone. We'd been like twins joined at the hip since my birth, sharing emotions and even a bed. But to her credit, she tried to be supportive about my decision. It was universally agreed that my father should not be told I was moving out, never mind with a woman!

"There's no way Dad will be able to handle it," Yolanda agreed, "and there's no way he's going to get any information out of me."

As far as Dad was concerned, the official family statement about me for the time being—and for the rest of my life, until further notice—was that I was living at home, taking care of Mom, and dating a lot (but not *too* many) of those nice Italian-Catholic boys. That's what we all told him, over and over, until we were blue in the face. Whether he believed it or not is another story. After all, you can't really con a con artist.

Dad was constantly interrogating my siblings to see if they'd slip up with any incriminating information about me. "Don't you have something to tell me about Rita?" he'd ask Yolanda, during her visits to LaGuardia.

"No, I have nothing to tell you."

And then, ten minutes later, in the middle of a different conversation: "What's happening with Rita—who's she dating? Tell me what's going on."

"She's dating a few guys."

"Who? You have something to tell me, don't you?"

"What do you want me to tell you, Dad? She's fine! Everything's fine."

Dad's house arrest was my freedom. It allowed me to do what I wanted to do without fear that he'd suddenly turn up in Jersey at 4 A.M. to give an impromptu inspection.

Once in a while, I did wonder if he'd go so far as to dispatch one of his crew to secretly follow me around and get the goods as to what I was up to. But that thought was fleeting, as I knew he didn't have the interest to go to that much trouble. My sisters and

I felt he knew the truth anyway and just hated being lied to. (Ha! Me, too!) At the same time, he didn't want to acknowledge the truth, so we all played this game for his sake and our own.

NOW THAT I WAS GOING TO SCHOOL IN THE CITY, I saw my father more than ever. Massage school was a ten-minute drive from Dad's place, so I was often summoned after class to come for a visit. It was always great to see Gram Crackers, but it was becoming more frustrating for me to be around my father. I was trying to live an authentic life as best I could, and he was getting deeper and deeper into his act.

Dad's longtime psychiatrist would sometimes pay him a house call while I was there, to do one of many psychological "evaluations" on him. They'd sit at the dining-room table, and Gram would make them strong coffees and try to feed the doctor lunch, all the while tossing her two cents into the medical exam. Her family background in the medical field made her an expert by proxy, she thought.

"How do you feel today, Vincent?" the psychiatrist would ask.

"I don't know," Dad would answer, deadpan, staring off into space.

"He's-a sick, doctor!" Gram would yell out from her station at the stove.

"What do you mean you don't know, Vincent?"

"God told me to say that."

"Is no good!" Gram would pipe in, shaking her head as she poured the coffee. "He's-a talking to God. Is not good."

"Do you hear God talk to you, Vincent?" the doctor would ask.

"I see pink elephants on the wall."

"You see what?"

"Spider, spider, on the wall . . . ain't you got no pants at all?" Dad would rhyme off, and then he'd giggle, or go into a Daffy Duck impression. Whenever he'd go that far, I'd have to leave the room. I couldn't stand it.

My own conversations with my father were slightly improved from our memorized, scripted days of my childhood because now he had two more topics he could ask me about (but still only vaguely care about)—massage school, and all that so-called dating I was busy doing.

I'd sit down with Dad, and Gram would feed me an awesome sandwich of roast beef, fresh mozzarella, steamed carrots with oil, vinegar, and garlic, on Italian bread. Even though I was following my strict eating regime, I didn't want to hurt her feelings, so I ate it. Plus, it was so fucking good. After lunch, Dad and I would do our revised shtick.

"How's your mother?"

"Good, Dad."

"You need anything?"

"No, I'm fine."

Pause.

"You dating anyone?"

Pause.

"Yeah. But no one serious."

Pause.

"How's school?"

"I really love it. I'm learning a lot, Dad. I really think I've found my calling."

Dad didn't want to hear about the details, though. He was pissed off when I first told him that I was going to study massage. "I don't want you touching people, especially men," he said. I wonder if he was also worried about the women.

But a staggeringly beautiful thing started to happen once I decided to take care of myself: I refused to let others upset or derail me. I especially wasn't going to listen to Dad—someone who, as far as I was concerned, had made a mess of his life and ours. He wasn't exactly a pillar of great life advice.

"Dad, I really enjoy it. I'll be careful with strangers."

Funnily enough, he didn't want me to go back to school, but he had no problem benefiting from my new skills. Some days when I'd arrive from class, fingers aching, he'd be sitting at the dining-room table waiting for me to practice on him. "Come over here and rub my shoulders," he'd say.

Other times, I'd just go up behind him and dig my elbow deep into his trapezius. For the amount of stress he lived with, his body was pretty loose and limber, but that might have been because he had the Rubber beating up on him regularly. What I remember most about working on Dad's shoulders was how he felt *energetically*. At massage school, I had begun to notice a tingling feeling of energy as I learned the techniques. But with Dad, it was one of the first times where I touched someone and could feel a strong energy force coming off of his body, like an invisible charge flowing back and forth through the tips of my fingers.

I could feel Dad's pure, unique essence, like a fingerprint, and I tried somehow to communicate with it. Maybe I was no contest for Joey the Rubber's 90-minute beatings, but I must have done something right. When I'd finish, it would be one of the few times he gave me a compliment. "You have good hands," he'd say. And then he'd repeat it to my mother: "Hey, Hon. She's got good hands!"

My father's doctors; his driver, Brewster; the Rubber; and my uncles were his main visitors while he was under house arrest. Dad had to be very careful about the crew since FBI surveillance was more scrupulous than ever, so Dom, Dom, and Dom stayed away.

Brewster drove Dad and Gram around to appointments when needed. He was a bald, roly-poly sort with a wide nose and a sweet disposition, and the family absolutely adored him. Yet Dad would just torture the poor guy. Maybe he was taking out his house-arrest restlessness on him, I don't know, but Dad was always calling him stupid names like "Flabber." Or he'd embarrass Brewster in front of us by smacking him in the back of the head for some little thing he had done that pissed him off. Dad was very, very good at embarrassing people.

Brewster would flinch every time Dad made a move because he never knew when he was going to get cracked. Whenever I saw Dad hit him, my body felt every blow and my hand clenched, wanting to hit Dad back for him. Of course none of us in the family dared to say a word when we witnessed Dad's cruelty toward

Brewster, for fear that he'd turn on us. Except for Gram, who was always the exception and always the brave one.

If Gram stood within earshot of the sound of Dad's slapping hand on Brewster's head, she'd rush into the room and go ballistic. "Vincenzo! *Basta!* Stop!" She'd pull Dad away from Brewster. She was the only one he'd listen to, and he'd stop.

And yet, Dad loved Brewster. Part of my father's demented psychology was that he often didn't know how to show love or channel his frustration. When Brewster was diagnosed with cancer after a few years working for us, Dad sent him to the best oncologists in the country, all expenses paid.

IF DAD WAS YOUR BOSS AND HE PAID YOU WELL, which he always did, you were at the mercy of his command and of his extreme moods. Not only did it work with his crew, but it worked with his family, too.

Every Christmas, each of us kids would receive a thick wad of bills from Dad, with an old rubber band wrapped around it. The holiday hand-off at his apartment usually consisted of him passing out the money, without saying anything. We'd say, "Thanks, Dad," and kiss his cheek. "Love you."

As for me, I'd go home to Jersey and stash the pile under a piece of hardwood on my bedroom floor, which had been pried loose with a crowbar specifically for safekeeping purposes. I also kept some of the money and any other valuables I was given in a special safe the size of a shoebox built into my bedroom closet. The lock had a miniature key, which I kept with me at all times.

At some point, it started to dawn on me that Dad was rewarding us for secrets kept and abuse taken during the year. If you kept the secrets, you could have money, a new car, or a diamond necklace. Once a year, my sisters and I went to Dad's apartment to look at jewelry. The dining-room table would be laid out with necklaces, rings, and bracelets. Yolanda got to pick first. Then Roseanne. When it got to me, I stood there, not moving.

"Rita, pick out some jewelry for yourself," Dad would say.

I didn't want to take anything because I didn't wear jewelry— and even though it was displayed there beautifully for our picking and choosing, it didn't feel free. Giving gifts and money was a way my father manipulated people. He was very smart about it because he gave a lot, but never too much. It was enough to make you dependent, but not enough to keep you from coming back for more.

By December 1996, I was working hard at two jobs—as a massage therapist, and as a personal trainer at the chiropractor's office —in an effort to build my experience and discern my spiritual vocation. For the first time in my life, I was self-sufficient. I was paying my own mortgage and car payments, and I felt great being able to rely on myself.

Dad was recovering from surgery to have his pacemaker changed, so a few days before Christmas it was Mom who handed out the traditional holiday "bonus." To our mother, this yearly cash was a generous Christmas gift our father was able to give to his children after the many sacrifices he made at work. She didn't think about where it came from; she just thought he was a hardworking man trying to take care of his family as best he could.

It was a Sunday morning, and I had just finished decorating the tree in my living room with colored lights and tinsel, and the house smelled of pine needles. As I sat at the kitchen table eating my perfectly proportioned Zone breakfast—40 percent carbs, 30 percent protein, and 30 percent fat—Mom came in and slapped down the envelope of cash on the kitchen table in front of me.

"Here, Ri. Merry Christmas from your father."

I looked at the envelope and my stomach twisted.

"What's the matter?"

What was the matter? *Everything* was the matter. I had spent the year pulling my body and soul together, trying to make all of me strong and pure, and now I was looking at a pile of blood money. I didn't have a problem taking it all those other years, maybe because I was in denial or because I felt he owed it to me for all the times he was invisible in my life and for all the pain his actions had caused me.

I didn't live in denial anymore. So now when I looked at Dad's money, all I could see was where it came from—from his lies, from his need for power, from his ugly world. Now I looked at his money not as a present, but as a bribe. And I didn't want to be under my father's thumb anymore. Taking this money meant that I'd be selling part of my soul, and I'd just got that precious part of me back . . . it wasn't up for sale or auction to the highest bidder anymore. The whole setup made me want to throw up.

I pushed the envelope away. "I don't want it."

"What?"

"Tell Dad I don't want it." *Fuck him and his money.*

"What's wrong?"

"Mom, I don't want his fucking money anymore. It always comes with a price to pay, and it's not worth it to me."

Mom looked at me in disbelief. "He's your father," she said, "and even though he's made mistakes, he still takes care of us and you should respect him. What would you do if he didn't help us?"

I still refused. When Mom saw there was no changing my mind, she took back the envelope, perplexed. I'm sure she made up some sort of story for Dad, or maybe she didn't even tell him at all. I have no idea what happened to that money, and I don't care. I knew myself, and that was good enough for me. Not taking my father's money was the best Christmas present I ever gave myself.

It was a time to let go of unhealthy ways altogether, so the second best Christmas present I gave myself that year was breaking up with Jessie. From the beginning, our romance had been tumultuous, and I knew soon after we moved in together that it wouldn't last. Jessie had a jealous streak that had grown worse the year we lived together. One night when we'd gone out, she saw me have an innocent conversation with a female friend and got so angry that she stormed home. Once inside, she threw and broke anything in our bedroom she could grab hold of, pushing the mattress off the bed in a rage.

Finally, her jealousy became too much for me. "Look, I can't do this anymore," I told her, at the risk of using clichéd soap-opera dialogue. I packed a suitcase and left, leaving most of my belongings behind.

After we sold the house, I met Jessie at the bank to get my share of the money, and I set up temporary camp back in my old room at Mom's.

THEN, THE UNTHINKABLE HAPPENED.

In May 1997, one month before my father went to trial after seven years of house arrest, Gram experienced terrible pains in her stomach. Uncle Lou took her to the hospital, and doctors diagnosed her with severe pancreatitis. Her blood wasn't filtering toxins, so the poison was rushing through her veins, spreading throughout her body. At first doctors thought she'd recover, but after a few days, they told us she wouldn't survive.

Gram wasn't afraid of death, but she had one request. "I don't want to die lying down," she told Uncle Lou, who sat by her side and propped her up with pillows. "Put me up in a chair."

For a woman as religious as my grandmother, it gave her a lot of comfort to have her son the priest by her side, saying all the official prayers and doing all the official priest stuff. He had brought her light blue rosary beads to the hospital for her, and she clutched them in her hands. A few days after she was admitted to the hospital, she was sitting up with Uncle Lou in the middle of the night when her breathing became labored and gurgled, and then she passed away.

I was in a deep sleep when I bolted upright in bed at 3 A.M. *Gram's gone,* I thought.

Around me, I could feel a tangible energy swirling about in the room like a breeze blowing in from the window. Seconds later, the phone rang, and I could hear Mom pick it up in her bedroom and speak quietly, then she was standing at my door in tears.

"Rita, Uncle Lou just called. Grandma passed."

For the funeral home, my brothers arranged a schedule with our half-siblings to keep the two families apart. So we stayed with Gram until 9 P.M., cleared out, and the other family arrived— and never the twain did meet.

The next day Uncle Lou performed a traditional Mass at Gram's favorite church, Our Lady of Pompeii, five blocks away from the dungeon and the neighborhood Gram called home her whole life. She wore a pale blue dress, her Sunday best, and the organist played "Ave Maria" as her casket was carried out of the church. Outside, dozens of reporters stood in wait. They had hoped to catch sight of my father, but he didn't come. My mother said it broke his heart not to attend his own mother's funeral, but he knew the FBI would be there watching closely, trying to catch him out of character, and that could cause problems.

As the organist played, I watched my grandmother's body being carried out of the church and was struck with a thought. *Gram planned this.*

She timed her exit perfectly. There was no doubt in my mind that Gram left this world on the eve of her son's trial, a trial that might put him in jail for the rest of his life. By age 95, she had already lost three children—her first Vincent as a baby; then Uncle Pat when I was a teen; and more recently, Uncle Ralph after a long illness—and she had lived and loved and lost and suffered enough for one full lifetime. She knew she couldn't bear one more loss, especially of the son who'd been right by her side for so long. And so, like I'd done with Gram's kitchen calendar 15 years earlier, Crackers had beaten me at my own game and picked her own death day.

I like to imagine that in the end, her good friend the Virgin Mary appeared to her once again in the hospital room, as she had done 60 years earlier, and this time, Gram said to her, "*Sì, sì . . . ora.* I'm ready now." Then, sitting upright like a queen, Gram happily followed her home.

There was no doubt in anyone's mind where the soul of Gram Crackers was going.

CHAPTER 15

METAMORPHOSIS

It wasn't until a few weeks later that the reality of Gram's death knocked me down like a sucker punch.

I'd come home after a long day of work to find sentimental reminders of Gram on the kitchen table: dozens of her hand-crocheted doilies, topped by her light blue rosary. I burst into tears.

Gram was the matriarch of our family, the one solid, true person depended upon by everyone, including my father. She was the cultural and spiritual backbone of this organization of ours. What would happen to us with her gone? Like the doilies, she lovingly stitched and restitched our family together as a meaningful whole. We were flawed for sure, just as the homemade doilies were. But with her handiwork, we were at least in one piece, linked together. Now I felt as though our world was unraveling . . . and I wasn't sure if I could stop it.

NOT LONG AFTER MY GRIEF FOR GRAM SURFACED, we got word that my father's trial was set to begin in late June. Dad had been found competent to stand trial and was finally going to face his judge and jury, and the tangled web he himself had woven would be unraveled in a court of law, for the whole world to see. At home, Mom was a nervous wreck and prayed for a miracle. But I've come to learn that miracles are mystifying—sometimes you pray for one kind, and God delivers you another.

I was now dating Jennifer, and it was a much more peaceful relationship than the one I'd had with Jessie. Even so, I realized after my time with Jessie that every relationship, no matter the difficulties, can yield goodness. From her I had learned that I must be honest as soon as possible within any relationship. I knew from the start I didn't feel right about moving in with her, but I said nothing because I didn't want to hurt her feelings. Honesty, I realized, is a better policy than politeness.

The other good that came of my time with Jessie was my introduction to my first laying on of hands, which opened up a whole new world for me. That world continued and grew during my brief time with Jennifer.

It began the afternoon we were swimming in Mom's pool on a beautiful summer day. Jennifer was lazily drifting on a blow-up rubber raft, and I was slowly treading water nearby, with my eyes shut and face tilted skyward. The water was warm and soothing, and I felt like I was rocking back and forth in a giant womb. I would have stayed there forever except that I was starving. I got out of the pool to get us something to eat from the kitchen, and as I stepped back outside, Jennifer looked up at me, shocked.

"What is it?" I asked her. "What's wrong?"

"Rita! Oh, my God. "

I recognized that tone in her voice. It was the one I'd had when I saw Jesus in the church window and on the shower door. *They're baaaaaack.* For as long as I live, I will never forget the look on Jennifer's face. Her mouth and eyes were open wide, like a fish out of water.

"Next to you . . . next to you . . . *angels!*" She told me that she saw four white angels—two male, two female—who were ten feet tall, with wings the size of our pool table downstairs. "They're walking with you as if they're guarding you!"

I spun around to either side of myself, but saw nothing. "I don't see them. Are they saying anything?"

"No. They're just giving off a feeling of . . . *protection*."

According to Jennifer, my angelic bodyguards walked with me for the 20 feet it took me to get from the back door to the pool, and then they vanished. We were both stunned, and then we had a little nervous chuckle about it. First Jesus, then Mary, now this? God's sending His angels down?

"Maybe Jesus was busy," Jennifer half-joked.

Despite our laughter, we both took this apparition seriously. It's not every day that a person sees Jesus or angels—well, not most people. For me, it was becoming a regular thing, as if my communion with Jesus that day in the church had opened up a portal between the spirit world and myself. It took a little getting used to, these visits from the Other Side, and I wasn't sure what it all meant exactly.

Jennifer was certain that the angels by the pool were here as reinforcements, perhaps to help in whatever upheaval was about to come for my family. I wondered if they were here for Dad's upcoming warfare or for my own. Either way, I couldn't imagine that having a legion of angels around would be a *bad* thing. Still, I made a mental note to call up some healers and mediums I'd met in the past year to ask their opinion of all my angelic visitors.

In the meantime, I went to sleep that night flooded with well-being, certain that the angels around me were my invisible "crew," watching over me during this transitional time. Dad had his crew on Earth, and I had mine in heaven—although you might say that mine were playing for the opposing team.

I fell into a deep slumber, dreaming of sunlight shining off pools of water and feathered wings brushing against my face and Mary hugging her baby on a glass door. Yet I woke up from the dream sweating and shaking, with the sensation of pins and needles prickling me from head to toe. I looked at the clock: 3 A.M. The same time I'd woken up knowing that Gram had died.

I was staying over at Jennifer's that night, and my body was vibrating so violently, it woke her up. She put her hand on my arm and gasped. "You're shaking! What is happening to you?"

"I don't know," I whispered, "but I feel like shit. Shittier than my usual feeling-like-shit feeling. And that's pretty damn shitty."

I didn't have a fever, and I wasn't cold. We couldn't figure out what it was. For the next few days, I was drenched with sweat and the shaking got worse. I grew dizzy and so tired, all I had the strength to do was eat and then go back to bed.

I went to the doctor and took a battery of blood tests and x-rays for everything, but they all came back negative. "There's nothing wrong with you," he proclaimed, and sent me home.

I went to a chiropractor, who incorrectly diagnosed me with Lyme disease and gave me a slew of herbs to take. When they almost killed me with an allergic reaction that made my throat swell, I flushed them down the toilet and threw up my hands in frustration. It was my childhood all over again: I was sick but didn't know what the hell was wrong with me.

As I lay in bed, shaking in my soaked sheets, it crossed my mind that maybe those well-meaning angels from the week before weren't a good sign at all; maybe they were here to finally take me away. *Maybe they'll put me out of my misery*, I thought.

I let myself think that for a minute or so, then got pissed off at myself and pushed the negative, useless thought away. That was the old me, the victim me, talking. The stronger, wiser me of today knew about the emotion-body intertwining, so it was time to get my ass in gear and put that knowledge into practice.

I sprang out of bed and, with trembling fingers, dialed up Anise, a local energy intuitive I had begun seeing a few months earlier. She worked with people's physical, emotional, spiritual, and energetic imbalances and specialized in a process she called "metamorphosis"—helping people shed layers of emotional hurt, like the silken layers of a cocoon, until they were free of them.

I blurted out my symptoms as I paced the basement floor, my face hot and flushed. She listened calmly and keyed into my energy. Then after a few minutes of silence on her end, and a lot more pacing on mine, she asked, "Rita, who hit you across the face?"

"What do you mean?"

"I keep seeing you getting slapped in the face, but it's in the past. Someone is hitting you, and it keeps coming and coming and—"

"Anise, I don't know what you're talking about. No one hit me."

"It has to do with your family. What happened to you ten years ago?"

I paced and sifted through my mind. *Ten years ago . . . ten years ago . . .* I stopped in my tracks. My stomach dropped, like I was in an elevator that plummeted down a thousand miles in one second.

Before I knew it, I was 19 years old again, back in Mom's kitchen with Sal, Roseanne, and Janet. In slow motion, I could see and feel Sal's hand coming at me with the force of a wrecking ball. I felt myself being smacked and lifted off the floor, then crashing down into a crumpled mass. Every detail was sharp and in Technicolor in my memory: the smell of Sal's sweaty T-shirt, the sound of his slapping hand against the veins of my neck, the terrifying gush of my bowels exploding down my legs, and the look in Sal's eyes: he wanted to kill me.

Thankfully, Jennifer was in the basement with me, so she was there to grab me as I almost passed out from the memory. Only it didn't feel like a memory at all—it felt like it was happening to me right there and then, all over again.

"You never dealt with it," Anise explained, as I lay down on the couch and painstakingly described that night to her. "The emotional and physical trauma has been locked away in your body underneath the surface all these years, causing you illness. I see that there are a lot of hurtful memories you've been holding on to, not just this one. But the time has come for you to deal with and then release them," she said. "It's a painful process, to be sure, but you must endure it to get to the other side."

"Endure what, exactly?"

"Everything you're feeling. And it's going to get worse—much worse—before it gets better."

"Where will it lead me?"

"To where you're supposed to be. To peace."

"How long will it take?"

"As long as it takes."

I hung up the phone, got back into bed, and surrendered to whatever was going to happen to me. I knew Anise was right. As she explained what she saw and I re-experienced the Sal ordeal, I felt the truth of the mind-body connection between my illness today and my emotions of that night so long ago like a lightbulb going on in my soul.

Sal had apologized to me over and over after that night, and I had said "I forgive you" in reply. I had mouthed those words to him, yes, but it was like an out-of-body experience when I said them. My body, heart, and soul hadn't really forgiven him at the time because they couldn't face the horror of that evening. I had put the pain on file and locked it away, trying to forget. But now I was strong enough, Anise assured me, to remember it and to face it. I had to. It was that, or remain the victim and get sicker.

A FEW DAYS LATER, JENNIFER AND I WENT TO my third laying on of hands at a local Catholic church. I barely made it to the pew because I was still shaking and sweating. We waited there until the priest gave us the signal to come up and get healed. At the front of the church, I saw a huge crucifix by the altar with stars of energy shooting off Jesus. It was beautiful; I couldn't take my eyes off it.

Father Fabrizio looked over at me almost immediately and rushed to us in the third pew. "You're next," he said, pointing to me.

At the front by the altar, he put his hands on my shoulders and started to pray. I went down like a feather. The priest knelt down beside me on the floor, took off his stole and put it on my forehead, and kept praying. When he was done, he looked at me, startled.

"God talked to me," he said, a little taken aback.

"Wha-what do you mean?"

"God told me to put my stole on your forehead and said to tell you that you would be healed emotionally in three years."

For the next few weeks, I tossed and turned in my bed. Did that priest tell me I was going to have three years of this? It was like my soul was combusting—any and every symptom I could possibly get physically and emotionally, I was aflame with. I'd get up in the middle of the night, drenched with sweat and spilling over with rage, rip a piece of paper from a notebook, and scrawl letters to my brother. I never sent them; I crumpled them up into angry balls and threw them on the floor. But I wrote them anyway, to release the pain.

> *Tuesday, June 24*
> *Sal,*
> *Fuck you.*
> *Fuck you for what you did to me. Fuck you for not accepting me. Fuck you for making me feel like nothing.*

> *Saturday, June 28*
> *Dear Sal,*
> *How could you break my heart like you did? Why did you make it impossible for me to ever trust you again? Why were you not a big brother looking out for me and protecting me instead of hurting me?*

> *Wednesday, July 2*
> *Sal,*
> *Fuck you for nearly killing me. Fuck you for kicking me when I was already so down, I was barely hanging on. Didn't I have enough to deal with without your betrayal as well? Don't you have an ounce of compassion in your soul at all?*

Anise had told me to call up an intuitive healer she knew named Julie Joy Johnston to help guide me through the process. I called up Julie Joy and described the hell-bent path I was on.

"Rita, you're going through a 'dark night of the soul,'" she said.

"The what?"

"It's like a death-and-rebirth process. It strips you of everything you know in order to rebuild you."

Jennifer and I looked it up in the encyclopedia at the library. The phrase *dark night of the soul* came from a poem written by Saint John of the Cross, a 16th-century Spanish Carmelite monk and mystic. His poem was about the soul's journey from the distractions and entanglements of the world to a place of perfect peace and harmony with God. According to the poet, the "dark night" is akin to the agony and spiritual growth Jesus endured before going to the cross.

But of course! That's when Jesus had gone to the garden of Gethsemane after the Last Supper and was in such anguish, praying to God that he didn't want to face the pain to come even though it meant salvation for the entire human race. In the end, he knew he had to go through it so that he, and we, could come out better people on the other side of it. My own dark night, I learned, had begun the evening the angels escorted me to the swimming pool. They were taking me to the diving board so I could take the leap.

"When you go through a dark night," Julie explained, "you rid yourself of the beliefs that were harming you so that new beliefs can enter. You've got to go through the dark to get to the light."

I braced myself for both the agony and the ecstasy of my upcoming metamorphosis. *Give it to me, God; I can take it.*

During this process—which lasted way more than one night —I visited Anise and Julie for dozens of hands-on healing and energy sessions.

Anise had a quaint little house filled with knickknacks, and shelves brimming with books on metaphysics. She was just what you'd imagine a healer to look like: she had a long mane of white hair and a big friendly smile. I half expected her to take out her Woodstock photo albums and tell me about her meditative romp in the field with Ravi Shankar.

Anise would lead me through her kitchen, up a winding staircase, and through a set of gauzy drapes to reach her healing room. There, we'd sit opposite each other in silence with our eyes shut until she could sense the part of my body that was "blocked" with the energy of past emotions. With her hands, she'd lightly touch the area—I could feel a tingling warmth as she did—and she'd begin to ask me questions.

"Tell me about that night . . . how did you feel . . . "

After a few minutes, I'd take a deep breath and Anise's body would shake. That meant that the energy had moved through my body, to her hands, and through her body—taking the blockage with it and releasing it completely. When I'd open my eyes, I'd feel lighter. With each session, a new layer of the pain cocoon was curling up and peeling off.

One morning at dawn, I woke up and went to my notebook. I calmly wrote:

Dear Sal. I love and forgive you.

And with those simple words, I began to say good-bye forever to the pain and hurt I'd been carrying around with me for a decade. It was to be an ongoing process, but I had set the course. I slowly tore up the note into ribbons and placed them gently in my wastepaper basket, to go out with the trash the next day.

When I finally emerged from under the cloak of my dark night, Dad's trial was well under way in Brooklyn. At home, we didn't watch anything about it on TV or read the newspaper stories. Yolanda had been going to the courthouse most days, though, so she'd give Mom and me daily reports on how it was going.

Sitting in the courtroom wasn't something Mom would have been able to handle. First, we knew the "other" kids would be there, which would have been awkward for her. Second, it would have brought back unpleasant memories of that one day in court almost 40 years earlier—Mom's first and only run-in with the other woman. Third, if she couldn't bear to watch Dad get hit in the boxing ring by a teenage boy 60 years earlier, how would she manage watching the FBI agents go at him like hungry wolves who finally got their paws on their prey?

Staying home also allowed Mom to drift in and out of a state of denial about the idea that her husband might be put away for good. On top of that, she was also worried about me. She'd seen me feverish and panicked in bed all those weeks and assumed I was having another one of my anxiety/depression attacks. I didn't tell her about the dark night or how I'd been, in my own way, fighting for my life.

Now that I'd gotten through it, I switched my focus to my father. I'd gone the distance fighting for my life and was bruised from the battle but still standing; it was his turn to fight for his.

As the trial was coming to a close, I finally went to the courthouse to show my support.

I had known about Dad's three other children for seven years but was the only sibling who hadn't met them, so I mentally prepared myself to do so. I was nervous and had my guard up, and didn't know what to expect from them—or myself.

Yo, Ro, and I arrived together on a steaming hot July day; the courtroom was packed with people mopping their brows with hankies. Yolanda led us to a bench in the third row, directly behind Dad. Our brothers and the other kids were already there.

To say that what happened next was one of the strangest moments of my life is . . . well, at this point, that's saying a lot. To say it felt completely normal—that's not saying much. What was normal in my world? The truth is, meeting my half-siblings for the first time as we stood 20 feet away from our mutual father on trial for his life was both the oddest and the most ordinary event of my life.

"Oh, hi, Rita! Good to see you," Cammie, the youngest of the other siblings, said to me as we all kissed and hugged like we'd shared Christmas mornings and Sunday-night dinners together our whole lives. This was just another family get-together, our easy hugs and kisses said.

"How are you?" I asked each one. We all knew each other's names as we went down the row, greeting each other.

On the scale of normalcy, it was the typical thing for an Italian family to do—hug, kiss, and show respect that way. But we do that with strangers we're meeting for the first time, too. Even after a seven-year buildup, that's what this meeting felt like. My three half-siblings may have had the same blood as mine coursing through their veins and the same DNA in their eyes, their hair, and their smiles—but looking into their eyes, I felt nothing. I didn't feel happy or upset, just neutral. We were intimate strangers.

There wasn't time to analyze these nonfeelings any further, though, because as soon as we sat down, the show began.

Dad's lawyers pushed him into the courtroom in a wheelchair. He was wearing black sweatpants, a white T-shirt, and a black jacket. He had arrived his first day in court wearing pajamas and a bathrobe, Yo told me, but the judge wasn't going for any of that and ordered him to dress more appropriately the next time.

I watched the back of my father's head and his profile while the judge listed off the charges against him: *extortion, racketeering and threats; interstate commerce, racketeering activity, and conspiracy; violent crime in aid of racketeering, murder first degree; and interstate commerce, labor payoff conspiracy.*

Inwardly, I shuddered. After 14 years of knowing what my father did, it still shocked me to hear it out loud. I still couldn't see him that way. I guess part of me was like Mom—wanting to cling to the best of him and hold on to that, untouched.

In fact, I had found out a bit of information regarding that other past infamous alleged murder attempt that soothed my soul. A family friend who was in Dad's business remembered talking to my father about the Costello shooting in 1957, the one Dad had supposedly botched when he yelled, "This is for you, Frank!" Everybody thought for the longest time my father had just made an inexperienced error when he called out like that, but our family friend told me otherwise.

"Costello was supposed to be alone when he showed up at his apartment," the friend told me, "but he arrived with a group of people. Your father didn't want to hit anyone else—he was worried someone innocent would get shot—and that's why he called out to Costello. He thought if he did, the others would get out of the way and be safe."

The new information stunned me. Did he mess up because he cared about those other people? Maybe he messed up because he wanted to? Sitting in the courtroom hearing Dad's murder charges now, I thought about his two "botched" attempts. My father was not the type to make mistakes. He was smart, he was methodical, and he was bold. If my dad did point the gun at Costello or order the bomb put in Gotti's car, maybe his innate, higher self would not let it follow through. Maybe his higher soul resisted the manifestation of his actions.

As the judge and the lawyers began proceedings, I couldn't take my eyes off my father. He knew that all of his children were together that day in the courtroom. In one glance, he would see for the first (and only) time in his life, all of us together. But for the longest time, he didn't look over at us. He looked anywhere else he could—up at the ceiling, out the window, down at his feet—and seemed disoriented. In other words, it was just like always when he knew he was being scrutinized and he had to put on the act.

I tried to key into his energy from where I sat—an ability I'd been cultivating with the healers—and it felt heavy and overwhelming. He looked strong but tired, and I felt sorry for him. I didn't want him to go to jail, but I had the feeling that they were not going to let go of him. I think he knew it, too. I wondered what my life would be like if my dad wasn't around anymore, if I didn't have to go to the city and see him or worry about hiding who I was from him. That part of me was excited, and I felt guilty about that.

I barely remember anything from the trial that day, except the sinking feeling that no matter what Dad's brilliant lawyers were telling the jury, and no matter what Dad's very credible witnesses were saying on the stand, he was doomed. Like John Gotti,

Vincent Gigante now had to pay a price for whatever he'd done, and there was no stopping it. (In 1992, Gotti was convicted of five murders—including the Castellano murder, thanks to testimony given by Sammy "The Bull"—conspiracy to commit murder, racketeering, obstruction of justice, illegal gambling, tax evasion, and loansharking and was sentenced to life in prison without parole. I silently prayed that my father's price wouldn't be so heavy.)

When the proceedings were finished for the day, Dad's eight children looked up at him expectantly from the bench. His lawyer stood up to begin wheeling him out of the room, but Dad reached down and clasped the wheel of the chair with his hand, halting the lawyer for a moment. That's when he finally turned his head around and took one sweeping glance at all of us, sitting there together for him. For a fraction of a second, he broke character and smiled. Then he was wheeled away.

A FEW WEEKS LATER, BEFORE OUR FATHER'S FATE WAS DECIDED UPON, I met my two half-sisters, Cammie and Lucia, for a drink in a funky little bar downtown. My cousin had Lisa set up the meeting and picked the place.

After I found out about Dad's second family I also found out that Lisa, who was very close to me, had known about them all along and had been seeing her "secret cousins" for years. That she had kept this hidden from me was another blow. But I had to understand the situation as if I was in her shoes: If I had been ordered to keep my mouth shut, I would have, too. She and I never talked about it after I found out, but I imagine she was now relieved that she didn't have to keep it from me anymore.

Mom said she didn't mind if I met up with the other kids, so I felt okay about it on that end. As for my father, I figured it would make him happy to know that the one lost, rebel sheep was inching her way into the fold.

In that dark little bar, I took a good look at my half-sisters' faces. In court, I'd been too focused on my father to take much notice. But now, sitting across from them in a little booth, I looked at these girls and did a brief scan of their features, searching for something familiar. I was shocked to realize that Lucia was the spitting image of Yolanda in her younger years. I didn't think either of them looked like me, but they both told me that their brother, Vincent, had been told countless times by family members that he resembled Sal.

After we ordered drinks, we had the kind of small talk you have when a friend introduces you to other friends of theirs. We talked about work, school, if we had any hobbies in common. We weren't sure how to really talk to each other, so we all tiptoed on a tightrope, trying to keep our balance and not jar anyone else with any quick movements. I asked them about mundane topics, but what I really wanted to know was: *How long have you known about us? What does my father say about us? Is he different with you? Why do you get more of him?*

At one point, we broke the ice and started comparing notes about Dad, joking around a bit, trying to lighten up a topic that was anything but light and funny.

"Does he ask you questions over and over," Cammie asked, "until he gets the answer he wants?"

"Oh, yeah."

I found out that Dad threw Cammie, Lucia, and Vincent parties when they graduated from high school. I flashed back on my own graduation: Mom and my sisters had come, and after it was over, a tiny part of me looked to see if Dad was waiting out there for me. I remember thinking, *Wow. You couldn't even show up for my graduation?*

I looked at my half-sisters now and flashed back on our divided Christmases when, I found out later, Dad would whisper to Yo, "We gotta be done by six o'clock," so that he could then spend the second half of the day with his other family. I remember how hurt Mom and Gram would be when we were ushered out. We were the early shift and they were the late shift.

I delicately brought up the topic of their mother. Cammie dug into her purse and pulled out a snapshot and handed it to me. I examined the photo and couldn't hide my surprise. The other woman was sitting at a table at what looked like a family party, with a small smile on her face. Her short dark hair hung flat against her head, and she looked plain.

"This is her?" I asked. She wasn't what I expected at all. I stared at the photo, lost in thought about my mother, thinking how beautiful she looked in her wedding photo with Dad. I can't remember how I brought it up, but I must have mumbled something about Mom and Dad being married for nearly 50 years now.

Lucia and Cammie looked at me blankly.

"What do you mean?" Cammie asked.

And just when I thought this whole Dad-has-another-family drama couldn't get any worse, one more lie was added to the pile, one more punch to the gut was thrown.

"You know my parents are still married, right?" I asked them. "They never divorced. They're still *to-ge-ther*."

Cammie shook her head adamantly. "No, no," she insisted. "He and *my* mother are married!"

"Not possible," I told her, putting my ginger ale down and looking at both of them squarely in the eyes. "Not. Possible."

I actually felt sorry for both of them in that moment. I could see by their crestfallen faces that they were not used to constantly discovering lies about their parents as I had become accustomed to over the years. Lisa didn't know what to say to ease the situation; she probably wasn't sure of the truth herself, so couldn't take a side.

Cammie and Lucia finished their drinks in silence, stealing glances at each other. I had ruffled their feathers, I saw. They had what Gram used to call *confidenza*—a sense of entitlement—and they were pretty pissed off that I had possibly taken away a big chunk of it. But I was only speaking the truth.

Our cozy girls' night ended quickly after that. I went home and told Mom that the girls thought she and Dad were divorced. That exchange produced an unfortunate domino effect that, once started, could not be stopped.

Mom sat down and angrily scribbled one of her break-up letters to Dad and sent it to him the next day using my sisters as reluctant courier pigeons. This one said: "Get the 'other' one to do your shit from now on!"

Dad, Yo, Ro, and Brewster were all sitting around the dining-room table at LaGuardia when Ro handed Dad the letter and he read it. He stood up and slammed his fist on the table so hard, the coffee cups rattled and everyone jumped.

"You did this!" he yelled at Roseanne, pointing at her. "You told them!"

"No! I knew you'd blame me for this! I didn't!"

"Yes, you did!"

My father was enraged and didn't wait for Ro to answer again. In one swift move, he shoved the dining-room table against her chest, pinning her against the wall, and swung at her from across the table and slapped her on the cheek.

"Dad, stop it!" Yolanda yelled, leaping up to pull him back as best she could. It was like Sal and me all over again, only a change in cast. Ro pried herself loose from the table, slipped underneath, and ran from the room crying and screaming hysterically to hide in the bathroom.

Brewster, sweet man that he was, rushed after Ro in tears himself and tried to console her as Yo held Dad back.

"I'm so sorry, Roseanne," Brew said, hugging her, as she sobbed on his shoulder.

Ro and Brewster spent at least 30 minutes in the bathroom before they came out, and by that time, Yo had calmed Dad down. When Roseanne walked out of the bathroom, her eyes were swollen red and her cheek was bruised.

"Roseanne, I'm sorry," Dad told her. He was full of remorse. But as Ro told me later on, she didn't care. "In that moment, I hated him."

Yet in that moment, *I* loved my sister Roseanne more than anything in the world. She had protected me by not telling Dad I was the one to divulge his secret. She took a beating for me and showed what true family loyalty could be.

MOM AND I WERE THE ONLY ONES in the family who didn't go to the courthouse on the day of Dad's verdict. Mom was too nervous and emotional to go, and I wanted to stay home with her to give her support.

On July 25, 1997, my father was convicted of all counts of the indictment.

From what my family told me, Dad's conviction was based on both direct and circumstantial evidence. In a trial that lasted four weeks, prosecutors presented mob turncoats who testified that my father was the head of the Genovese crime family and relayed face-to-face discussions they'd had with him about mob business, including those murder plots and various rackets.

Making the biggest splash of them all was Sammy "The Bull" Gravano, who testified to attending a Commission sit-down meeting with my father years earlier where Dad conducted business sanely and with authority. He also added that when he and John Gotti plotted to kill Castellano in 1985, they purposely didn't reveal their plan to my father for fear of retribution.

Gravano had only met my father maybe twice in his life, one relative complained to me after his testimony. "People are getting up on the stand and making shit up," I was told.

Yet other witnesses included FBI agents and detectives who had been watching my father for years as he used public telephones in the middle of the night, and they had recordings of other associates —including Gotti and former Genovese boss Anthony Salerno— that made references to Dad as the Genovese boss. While Dad never incriminated himself on the phone or from planted bugs— and never acknowledged that he was the boss of the Genovese crime family—the evidence from his former associates and the FBI combined was enough to put him away for a while. Dad was then remanded to custody in a secure ward at Beekman Hospital in New York, pending a decision by the court as to whether he was competent to be sentenced.

After Dad was convicted, Yo called us from a pay phone outside the courthouse in tears to give us the news. We were stunned, but remained hopeful. There was still time for Dad's lawyers to pull a few rabbits out of their hats, which they did.

In September, according to the record, the charge of conspiracy to commit murder in the first degree (conspiring to kill John Gotti and his brother, Gene) was dismissed by the court following a motion made by Dad's legal team to set the verdict aside. The court also granted a mistrial on some racketeering acts as well.

In December, Dad was found competent to be sentenced and was given 12 years in prison, to be followed by five years of supervised release after his incarceration.

I HAD ALREADY SAID GOOD-BYE TO MY FATHER before the day of the verdict. My mother had implored me to visit him, just in case Dad would have to "go away" for a long time, so I did. He asked me to meet him at the other woman's brownstone and I agreed, with the guarantee that she wouldn't be in the room. I couldn't bear the pretence of having a pleasant conversation with this woman as if everything was normal.

"If she shows up, I'm leaving," I told Roseanne, who came with me. "I'll take a cab home and you can take the car."

Even though Ro was despairing after my father's recent beating, she wanted to see him, too, and figured she was safer if I was with her. Dad met us at the front door wearing his light blue pajamas and a black robe, and we all rode up a basement elevator to the first floor.

Dad had spent time convalescing at the brownstone earlier that year after having his second heart surgery in six months. At that time, he had asked his cardiologist to tell Mom that he needed to recuperate uptown, to be near Lenox Hill Hospital, which was only a block away. But really, Dad just wanted to stay with the other family as he recovered. Yolanda told me later that the doctor had refused to lie for him.

He was happy to see us, and led us to the dining-room table as I scanned the house—on the outside, it looked like an expensive brownstone, but on the inside, it wasn't much to speak of. It was dark like the dungeon (I guess you take your inner dungeon wherever you go), and the floors and a nearby stairwell were covered with paper, as if they were renovating or painting.

Considering Dad's pseudo-freedom and fate hung perilously in the hands of a group of strangers, he was strangely talkative and in a good mood.

"How's your mother? How's school?"

He started asking all the usual questions, but I stopped him. Only God knew if I was ever going to see him again; this was no time for our usual, meaningless banter. I wasn't a frightened ten-year-old anymore. I hadn't intended to confront him, but it just came out.

"Dad, does *she* know the truth about Mom?" I pointed my finger upstairs, where I knew the other woman was. "Does she know that you and Mom are still married?"

He looked uncomfortable, and annoyed. I didn't care. "Rita, it's complicated."

"Dad, I think everyone needs to know the truth. Have you told her or not?"

Roseanne shifted in her chair across from me. She looked like she was about to dive under the table for cover. But I was calm as could be. I'd spent a month facing down demons and looking at truth unflinchingly—I'd already walked through the fire. Asking my father questions and demanding an answer like a normal human being, for once in my life, didn't scare me anymore.

So I asked him again, "Dad, does this other woman know the truth?"

My father actually giggled. I think he was so taken aback that one of his children was showing such balls that he was like, *Holy shit!* He shook his head like he could not believe I was talking to him this way, and worse—that he was letting me get away with it.

I asked him again, and he giggled again. I kept going until I broke him.

"Rita, she knows the truth," he said, solemnly, looking down. And I could see he was being honest.

I sighed with relief. I was glad I'd be able to go home and tell my mother one bit of information that might make her feel better, after all she'd been through with him.

It was my last heroic gesture for Mom to help her in their confusing, tortured, fated relationship. From that point on, I made a vow to myself that I wasn't going to fight anyone else's battles anymore except my own.

It wasn't a long visit, maybe an hour. But for me to be semi-alone with Dad for that amount of time without Yo, Mom, or Gram there as a buffer, it was a lot. When it was time to leave, he kissed Roseanne and me good-bye, same as always.

"I love you," he said.

"We love you, too, Dad," we both answered. "See you soon." We started to make our way to the elevator.

"Rita?"

I stopped and turned. Ro was already out of the room.

"I'm not scared, ya know."

I walked back over to him and put my hand on his shoulder. "I'm glad, Dad," I said, then hugged him.

Outside on the street, I looked up at the window just in case he was there, waiting to wave good-bye to us. He wasn't, but I waved anyway at the empty window as Roseanne went to get the car.

Dad and I had both stood trial that year—mine was in the spirit world, and his was in the mortal one. They weren't really that different of a fight, but we would have different outcomes—I'd be set free, and he'd be put behind bars. Maybe that was because I had ultimately faced the truth, and Dad kept trying to dodge it.

I put my baseball cap on backward and waited on the sidewalk under the lamplight for my sister to come get me. I wasn't scared, either. Looking westward toward Central Park, up to the lights shining in from the Jersey shore across the river, the road looked clear.

CHAPTER 16

HEALING HANDS

"Chop it all off," I ordered Ramon, the gay, Latino stylist who'd been cutting my hair for years.

"*All* of it?" he asked, incredulous.

"All of it. Buzz it."

I was sitting in a swivel chair at the hair salon getting my usual inch trimmed off when I decided it was time to slice off yet another layer of my emotional cocoon as part of my metamorphosis. As Ramon's hands buzzed around my head and chunks of my curly, shellacked hair fell to the floor, I stared at myself in the mirror, riveted.

"Cut more," I kept telling him. "A little more . . . "

Like when a sculptor with a vision chips away at a slab of marble to uncover the true shape underneath, I watched myself transform. With each flash of Ramon's scissors, I became more me. Samson may have gotten his strength from his tresses, but for me my long hair was a symbol of captivity, part of the costume I was sentenced to wear to play the part of someone else—*wear dresses, grow your hair, walk like a lady.* I had turned 30 and, as a present to myself, wanted the outer me to match the inner me.

When Ramon was finished, my hair was a cropped, sleek, shining cap. I leaned into the mirror, turned my head left and right, and laughed—I looked just like my father's Elvis-style mug shot, circa 1957.

Out on the street, my newly shorn hair—combined with my natural baritone voice—had a surprising effect on strangers.

The following week I was waiting in a long line at the bank, wearing a big sweatshirt and my baseball cap on backward, and struck up a lengthy conversation with an older gentleman standing next to me. "I'd love to introduce you to my daughter," he said, when the line started to move. "You'd be perfect for her."

He was so excited about his matchmaking, I didn't have the heart to tell him he'd mistaken me for a boy.

"Oh, thank you, but I'm with someone already."

A few weeks after that, I went to a funeral-home viewing of a friend of the family. As I stood in the hallway with Mom, Ro, and Sal, an old woman walked in who knew my mother and started doing a round of kisses with all of us. I was wearing a black suit and had my hair slicked back. She kissed me on the cheeks and then grabbed my face between her two hands.

"Olympia! Your son! He has such a beautiful face!"

Ro, Sal, and I looked at each other and almost bust our guts trying not to laugh. Poor Mom nearly passed out from embarrassment. At least if I was being mistaken for a boy, I was being mistaken for a *pretty* boy.

Every time I passed a mirror, I smiled at myself. My reflection looked like the inner me, the real me—like that day at Immaculate when we'd donned the boys' uniforms and I couldn't pull my gaze away from the mirror.

The mirror soon became another teaching vehicle for myself. As I continued my exploration into the healing of my body and soul, a spiritual counselor gave me a homework exercise that was brilliantly simple. Yet at the same time, it was almost impossible for me to do. She told me to look at my face in the mirror every day and tell myself, "I love you." It sounded crazy to me, but the next morning when I went to brush my teeth, I remembered her instruction and gave it a try.

With toothbrush in one hand and a tube of toothpaste in the other, I squinted at my reflection. "I loooooo . . . I loooo . . . " I sputtered. I felt like Dad muttering to the parking meter on the street. *This is ridiculous. Ah, shit, no. I gotta do it.*

"I looo . . . " and then, laughing my ass off, I yelled it out loud: *"I love you!"* And then again for good measure, "I loooooooovvvve youuuuuu!"

I laughed some more, wondering if my mother could hear me from down the hall. It was surprising how difficult it was to say those words. I guess I wasn't used to feeling that way about myself, never mind saying it out loud. It felt good, though, and I intended to talk to myself like that more often.

It was all part of my ongoing healing process, which I stepped up when my father went away to jail. Like my hair, he'd been suddenly severed from my life. But while I missed him, his incarceration gave me even more freedom to become the person I was meant to be.

During the first few years Dad was away, I continued with my massage-therapy classes and graduated from the Swedish Institute. Then I followed that with something else I had always wanted to do: go to college. I enrolled at William Paterson University in New Jersey to get my bachelor's degree in science, concentrating on exercise physiology. I was in my early 30s and at long last was finally figuring out what to do with my life. As the first girl in our family to dare venture away from tradition and go to college, I studied my ass off to prove that just because something was sacred tradition, that doesn't mean it's right. Some traditions evolved to be broken.

I wish Gram Crackers could have seen me when I graduated with highest honors—*summa cum laude*—in my cap and gown. I was proud of myself for finishing both massage school and college, working hard and seeing both to completion. Mom was the only one who came to my graduation, but she had the biggest smile of all the mothers when she saw me hurl my tasseled cap high into the air.

My relationship with Jennifer ran its course during that time, and I began dating one of my professors, Nicki. She was 12 years older than I was, had two children, and had been separated from her husband for several years. In many ways, the relationships I was having back to back since I came out were about me making up for lost time. Because I'd kept my sexuality a secret for so long, I didn't experience regular dating like others in high school and into their 20s. Now that I was out, I was doing what everyone else was doing—trying to find true love, but still looking in all the wrong places.

Nicki and I began as friends, talking in between classes and over lunch for several months, until it got serious and we decided I should move in. If the time I moved out with Jessie was a dip in the ocean of freedom, this was a solid dive into a new world and a new family.

I moved in with Nicki and her kids in their house an hour away from Mom's—and for the first time in my life, I saw my mother only once a week. It was very liberating for me to not be in constant contact with her or responsible for her on a daily basis. It freed up my energy and emotions so that I could direct them toward my own growth and healing.

As I did, I made an unexpected discovery. The more I healed myself, the more I was able to heal others. The more I gave to myself, the more I was able to give, period. The more I rid myself of dark energy and let the light in, the more I was able to share that illumination.

MY DESTINY IN THE WORLD OF LIGHT began to reveal itself during my work as a massage therapist. As I worked with clients, something strange began to happen. My clients would rise from my table with a relaxed neck or an eased back and an odd look in their eyes.

"You have healing hands," they would say. "My whole mood feels different."

I took it as a great compliment, of course. I had personally experienced the powerful effects of loving hands and what can happen when a pure and good energy is sent through one's body like a positive charge. Anise had shown me that, and with a touch of his hand, the priest at the laying on of hands had, too. They both taught me that the love energy was coming from a place of light, a place of God—"Spirit," Julie called it, meaning a positive God-force that included and embraced all beliefs and religions.

"Jesus was a great healer," Julie told me, "because he saw each person as whole and without illness. And as long as a person had a speck of faith—even as small as a mustard seed, as he said—that person could be healed."

Faith, energy, and God were a trinity of thought I'd drift into during a massage, imagining my clients on the table as healthy and whole while I worked on them.

One afternoon a regular client of mine named Dennis came in for a session. We usually worked on his right rotator cuff, but this time he was complaining about pain closer to his neck. As soon as he lay down on his back, my hands wanted to go to the area of his throat chakra—the area of truth. Sure enough, I could feel heat radiating from that spot, which meant he had words and thoughts that were stuck.

I shut my eyes and started seeing images in my mind of a black cloud of blocked energy above Dennis's throat. Then I saw Jesus standing in the corner of the room, observing us . . . then a moving image of Dennis from another era, the captain of a ship that was going down in the water as the beautiful woman he loved stood ashore, crying. It was like watching a movie.

"I had a big fight with my wife today," the Dennis on my table suddenly said, out of the blue. I held my hands steady over the black cloud above his throat.

"She asked me if I'm in love with another woman."

As he spoke, I felt energy shooting out from my fingertips and into the black cloud. He had never, ever, talked to me so personally before.

"I couldn't admit it. But the truth is, I met another woman four years ago, and she's the love of my life. I want to be with her. I don't know what to do . . . "

At that moment, I felt an instantaneous shift in the energy between my hands and his body. Dennis gave a choked-up, emotional sigh. It was like a key had been found that had opened up a heavy door. I saw a fleeting image of Captain Dennis kissing the beautiful woman onshore, and they were smiling—he had found a way to be with her.

Dennis got up from the table and had tears in his eyes. "What did you do?" he asked me. "I don't know why I told you what I did . . . I haven't told anybody about that. But I feel great. What the hell did you do to me?"

I wasn't so sure myself. I felt emotionally depleted, but in a good way—like we'd just been through an intense, life-changing therapy session together. I knew that Dennis's release from pain had something to do with his speaking out loud his inner truth, but I didn't know how I had accessed that for him.

A few weeks later I went to my fourth laying on of hands with Father Fabrizio, that same Italian-Catholic priest I'd been working with for a while, and I got my answer.

After the usual group prayers at the back of the church, we all lined up by the altar to get the healing touch. The priest explained how everyone gets healed in the way they need and can handle at that time; it was nothing he or we could control but was more about surrendering to one's destiny.

When it was my turn in the line, Father Fabrizio gently tapped my forehead with his index finger, and I floated to the ground like a leaf falling from a tree, buoyantly and effortlessly. I lay on the church floor for a good 15 minutes, feeling close to God and grateful for the peace I felt. I thought about how fulfilled it made me feel to use my hands and help people on my massage table, like I had for Dennis and like Father Fabrizio had just done for me.

After I got up from the floor, I approached the priest when he'd finished with the rest of the group. I needed to speak to him about my *destino.* "Father . . . I want to learn how to do this," I said.

"I want to be able to do the laying on of hands, like you do. Can I learn it? How can I learn?"

Father Fabrizio put his hands on my shoulders and smiled. "My dear, you already know how to do this."

I was shocked. "I do?"

"Yes, you do. Now go out there and do it."

The irony didn't escape me that as I got out there and did it— as I helped free people from their emotional and physical pain— my father was living in a dreary place of no escape.

THE FIRST PRISON DAD WAS SENT TO was in Butner, North Carolina. But after that, he made stops in Illinois, Minnesota, Texas, and finally, Missouri.

Because of his heart condition and pacemaker, he was sequestered in a special hospital-like unit and didn't have to do the hard time you see in the movies where the guy sits in a tiny, barred cell all day like a caged animal. Dad often lived in a very big room with 14 other inmates, much like a hospital ward, closed off by a door with a window that looked out into a busy hallway. He was somewhat free to come and go as he pleased, whether it was to go to a common lounge area to watch TV with the others, or outside to stroll the grounds and do some stretching and calisthenics— as long as he checked in and out with the guards.

Of course, everybody knew who federal prisoner no. 26071-037 was—the inmates, medical staff, and even some of the guards were in awe of him. In fact, a few days after arriving in Butner, he'd already charmed (or intimidated?) the lot of them. Imagine if you were in jail with my father . . . you'd want to be on his good side. Just because he was in prison, that didn't mean he had lost one ounce of the power he wielded outside. No one was going to fuck with that.

His main worry on the inside was the food. Not because it tasted bad—which it did. And not because it wasn't healthy—which it wasn't. No, Dad didn't eat the brown high-school-cafeteria slop they served because he was paranoid it would kill him.

"They're going to poison my food, I know it," he'd tell my mother, on her monthly visits to see him. "They're gonna screw with my pills."

We regularly deposited money into Dad's jail bank account—he was allowed a small amount per month, which he'd use to buy turkey sandwiches, fruit, and cans of tuna from the commissary. Because we weren't allowed to bring him food from the outside, it was impossible for him to stick to the disciplined, low-fat, low-salt, low-sugar, no-chemical menu he had adhered to for two decades. Soon, he gave in to the treats he'd denied himself for so long—doughnuts, pound cake, jars of peanut butter, and Hershey bars.

All that sugar hyped him up plenty in order to torture my mother and sisters about how they planned to spring him out of the joint.

Every weekend Dad would have amassed a certain number of points for good behavior, so he'd be rewarded the maximum number of visiting hours. Our family alternated with the other family so that every other weekend at least one of us would go. The visits were long and agonizing—eight hours a day for two days in a row. The visiting room was a bare white room with tables and straight chairs and a vending machine. Four cameras were mounted on the wall recording everyone's movements from all angles. It would be impossible to say or do anything without those guards knowing.

Mom, Ro, and Yo had gone to visit Dad one weekend and were waiting to go through the full body–scan machine before entering the main prison area. The machine sounded an alarm if you were trying to smuggle anything in, even a stick of gum. It crushed Mom's heart that she wasn't allowed to take Dad his favorite apple pie or cookies.

As my mother and sisters checked their personal items in at the desk, Ro looked up and saw a tall woman with big, blonde hair, wearing a black suit and stilettos.

"Shit, is that who I think it is?" she spoke out loud to Yo, but in Italian, so the woman wouldn't understand. Yo looked over at the woman and recognized her immediately.

"Don't you think she might understand Italian?"

My sisters looked at each other and both started laughing their asses off. The woman in question was Victoria Gotti, John's daughter. If Victoria saw them, she didn't recognize them. But they surely knew who *she* was, even Mom did. They all stared as she walked through the body scan—and then they realized that she must be there to see her father. Which meant that John Gotti was in the same jail as my dad!

Once this oversight was discovered, Gotti was rerouted to an alternate visiting room. A few weeks later, I heard that he was whisked away in a midnight maneuver to another jail. But until then, we had to notify the guards if any of us were coming to visit so that they could make sure the two men never crossed paths.

Anyway, during their visits, Mom and my sisters would try to keep Dad's fighting spirit up.

"You can't give up, Dad," Ro would tell him. "You've got to keep fighting. We're setting up an appeal."

They knew there was only so much they could talk about because every word they said was being recorded. So they'd update him on every family member, going through the long list one by one, and move on to friends and neighbors if need be. That's about the time when Roseanne would doze off in her chair . . . and sometimes, my father would, too.

Eight hours in the visiting room two days in a row was like a whole other jail in itself, the family package deal. But try as they might to divert his attention, Dad's mind was fixated on one topic only: What were you doing to get him out of this place? One of his favorite films before he'd gone away was *The Shawshank Redemption*, in which Tim Robbins's character tunnels his way out of jail over a nearly 20-year period. Dad had no intention of waiting that long.

"Did you talk to the lawyers?" he'd ask. "Did Uncle Lou talk to the Archbishop? I'm going to die in here. Tell Uncle Lou to talk to the Archbishop."

My uncle Lou knew the Archbishop of New York from his Catholic circles and, of course, the Archbishop knew who my father was—not just for his notoriety, but also because Dad had donated a lot of money to the Church in the past. Now he wanted a favor in return. Dad wanted one of us to speak to the Archbishop and plead his case, so a meeting was set up for one of our family members.

The Archbishop's residence was nestled behind the main sanctuary of the grand St. Patrick's Cathedral in midtown Manhattan. The relative chosen for the task was led down a hall decorated with thick red carpeting, deep oak paneling, gilded frames, and antiques. Once they reached a small salon, they were told to sit and wait on an ornate, narrow chair as a grandfather clock ticked loudly from the next room. Soon, the Archbishop arrived, moving slowly. He was nearing 80 and was pale after being recently diagnosed with a serious illness, but he was still the head of the diocese until God decided it was his time not to be. Just like Dad, he was the boss until they took him away in a box.

The family member explained the situation to the Archbishop, imploring him to help. Dad faithfully prayed his rosary morning and night in jail, they told him—surely those prayers traveled from his mouth to God's ears, then back down to His Excellency's own?

The Archbishop sat there, hands folded, shaking his head.

"There is nothing I can do," he said. "My hands are tied."

WHEN THE ARCHBISHOP'S RESPONSE was described to me later, I looked down at my own hands. My hands were *not* tied.

For the first five years of Dad's incarceration, I had refused to go see him, even though my mother had pleaded with me at least once a month to accompany her. But like my ten-year forgiveness process with my brother Sal, I had needed time to work through my feelings about my father. Seeing him would have only interfered with that. The family wasn't so happy about my decision— "What do you mean you're not going to take your turn?!" I heard, over and over. But I remained steadfast; I was not going.

During those years, Dad and I kept in touch on the phone and with letters. From a safe distance away, I was able to "exchange energy" with Dad like when I used to massage his neck, only I was doing it hands-free. I was learning from my healing teachers

that you didn't need to be beside someone to send them energy—
it could be done from a thousand miles away without ever touching them. With just a thought or intention, you could create a
seismic shift and move mountains. That was what we did when
we prayed for someone or even thought good things about them.
Prayers, thoughts, love, and energy have no boundaries of distance, time, human-made laws or even mortality.

Dad's ward had one phone for the prisoners to share, and only
two hours a day when they could use it. My father lined up every
day to call his family members, even though I couldn't imagine
him lining up to use a telephone, never mind *using* one! He only
had five minutes to talk when he called, and I'd be allotted one of
those minutes. But one minute was more than I'd ever had before.
Up until then, I'd never spoken to my father on the telephone. It
was a shock to hear his voice travel along a crackling phone line
and spill out of a mechanical device into our kitchen.

"How are you feeling, Rita?" he'd ask. "Are you taking care of
your mother? Tell everybody that I love them and I'm praying for
them. Tell them to pray for me."

That took up the first 30 seconds. The second 30 seconds, he'd
make me cry. "I miss the family," he'd say, in a sad voice. "I miss
you and your mother. I wish I could be home with you."

I drank it in. How many times had I lain in Mom's bed as a
child, looking out at the weeping willow, wishing my father would
say those exact words to me?

On the phone and in our handwritten letters to each other, we
started saying words we never could face-to-face.

Dear Dad,

*Hope all is well with you. I have been so busy lately. Work,
work, work. I am doing more massage and loving it. Thank
God. I got a referral from the massage school to work on a
woman who is 90 years old. She has a lot of physical problems,
but I am looking forward to the adventure of it. I figure if nothing else, she will have a lot of wisdom behind her years to share.*

Mom's birthday is coming up, and we are all going to take her out to eat. This year her birthday falls on Father's Day so we will be able to celebrate the both of you. I bought her a massage table for her birthday—this way she knows she will always get a massage one way or another. She looks forward to them. She has gotten many massages since you left, so you are going to have to make up for them when you come home. The table will be waiting for you.

Anyway, Mom decided to open the pool this year. I am looking forward to swimming and relaxing a little. Roseanne did a great job on the backyard. They put in a swing, some new lounge chairs, and a tent so that Mom doesn't have to be in the sun. They also put in a lot of flowers, and it looks beautiful. Ro painted the cabana white and green. It looks much nicer. The backyard has never looked better. You will enjoy it when you come home. It will feel very peaceful, and you will finally enjoy life the way you deserve to.

I forgot to tell you something. I decided to take singing lessons. So far I have taken six lessons, and the lady said that I have a good voice. I'm not sure why I decided to do it but I just wanted to do something for myself that I thought I might enjoy. I'm having a lot of fun with it, and that's all that counts. I also thought about taking piano lessons. I think when I'm a little further along with the singing, I will do that. If I ever have a recital, I will send you some pictures. By the way, can I send you pictures of me and Mom? I wasn't sure if I could.

So, I guess I have you all caught up. I'll write soon. Please take care of yourself and pray, pray, pray. Look at the bottom for some more enjoyable reading. Before I forget to tell you, thank you for the stuff that you sent me. Mom and I enjoyed reading them. If you have anything else, please send them.

Love, kisses, hugs, and more,

Rita

HAPPY FATHER'S DAY

P.S. Each experience in your life was absolutely necessary in order to have gotten you to the next place, and the next place, and the next, up until this very moment. So each moment that passes, brings you closer to home.

> *Dearest Rita,*
>
> *I loved the cards you sent me very much. What you said about the Blessed Mother was beautiful and your words so true. I am sending you these two books, one for you, and one for Mommy. I know you will both love them.*
>
> *May God Bless and keep you and Mommy always safe. You are both in my prayers.*
>
> *All my love always,*
>
> *Daddy*
>
> *P.S. Colin helped me with this letter. He is my friend.*

> *Dad,*
>
> *I picked this out for you. It comes from the book of Isaiah in the Bible:*
>
> *"In quietness and trust is your strength."*
>
> *God says, "Quiet your heart. Listen for the small desires of your heart and Mine. Listen for our thoughts to melt together, forming a perfect union. With Me, you will discover untold joy in the smallest sigh of life. Nothing is insignificant to Me. Listen to the sweet urgings of My Will for this new day. It is the restless heart that demands grand and monumental events. Listen for the silent things. Cherish the simple. I work slowly and do a work perfectly in you. If you do not love the minute, the almost imperceptible, you find yourself fermenting in impatience and frustration. It takes many years of discipline to turn a mortal being into an immortal one. Enjoy each moment as a gift."*
>
> *Love,*
>
> *Rita*

> *My Dearest Rita,*
>
> *I wanted to let you know I cannot use the phone. I hope everyone is well. Please make sure you take care of your mother.*

I am praying the rosary every morning. I hope all turns out the way it should. I miss you and Mommy, and I can't wait to see all of you.

All my love and prayers always,
Your Daddy Forever
P.S. If anyone wants to write, you can write me.
P.S.S. My friend Colin wrote this letter for me.

Dear Dad,

I am sorry I didn't get this out until now, but I searched and searched for the right card and could not find one that said what I truly felt. So I decided to make my own card.

I hope you are doing well and keeping healthy. It has been a little hectic lately, but I am trying to take more time for myself. I have been doing a lot of massages, and my name is starting to get out there.

I don't know if you know this but I am a healer.

I have been called by God to do His work here and have accepted the job. This means that God places people in my path who need help in all kinds of ways. I have worked on people who have physical ailments, emotional and psychological problems, and spiritual issues. I am grateful for this and know that it's my purpose. Each time I do a massage, it is an opportunity to help someone transform themselves. This is a tremendous reward for me. To know that I am part of helping another human being transform their lives is more than I can put into words.

Anyway, Mom is doing well. She had her eye operation and is recovering nicely. I've been helping her bake for the holidays and am getting really good at it. I am trying to keep tradition with her and at the same time make great memories. I ate at Yolanda's house for Christmas Eve and Roseanne's house Christmas Day. We had a wonderful time. I hope to get to speak to you soon, and I am praying for you.

Love,
Rita

After five years of buildup, I finally went to see my father. As always, I had mixed feelings about seeing him. Even though we'd shared loving words in the letters, I had no idea what to expect in person. Seeing Dad was like playing a game of emotional roulette: you never knew what mood you'd get. Yo warned me that he was pissed I'd waited so long to go visit, so I prayed for the best and prepared for the worst.

At the scanning machine with Mom and Yo, I emptied my pockets—my keys, gum, a pen, a health bar, lip balm, some vitamins, and Kleenex all had to go in a little bag and would be returned to me when I left. We were led to a holding area where we waited for more visitors to arrive, then the whole group of about 20 followed a guard to the sparse visiting room.

"Do not forget," the guard reminded us sternly, as we filed down the hall behind him like schoolchildren, "you can embrace the inmate hello and good-bye, but that is it. You cannot under *any* circumstances touch the inmate any other time. If you do, they will lose visiting privileges. Do I make myself clear?"

My heart sank. I hadn't known about the forbidden act of touching. And I was so desperately hoping to touch my father and see if I could use my hands to unlock a heavy, painful door for him, like I had done for my client Dennis. But it was not to be!

In walked my father, wearing an orange jumpsuit—they almost could have passed for his usual pajamas—looking as he always did. We hugged briefly, and I took an immediate energy reading. He was closed off to me, like an angry child. He was punishing me, I could see, but at the same time he also wanted my attention.

That was my first revelation during my visit. It had been five years since I'd seen my father, five years in which I did a lot of growing up and learning. And in the first five minutes of my visit, I was startled to understand a truth about him that I had never noticed before: he was like a little kid. Even with his title and power, with all the people who were afraid of him and did what he commanded, and with all the lives he held in his own hands . . . he was a hurt and confused child, like the rest of us. I felt sad for him.

Soon enough, he warmed up and gave me a smile. But my second revelation of the day was that if I was expecting some sort of dramatic and tearful confession and reconciliation with my father—or anything different from the ordinary procedure of the last 30 years—that wasn't about to happen, even after our intimate letters.

"How are you?" he asked. "Are you taking care of your mother?" Blah, blah, blah. Same old, same old. I saw that he was keeping up some of his "I'm insane" act, with his whisper and groggy demeanor. I don't know if it was because he was used to talking that way for so long he didn't know how to stop, or if he was doing it for the benefit of the cameras and the guards.

For the rest of our eight-hour visit, Dad mostly talked to Mom and Yo, and I watched him. It was strange to see someone you love in a place like that, especially someone like him. He looked like he didn't belong there, yet it was exactly where he belonged. After so many years of our family living in denial about who Dad was and what he did, there's nothing like seeing someone in his position in an ugly orange jumpsuit eating old Ding Dongs out of a vending machine to give you perspective and help you face the truth.

When it was time to leave, we hugged again briefly, and then standing two feet away from each other, we both said, "I love you." That I couldn't touch him more was so symbolic of our relationship. He was right there in front of me, but I couldn't reach him.

I had forgotten what I had learned over the last five years, though, which was that the farther away my father was physically, the closer we could be spiritually. While I had worked hard to break down barriers of communication in my life, he was way behind me in that area. Unlike me, he was not ready to face and speak truths yet. Unlike my client Dennis, he could not speak his truth out loud yet. And that was okay. Everybody had to learn lessons in their own time, and you couldn't force it. People were ready when they were ready.

A FEW WEEKS AFTER I GOT HOME from the prison visit, I woke up one morning in a state of intense "readiness." I felt energy bouncing around in my body, as if it wanted to release something. It was a similar momentum like the day I awoke and wrote the final forgiveness letter to Sal. The wind was gusting through my open bedroom window, making the curtains dance like crazy, and my fingers were tingling.

Maybe my father wasn't ready to face who he was and what he had done in his life yet. Maybe the Archbishop hadn't heard God's whisper that my father's heart was aching for help and forgiveness. But I sure did, and I was ready.

I sat down at my computer, in my pajamas, and started typing:

Dear Dad,

I am writing today to tell you who your daughter really is. I don't think you know me very well because of all the things that have been in both our ways for most of my life. Before I begin— first and foremost, I forgive you. I forgive you for all the things you couldn't do; for the father you couldn't be; and for anything that was said, done, not said or done. I also forgive myself for all the anger, rage, and resentment—and for anything I said or did that hurt you in any way.

You see, I am choosing to let go of all of the lies, deceit, betrayal, hurt, and pain because it does not feel good to carry it around anymore. It affects every aspect of me, physically, emotionally, mentally, and spiritually. I have come to a place in my life where I desire more freedom, and I realize that the only way to get this is to forgive anything and anyone who has hurt me, knowingly or unknowingly.

So let me tell you a little bit about myself. I have come a long way since the days of anxiety, deep depression, and panic attacks. These are most of your memories of me because that is how my body responded to the stress in our family life. I have very sensitive energy and can feel and sometimes take on (although I'm getting better at this) other people's stuff (feelings, emotions, etc). So whenever Mom was feeling anxious, depressed, worried, sad, angry, etc., I would feel it, too.

*Mom wasn't the only one I could feel but she was the clos-
est to me, and I took on a lot of her stuff. Most of the time it
felt like it was your fault as to why she felt this way, so my
emotions toward you seemed justified. But then I realized that
you weren't the only one I was angry at. That it wasn't all
your fault. That everyone in this life is responsible for their own
happiness, and that included me and Mom. So I learned how
protect myself from other people's "stuff." I learned how to let
go of people's pain, sadness, loss, etc., and allow them to take
responsibility for themselves. This was a profound knowing for
me. It changed me to the core.*

*I am very proud of who I am today and continue to work
on myself to be more aware. My anxiety is minimal now, and
I no longer have panic attacks. My depression has decreased
dramatically, and I feel that I can deal with things much easier.*

*I told you previously that I am a healer. I am committed to
helping people find their way. I am committed to Spirit and look
forward to learning from other people and working with them.
By the way, I need you to understand who "Spirit" is. I work
mostly with the energies of God, Jesus, Mary, the Holy Spirit,
and the Archangels. It is where I feel most comfortable. I see
miracles every day, small and large, in my life and in the lives
of my clients. I am forever grateful for this opportunity.*

*Dad, I know that when you read this, you will understand
what I am saying because it will resonate with your soul. I
will continue to pray for you and send you good energy. Thank
you for being my father and for helping me learn my lessons
in this life.*

In gratitude and love always,
Rita

Was I telling him that how he had lived his life was accept-
able? No. Was I absolving him? No, that's not for me to do; I'm
not the judge. With my words, I was relieving myself of my own
pain and forgiving him for whatever part he took in it. I was also
forgiving my mother, my siblings, and myself, because we were

all responsible for our own choices and how we reacted to them. My days of blaming others or living as a victim or fighting other people's battles were over for me. It was time to move forward, own what was mine, and let go of what wasn't.

After a few hours glued to my computer typing, I got dressed, went down the street to mail the letter, and let go of the outcome. It didn't matter to me if he responded or not; the energy was set in motion, and it was up to him to understand it or not. I had complete clarity for myself—I didn't need his approval, and I didn't even need his response. For me, writing that letter filled a deep, black hole in me that I'd had since childhood, but didn't know how to fill until that morning. As I wrote the letter, the cavern in me filled with light so bright, I could barely contain it.

Two weeks later, I went to visit Mom one afternoon to find her in an excitable state.

"Ri, what did you say in your last letter to your father? I just got off the phone with him and he was so *emotional*. I've never heard him like that before!"

"What do you mean?"

"His voice was shaking. And he said, 'Rita wrote me the most beautiful letter I've ever gotten in my entire life. Can I speak to her? Is she there?' What did you say to him?"

I was blown away.

"Mom, I just told him about me. And I wrote about forgiveness. What else did he say?"

"He said, 'Tell Rita that I love her very much and that I tried to reach her. Please tell her that I'm *trying to reach her*. And tell her . . . tell her *I understand*.'"

I pressed my hands to my face; my cheeks were radiating heat. I could feel it, I could feel the energy shifting and traveling. And five hundred miles away in a dreary jailhouse, I could feel the heavens and earth move.

CHAPTER 17

A SPIRITUAL
CONTRACT

Scientists say that the flap of a single butterfly's wings contains the power to change the course of events thousands of miles away. From far away, I could feel a change happen inside my father, the kind that starts with the subtle flutter of a delicate wing and leads to a tremor that becomes an earthquake, altering our landscape forever.

The day I woke up and felt that electric energy rushing through me, I translated that energy onto paper and sent it to my dad. I also sent my message of understanding and forgiveness in a way that could not be seen—hurtling my thoughts and feelings toward him from my mind through the universe like I would aim a football toward the end zone.

Whether he was going to understand my message or not, or be willing to receive it or not, I didn't know. Much like when I worked with someone on my massage table, I had to believe that they could be healed so that I could open myself up to universal love, truth, and God. In turn, their energy had to want to be healed and be open to what I sent them. It's a sacred, nonverbal agreement made between healer and receiver—an invisible contract of love, soul to soul.

The question was, was my father ready and willing to sign on the dotted line?

Judging by his phone conversation with my mother, I thought so. When he said, "Tell her I understand," I felt like it was the first time he was really hearing me, the first time he listened. We had unlocked that heavy door of fear and he was now standing on the threshold, waiting to step across toward a new life.

By THE SPRING OF 2003, DAD HAD SERVED nearly six years of his twelve-year sentence, and a possible parole was coming up. He was desperate to come home, and he told me so in every phone call and letter. But while he was behind prison walls, the feds feverishly worked on gathering evidence to build a new case and keep him there for good. They had chased him for decades, and he had outsmarted them—and they knew it. So as his parole date neared, their next move was to go after Dad's Achilles' heel, the one spot that made him weak: his family.

Yo was making lunch for her kids one afternoon when she got a phone call from Sal's wife, Janet.

"Yolanda, my God, did you read the newspaper this morning? It said that the feds are coming after the family!"

"What are you talking about, Janet?"

Yo hung up on her and urged her husband to rush out and get a newspaper, then she called me to get over there pronto. Together, we laid out the dailies and read them.

In an effort to present more evidence against my father on charges of racketeering and obstruction of justice, the papers reported, it appeared that prosecutors intended on involving family members as well—specifically Yolanda, Mom, Sal, Uncle Lou, and my half-brother, Vincent—and there was the potential that they could even face obstruction of justice charges, for helping Dad knowingly feign mental illness.

"This can't be happening," Yo said, petrified. "Dad has got to do something about this!"

I tried to calm her down, but part of me was thinking, *Holy shit! Can they really do this?*

I went home worried for the future of my family. That night, I had the same recurring nightmare I'd had since I was a child, but it was to be the last time I ever had it.

In the dream, I was looking out of Mom's basement window and watching a tornado rip apart our backyard and our house, spinning our lives out of control and uprooting everything we had. It was the same dream I'd had for 30 years down to the last detail, except for one difference. All the other times I'd dreamed this, it would leave me with a feeling of dread, knowing that I was going to die. This time, the dream meant survival: It meant that I was still standing strong and alive. I remained looking out the window, untouched, no matter what violent storm swirled around me.

When I woke up I knew that no matter what craziness was going on, I'd be protected, and so would my sisters and mother. It was my father they wanted.

The next day, one of Dad's lawyers went to visit him in jail. He was now at the United States Medical Center for Federal Prisoners in Springfield, Missouri. It was the same prison where John Gotti had died a year earlier of throat cancer at the age of 61. Over the years I've heard bits and pieces from the family, who got it from Dad, as to what went down that day.

As they sat in the bare visiting room with crying kids and weeping spouses a few feet away, the lawyer gave it to him straight. "They have audiotapes of your phone calls to the family when you sound sane and lucid," he told Dad. Specifically, the lawyer was talking about Dad's concerned calls to us after he saw the planes crashing into the World Trade Center on September 11, 2001. All the inmates rushed to the phone to reach loved ones, and Dad pushed his way to the front of the line to get through to Mom and make sure we were all safe. It was one of the rare moments in his whole "acting career" when Dad dropped character for several minutes, and now it was coming back to haunt him.

Then the lawyer gave Dad the second part of the ol' one-two punch: "They're going after your family, Vincent. I don't know if they have any evidence or not, but . . . "

Dad put his hand up as if to say, *Enough. I don't need to hear anything else.*

He understood what was happening, and he knew what to do about it—he didn't need any time to decide. He'd already had every day of six years to think about what he'd done to his family and to his life. As desperate as he was to get out of jail, he didn't want to inflict any more pain on us, and he was tired of the lies. He wanted it over. He was done with it. If Dad was going to go down, he was going to go like a man and not sacrifice his family.

Dad and I had never spoken of the letter I'd written to him the year before—he never mentioned it after that day on the phone with Mom, and I didn't bring it up. Neither of us felt a need to. But like the morning I woke up and felt that insistent readiness to speak my truth to Dad, he too was finally ready to speak his to the world.

"Tell them to leave my family alone," he told his lawyer, as he stood up and signaled the guard to let him know the visit was over and he wanted out. "I'll admit everything. I'll tell them anything they want. I don't care what happens to me; just don't touch my family. They've been through enough."

About two weeks later, my father signed a plea agreement in Brooklyn court in which he basically agreed to admit that he had faked mental illness for the seven years leading up to his trial. And then he admitted it in front of the judge, in person, on the record.

I wasn't in the courtroom that day, but other family members witnessed the big moment.

"Please raise your right hand," the court clerk said.

Dad started to raise his left, then corrected himself. After all, he didn't have to pretend he was confused anymore.

"I'm going to ask you, Mr. Gigante," said the judge, after Dad was sworn in, "whether it's true that between May 1990 and

December 18, 1997, you knowingly, intentionally, misled doctors who were evaluating your competence to stand trial, and you misled those doctors with the intent to influence their testimony regarding your competence in connection with those trials. Is that true?"

"Yes, your honor." Dad said softly.

"Mr. Gigante, anything you want to say to me before I impose sentence?"

"No, thank you."

And that was the end of that. In return for his admission, Dad got three years tacked on to his current sentence and a promise that they'd leave the rest of his family alone. It was a good deal, yet bittersweet. He had made it for the greater good of his loved ones, but he was the leverage, the sacrifice. And while they say the truth will set you free—and it certainly did that for us, and for his conscience—it locked him up for good physically. Signing this agreement was the same as signing his own death warrant, and he knew it.

Soon after, the press had a field day with Dad's confession. For example, here's an excerpt from one of the articles that ran in the papers (this one's from *The New York Times*):

Analyze This: Vincent Gigante, Not Crazy After All Those Years

By ANDY NEWMAN
Published: April 13, 2003

An enduring urban mystery was solved last week when Vincent (The Chin) Gigante, the Mafia leader who spent decades slobbering, muttering and wandering Manhattan in his bedclothes, admitted in a Brooklyn federal court that he had deceived the teams of psychiatrists who had evaluated his mental competency from 1990 to 1997 and found him to be suffering from various forms of dementia.

Mr. Gigante, 75, was sentenced to three years in prison, to be served, if he lives, after he completes his current racketeering sentence in 2007. He pleaded guilty on the eve of a trial at which prosecutors were prepared to play audiotapes of numerous phone calls he has made to family and friends since being imprisoned in 1997.

Another mystery remains: How did some of the most re-spected minds in forensic psychiatry and neuropsychology—including a prominent Harvard psychiatrist, five past presidents of the American Academy of Psychiatry and Law, and the man who invented the standard test for malingering—get it wrong? For Mr. Gigante's 1997 trial and sentencing, at least six doctors declared him mentally incompetent. . . .

Back at home, Mom, Ro, and I convened at Yo's to discuss the surprising turn of events. We were all in a state of shock, relief, and confusion. We were shocked by Dad's admission, at what he said and how it came out of the blue like that. We were relieved that the family was safe, but we were also confused. How were we supposed to act now? We'd been saying the words *He's sick* for so long that they came out of our mouths like outgoing messages on an answering machine: *Hi, my name's Rita, my father's sick, please leave a message . . .*

I'm sure my mother and sisters had even incorporated it into their belief system as if it were true. If you say something to yourself and others enough times, you can convince yourself of anything —your body and brain have no choice but to agree with you be-cause they have to, for your own mental survival.

Now we had to dismantle the whole fabrication in our brains. As we spoke about it, we were gentle with each other, like a death had just happened in the family, but of someone so sick that it was welcome—the sudden death of a relative on whom Dad had pulled the plug. It was an odd moment. After so many years of half-truths, we were now sitting in a room together with reality staring at us in the face. Who was going to say the first word?

"He did the right thing, doing what he did," I said, tentatively. "It was a big step, to admit something like that."

"We'll still get him out," Mom said, quietly. "We've got to keep hoping and praying."

Yo and I nodded for Mom's sake, but who were we kidding? Dad was now due for release in nine years, but we both knew that wasn't going to happen. The feds would either find another way to keep him in jail, or he'd die in there.

Even though my father's legal contract said he'd get out, I knew he never would because it wasn't part of his *soul* contract. I had learned from Julie Joy about soul contracts, and that we all come into this world with a list of what our soul wants to accomplish and how we are going to do it. Before we get here, we choose who will be our family, friends, foes, and allies. We choose our bodies, talents, looks, and place of birth. All of these choices help us learn what we're supposed to learn here.

Julie explained to me that I'd chosen my family to be born into so I could learn to create freedom for myself in this lifetime. And I, in turn, was to give my family an opportunity to embrace the truth and set them free. My writing the forgiveness letter to Dad, she said, helped him confront his lies and let go of them. My mother had a contract with my father to show him unconditional love no matter what, and she held up her end of the bargain for sure. And I had a contract with Mom to take care of her.

"Sure, Mom," I said now. "Of course we can't lose hope."

But I'd also learned that in our contracts, we have escape clauses —we get "outs" along the way, and if we decide to take one of them and continue on to the next spiritual realm (what some people might call heaven), we can. Dad couldn't escape from jail, not physically anyway. But there was always that escape clause for the soul to leave and move on. If he chose, he could decide, *Okay, I'm outta here,* and will himself onward to the next phase. Whether Dad chose that kind of get-out-of-jail-free card was up to him.

IN EARLY DECEMBER 2005, we were getting ready for Christmas and trying to keep our spirits up. Mom and I were sitting at the kitchen table making a menu list for the holiday supper. Easter meant a big leg of lamb—traditionally the "sacrificial lamb"—but the Christmas Eve meal was always fish. In Italian-Catholic culture, it was called "the Feast of the Seven Fishes," or *Festa dei Sette Pesci,* and it included at least seven seafood dishes.

The number seven was symbolic in a religious context. In the Bible it is the most repeated number, appearing over 700 times—for example, it took God seven days to create the earth, and on the seventh day He rested; there are seven sacraments in the Catholic Church; Jesus divided seven loaves of bread into seven basketfuls. And according to the Gospel of Luke, Jesus is 77th in direct generational line from Genesis's Adam. In the Bible, the number 7 represents perfection and the number 77, the forgiveness of all sins.

That's a hefty history to keep in mind while planning a grocery list. And on this day, the number 77 took on a whole new meaning. As we went over our items for the fishmonger, Mom began telling me about the strange premonitions she was having.

I always believed that my mother was psychic, though she'd never put it that way. Her Catholic upbringing categorized that kind of intuition as being occult, even though the Bible describes many examples of it—for example, when Saul visits a medium in the first book of Samuel. Whatever you want to call it, Mom sometimes saw signs in front of her that foretold the future.

"Everywhere I look, I keep seeing the number 77," she told me now. "It is so strange. If I open a book, it's page number 77; if I buy something, it's $7.70; if I'm driving, I see it on the license plate in front of me."

Mom was 76, and her birthday was six months away.

"Do you think it means I'm going to die next year? That my number is up?" *Again with the death days in this family*, I thought.

"No, of course not," I told her. But I was concerned. "Ma, I wouldn't mention this to Dad. You might worry him."

The next day Mom left on her own to visit Dad in Missouri. As soon as she saw him, any worry for herself vanished.

"Ri, his legs are swollen and his face is gray. He told me he felt sick. He's all blown up," she told me on the phone, panicked.

"Is he taking his medicine?"

"I think so. But he thinks that they're doing something with it. He said, 'They're screwing with my pills, I don't feel right.'"

My siblings called Dad's lawyer right away to look into it . . . other than that, what else could we do?

"Let's pray for him," our mother said. And like old times, when she got home we went to her bedroom and took down her rosary and prayed.

Two weeks later, Mom was getting ready to leave for the airport to see Dad again when I got a hysterical call from Ro. I was at my office at my new holistic healing center, Nature's Remedy, and had just finished giving a session. It was the end of the day, so I was alone and closing up shop.

"Ri!" my sister shrieked through the phone. "Ri . . . d-dead . . . "

I thought she was telling me that Mom's premonition had come true and she'd had a heart attack or an accident.

"Mom? Are you saying that Mom . . . ?"

"No, no . . . it's *Dad*. Daddy died!"

I stood up from my chair, not believing my ears.

Between sobs, Ro tried to explain: " . . . congestive heart failure . . . his lungs filled up . . ." But all I could hear was my mother wailing in the background. I was in shock. I hung up the phone, dropped to my knees, and broke down in tears.

"Dad! What did you do? *What did you do?!*"

I had spoken to him a few weeks earlier—we'd had our usual one-minute quickie—but I hadn't seen him since my visit two years before. There was still so much left to say to each other.

"Dad, where are you?!" I cried, crouched on the floor. It was the same sad question I used to cry aloud as a child and never got an answer.

This time, I did get an answer. Two minutes later, I had the urge to call my psychic friend RoseMarie Cappiello. In psychic-medium-channeling-healing circles, she was one of the best and could connect with people who had crossed over to the Other Side as clearly as if she were having tea with them in her living room.

"Ro, you're not gonna believe it," I said, when she picked up the phone. But I didn't have to say any more—she was so good, she already knew.

"Ri, your father's coming through!"

Both Dad and Ro-C, it seems, were already on the job together in the land of Spirit. I started hyperventilating. Yes, I'd stared into the eyes of Jesus and walked with angels. But the idea of talking to my father three hours after he died was freaking even me out. This time, it was personal.

As soon as Ro-C picked up her ringing phone, she told me, my father's energy barged into her kitchen where she was cooking and urged her to be his telephone operator between the two worlds.

"Okay, listen . . . he's here," she told me. "And he wants me to tell you . . . that he feels free . . . that he doesn't feel confined anymore—in body or in spirit. Hold on, hold on . . . he's talking so fast and so loud . . . just a minute, Vincent! Slow down! He's all excited to talk to you. And now he's . . . wow, what a handsome man!"

Ro-C had never met my father, and apparently he was making his first appearance in spirit form for her in fighting shape and wearing his Sunday best.

"He says he's wearing a suit to make up for all the pajamas he wore . . . he could never dress up nice, like he would have wanted to."

"Yeah, yeah," I said with a laugh. "Oh my God, this is nuts."

"He's showing me what happened when he died. Yes, I see . . . "

"Was he afraid?" I asked.

She paused, as if she was asking him this question in her mind. Then she told me, "He had a split second of fear, because his lungs were failing and filling up and he couldn't breathe. Then his heart failed, and the rest was quick, so then he was gone. But he's okay. He wants me to tell you he's okay and to please tell your mother. And that he's got to go now, but he'll be back."

"Wait, wait . . . where is he? Can you ask him . . . "

"He's gone."

We both were silent on the phone for a minute, then I took a deep breath. I was devastated and elated at the same time—the usual contrasting feelings I would have during a Dad visit when he was alive, only more intense. My father was dead . . . but he wasn't.

My father was gone . . . but he was right there, I had just spoken to him. How exactly was I going to relay all this to my mother?

I thanked Ro-C for passing along the incredible message. My pain a few minutes earlier was now turning into a feeling of peace. He was okay, and he was where he was meant to be. His spirit had been freed over a year earlier, and now his body followed, that is all.

As Mom would say, his number was up. And then I realized, as I drove to my mother's house to see and comfort her, that she had unknowingly predicted Dad's death. He was 77 years old.

THREE DAYS BEFORE CHRISTMAS we had a small, private, simple Mass for Dad at Immaculate Conception, a small church in New Jersey, just for family and a handful of friends. As it turned out, my father didn't make it to his own funeral—the one we had for him, anyway. Even in death, my father's body was torn between two sets of women and children.

It had been decided that each family would have a separate funeral for my dad—we had spent a lifetime keeping the two Olympias apart, and to bring them together for his farewell would have been too much for anyone to take. Like Gotti and Dad coming face-to-face in a jailhouse hallway, God knows what would have happened if these two women came face-to-face in the church.

However, there was the question of what to do with Dad's body. For some reason my brothers were trying to convince my mother, who was alternately crying and in shock, to "let the other family have him" in order to keep the peace and avoid a media circus. At least, that's the reason they were telling her. I was in the room as they were coaxing her, and I was furious on her behalf— taking this as just one more insult to her.

I went over and spoke to her in private for a minute. "Listen to me, Ma," I said, holding her hands in mine and squeezing them. "You are the wife. You get to decide where you want his body. If you want it with us, so be it. If you don't, so be it. But please make this your decision and no one else's."

I exited the room and left it up to her, as she had to be re-sponsible for her own decision. In the end, my brothers persuaded her to let the other family assume Dad's body. Maybe she had finally grown weary of this schizophrenic, two-city existence for my father. He had been pulled in two directions—between two homes and two families—for so long, it was time to stop playing this tug of war and let him rest in peace. So as we had our mass in Jersey, the other family had a private viewing and mass in the city, which most of Dad's friends and his brothers attended because they wanted to be where Dad's body was.

After Dad's city funeral he was cremated, and the other family took one half of the ashes and kept them in the city, while the other half went with Sal in New Jersey. *Dad never has to cross the George Washington Bridge ever again,* I thought. *Now he can be in both places at once.*

The days following my father's death are a blur to me, but the vivid image I do recall is of my mother inching her way down the aisle of the church with my brothers on either side, propping her up. She was crying and her head was bowed, to the point that she looked as though she was going to topple over.

We all sat in the front pew, and as I listened to the priest talk about my father being Catholic and being in heaven, I wondered, *Is that where he is? And if so, what is he doing in this world of Spirit, this place that has become such a big part of my world, my work, my life over the last few years?* It was a little odd to me that I had been in contact with the energy of the spirit world so often, and now he was there, at home base.

I looked over at my mother, who was crying quietly but looked so beautiful. She always looked beautiful. In my last phone conversation with my father, he had ended it with his usual sign-off: "Take care of your mother." I had, indeed, tried to take care of her my entire life. It was my job description from the moment I came into this world, and I guess my father knew it, too.

Don't worry, Dad. I'll take care of her, I assured him in my mind. I was surprised to hear a follow-up order, a whispered reply, and I wasn't sure if it was my father or myself talking. The voice said, *Take care of yourself, too, Rita.*

I SOON LEARNED THAT WHILE MY FATHER might have been at peace wherever he was, he had no intention of resting. A few months after he passed, I was in the middle of getting a chakra balancing on my back from Ro-C at her home, and he popped right in. (Though "popped" isn't really an accurate way to describe how my father entered a room—dead or alive, on Earth or in heaven, he wasn't the popping type.)

I was lying on Ro-C's table explaining how I'd twisted my back when I saw her body lurch forward. "Your father's here!" she announced. "Oh, man, is he *ever* here. Okay, okay . . . I will, I will. He wants me to tell you something important."

I gulped and sat up. *Okaaaay.*

She was quiet for a moment, nodding, as if she was listening to him. "Okay, yes, I got it . . . he wants me to tell you . . . that you were the 'smart' one. He's saying, 'You were the smartest of all of us. You took a different path than everyone else, and you had the strength to live your life as your true self, without worrying what everyone else thought or if they judged you.'"

"You're hearing him say this?"

Ro waved her hand and shushed me. "I can't listen to both of you at the same time," she scolded.

"Okay. Now . . . he's saying that he admires you. He's proud of you. You stuck up for yourself against all odds. Yes, *yes*, I will tell her word for word. He's saying, 'I couldn't see how wrong I was and how right you were while I was alive because my ego got in the way. But I'm sorry. I'm sorry for not understanding and not seeing it . . . '"

And then, as quickly as he'd arrived into the room, he exited. Ro-C said that she felt a tornado of energy swoosh past her and out the door, like a bull charging out. "He left," she said.

We looked at each other, speechless.

"He sure is, um . . . the pushy type, huh?"

I laughed; she had no idea. I'm sure he'd be the kind of guy who'd haunt someone until he got a message through. Sure enough, after he saw that he could reach me through Ro-C, Dad started making the rounds of my psychic friends over the next few months—sporadically delivering messages to me and hanging out with the girls. He affectionately called them his "new crew," and he called them at all hours of the day and night. You might say he was like the Patrick Swayze of the Other Side—he was so charmingly insistent, like Swayze's *Ghost* character. And like Whoopi Goldberg's psychic character, my friends couldn't resist him.

"Rita, your father woke me up again," my friend Nancy called late one night, her voice groggy. "He was very sweet. He wanted me to tell you to tell your mother that she was his one true love. And he messed up because he got himself trapped. He said, 'I see how much I hurt your mother, and I didn't want to hurt her.' Then he said something about apple pie and I got confused, but do you get it? He wouldn't let me go back to sleep until I called and told you. Now, can you tell him to . . . you know . . . back off a little?"

"I will, I will. Sorry, Nancy. And thanks."

Then Dad started showing up at my various holistic healing appointments because he knew I'd be with practitioners who'd be able to sense him. When he appeared at my reflexology session with Monica, a petite, waiflike woman, he nearly knocked her over.

"Rita, he's standing on top of me! Can you tell him to calm down a bit?"

"Dad, please . . . " I'd beg out loud. He'd soften his energy, but he'd never leave. He'd waited his whole life to talk to me, he said, and now that he could do so with nothing in the way—except my mortality and his death, two minor obstacles—he wasn't going to waste one minute or lose one more opportunity. It was just like my father to have an easier time talking to me in death rather than in life. This was probably the case, Ro-C told me, because he didn't have his ego attached to him anymore to get in the way. He was communicating from his soul now. And now that he was dead, we'd never been closer.

Every time he came through, he had a new message for me that he was excited to give, like a kid coming home from school bubbling over to tell what he'd learned that day.

"He's saying it is like school where he is," Jane, my cranio-sacral therapist, told me one day, as she dug into my head with her fingers. "He said that Earth is like kindergarten, and where he is it's like high school. He's learning new lessons and moving up the grades . . . "

"Can you ask him if Gram is with him? Where *is* he?"

He'd always make a getaway before I could get that last question in.

NEARLY TWO YEARS AFTER DAD TRANSITIONED to the Other Side, I had just finished with a client at my new healing room at home, and my whole being felt wide open to the universe. It was a golden autumn evening, and I had sent the woman off into the twilight feeling elated. After months of sessions, she had made a fundamental breakthrough on the table that day, and divulged a locked-away secret that needed to be spoken out loud and honored.

"Rita, you are the only person I've told that to," she said, giving me a long, tight hug before leaving. "But I know you keep all my secrets."

After years doing this work, I'm still amazed by how quickly the body can heal once truths are finally faced and embraced. My client skipped out of the room lighter than she'd felt in years, and I was feeling just as joyous.

As I put away my essential oils, I had a revelation that was so amusingly full circle I had to laugh out loud. It occurred to me that all the years I spent keeping family secrets had actually groomed me well to become a healer. I had now become a treasured, different kind of secret-keeper for my clients—the kind that involved trust and love.

I blew out the candles, stuck my head out the window, and closed my eyes, breathing in the rose-scented air.

I was happy. I was so, so happy.

I had found what I wanted to do in my life, and I was good at it; I loved helping people and feeling close to God in the process. My little visits with my father since he'd died made me feel connected to him and gave me hope that our communication would continue and maybe even grow.

I had ended my relationship with Nicki a few months earlier—it just wasn't right for me—and for the first time had bought a beautiful little home of my very own to start afresh. I was getting my life in order and, long after my death days of childhood, I now had "a knowing" that my future looked bright—great, in fact. I even had a knowing that there was a love of my life waiting for me, just around the corner.

I breathed in the evening air deeply and laughed.

I was Ebenezer-Scrooge-waking-up-on-Christmas-morning, dancing-on-tiptoes happy. I was George-Bailey-getting-a-second-chance-in-*It's-A-Wonderful-Life* happy. I felt my whole life opening up in front of me and . . . then I sensed someone behind me.

I swung around and called out, "Hello?" I thought my last client had come back, perhaps having forgotten something. But no one was there.

And then I felt his unmistakable energy stride into the healing room; march right up to me; and wrap his big, strong, Daddy arms around me with the bear hug of a boxer.

Dad?

"Is that you, Dad?" I asked out loud.

The answer came to me first in an image. In front of me stood my father, tall and handsome, wearing a dapper pinstriped suit and a crushed wool fedora. I froze in my spot and held my breath.

"It's me, it's me," I heard. Not like a regular voice and words, like Ro-C would have got, but more telepathically, like that "knowing" feeling I get sometimes.

Dad!

I didn't know what to do next—at the time it was only my second experience channeling someone from the Other Side. So I stood there and swayed with the hug and breathed in his energy, and I let him do all the talking.

"I came to sit with your energy and be with you," he said. His own energy was different from the other times he'd come through to my friends. Before he had been like a bull rushing through the room, bold and untamed. Now he tread as though he'd found his footing.

"It was too soon for me to come to you before, and I had a few things to do first. Now we're both ready."

"Okay, good," I answered out loud. I was in a woozy lull. I was drunk with the smell of candles and roses and the feel of my father's arms around me. What was the protocol for talking directly with one's dad in spirit form? I wasn't sure. We had our old script we used to follow, but I had a feeling we were about to write a whole new one, a whole new chapter.

"I want to tell you two special things," he said.

I answered him in my mind. *Okay.*

"I'm sorry, Rita. I'm sorry I wasn't able to accept who you were when I was alive. I had no right to judge you, not with the kind of life I led. I misunderstood. I was judgmental because of what I was taught, but what I was taught was wrong. Now I know that none of those things matter and you love whom and how you love. And your heart is as big as all outdoors."

Oh, Dad . . .

"When I was there, I chose the wrong path in work. I had a chance to get out when I was younger, but I got caught up in it and then it was too late. From here, I watch you work and can see the love and compassion in what you do. You took a path I would have wanted."

Then my father told me the second special thing. It was more of a deal he wanted to make, really—a kind of plea bargain where everybody wins.

"Rita, I hurt a lot of people in my lifetime, and you heal them. Now I want to humbly make a request. I'd like for us to work together."

How?

"Do you remember how I used to tell you that you had good hands, when you did my shoulders? We had a strong energy connection together, even then. I felt it and so did you."

Yes.

"Remember when you were little . . . I used to rub your back for you when you were sick and it would make you feel better? It would heal you?"

Of course, Dad.

"We can put our energies together. From where I am, I want to help you heal people. And from where you are, you can help me make up for some of the hurt I caused. We can do it together, side by side, like a father-daughter team."

I stood perfectly still and silent for a moment. The setting sun streamed in through the window, filling every crevice of my heart and healing room with a warm, golden light. I was surrounded by a world and a life that I loved, and it even included my father's embracing arms. He was asking permission to join my own healing crew, on this mortal side—and on the side of the good guys.

I looked at him in front of me, standing tall in his suit and fedora—young and earnest, the way he must have been when Mom first fell in love with him.

I realized, *This is all too perfect. How could I possibly tell him no?*

I didn't even have to ask him where he was again. I knew. I had tossed him a Hail Mary pass before he died, and he had caught the ball and run with it.

And now, my father had come back to me from heaven to make me an offer I couldn't refuse.

EPILOGUE

We Are Family

Every Sunday night, I crank up the Bee Gees and Sister Sledge on my iPod, and we dance barefoot in the kitchen. Leading the floor show are our canine mascots: Tripod, the three-legged, snow white, spaniel-mutt wonder dog, whom I adopted from Chile after he lost his leg in the earthquake of 2010; and Tripod's new sister, Sarah, a German shepherd–terrier mix who hails from Rockland County, New York.

I like to belt out the lyrics to "We Are Family" until the dogs howl, singing about having all my *sistuhs* with me—and I do.

As Italian traditions go, Sunday-night dinner with the family is sacred. And my newly extended family, which now includes the love of my life, Bobbie; her son, Joe; and a handful of dear friends, can be a boisterous bunch. We open up some vino, let our hair down, and let loose—a bunch of goddesses (and a few teenagers) on a mission to spread loving energy.

As I write this, it's May 2012. I've been a healer now for over a decade and in that time, I've seen more miracles happen, large and small. I've touched what some think is the impossible, but as I've learned—and as Gram taught me—nothing is impossible. Last week, a woman crawled onto my table crouched over in pain. An hour later, she walked out my front door standing upright, feeling great. One woman with stage III cancer came to a group healing

I was part of, and afterward she went back to her doctor and got a perfect bill of health and a clean CAT scan. I'm working hard to help these people, as I felt inspired to do long ago, but I'm not alone in doing it.

Last year I gathered together an amazing group of healers: chiropractors, Reiki masters, yoga instructors, spiritual counselors, herbalists, hypnotherapists—you name the practice, we've got the expert. We call ourselves "the Collective Healing Network" and our common goal, with the help of Spirit, is to help people heal themselves and find their own space of grace.

To call someone a "healer" is a bit misleading, though. We don't technically heal people; we act as a vehicle for the healing. It's Spirit who does the healing, who sends the energy through our bodies so that we can then send that energy to the person in front of us. As healers, we merely "hold the energy" for people—it's why many call it "energy work." Completing the process are the individuals themselves, who must want to be healed. Because ultimately, everyone is responsible for their own health.

ALSO ON THE JOB WITH ME since our spirit pact of 2007 is my father, who has lived up to his end of the bargain. At least once a week, I'll feel his unmistakable energy fill the room when I'm with a client. After a quick "hello" to me, he'll survey the situation and give me his Other Side input. Sometimes he'll whisper a bit of advice—"Ask them about what happened when they were ten years old"—sometimes he'll inspire my hands to move to a certain spot on their body. Other times, he'll just hang around and watch me and "sit in my energy," as he likes to say.

"I didn't come to watch any of your softball games or see you graduate," he said to me during one visit, "so I'll watch you now."

For the first time in my life, I feel safe in my father's presence, and I can feel his protection. I know he's watching out for me.

A few months ago I was working on a friend, Mark, who knew my father from the street. Mark had endured several months of aggressive chemo the year before and was due to have a CAT scan to check if the cancer had returned, so he came in for an overall body healing beforehand.

As I worked by Mark's feet, I could feel Dad stride into the room to help. First, he gave me his diagnosis: "Mark's okay. There's no more cancer in his body." Then he went directly to Mark.

"I feel like your father is in the room with us!" Mark said, ten minutes into our session.

"Um, yeah . . . I know. He's here. I didn't know if I should tell you or what."

"His face is right in front of me and he's talking to me! He's saying . . . "

Mark stopped, and chuckled.

"What?"

"He's saying, 'Marky, do me a favor and keep an eye out for Rita. She's going to have a lot of people around her with this work, and I want you to watch out for her, make sure she's safe.' I told him I would."

When I started getting messages from Dad on the Other Side, I'm not sure if my family knew what to make of it. My sisters were open to it, but my mother had been so limited in her framework of thinking because of her rigid Catholic upbringing that I had to move her along gradually. Sometimes if I thought she was ready, though, I threw her into the water.

One afternoon after I had explained to her about the laying on of hands, I dared her to give it a try. We were at my niece Allison's house, Yo's daughter, and I was telling her how people drop to the floor once I touch them.

She shook her head in disbelief. "That would never work with me. I'd never go down."

"Oh yeah, Ma. You would."

"No, Ri. I find it hard to believe . . . "

"Well, why don't you let me try it on you right now?"

She hesitated for a moment, wondering what she was getting herself into, and then agreed. I think she said yes because she thought nothing would happen. Maybe a small part of her also wanted to know for sure—did her youngest *really* have the gift of healing? She had a smidgen of belief, and that's all it takes to make a leap of faith.

"I ain't going down, I'm telling you!" Mom repeated, as I instructed my niece to get behind her. We were in the kitchen, and I didn't want her to bang her head on any countertops or appliances.

"Allison, have your arms out ready. It will be fast."

It only took a second, not even that. I stood in front of Mom, eye to eye, and barely touched her forehead with my finger. She gently sunk into Allison's arms, dissolving into tears on the way.

"I can't believe it," she said, over and over, as my niece pulled her up to her feet and held onto her. "I just can't believe it!"

Mom felt light as a feather for weeks after that, as if she'd released something heavy that had been weighing her down. "You had buried pain and emotions to let go of," I explained to her. We didn't go into details, but I suspect that they were linked to my father.

Since that day, Mom's been my biggest fan and cheerleader. Not just in the healing realm, but in my personal life, too. Gone are the days when she worried that my being gay would send me to the eternal fires of hell. She changed her beliefs, and that was brave of her.

"I didn't understand before, but I do now," she explained to me, sounding just like Dad from the Other Side.

"These beliefs are designed by men, not by God," Mom reasoned. "They don't make sense, and they needlessly hurt people. We were scared of gay people back then; it was an unknown. We were taught to be afraid and judgmental."

My mother's relationship with religion has obviously changed since the days when she'd chastise me for missing confession. And while it has been interesting to watch her shift, I've come to learn that there are many people in the world who need and want the structure of an organized religion to tell them right from wrong as she once did, and make them feel close to God.

The concern is when folks get stuck in an inflexible set of beliefs and are too afraid or closed off to think for themselves and allow their beliefs to evolve—even if reality, logic, experience, or feelings show otherwise. Faced with a new set of truths in front of them, people can either choose to hold on to the old ones or open up their minds to new ideas and thoughts, as my mother has.

In my experience, once human beings understand a new "truth" or have a new awareness, there is no going back to un-knowing it. Even so, there is no right or wrong direction to take—just the right one for each of us, at our own pace and time. We choose what we are capable of, and no one should judge another's journey.

The Catholic religion taught me the compassionate teachings of Jesus, introduced me to the all-loving Blessed Mother and the angels, and gave me the rosary . . . and I keep these treasures close to my heart. I pray the rosary every morning, and even though I rare-ly go to church, Jesus and Mary are right beside me every minute of every day—once they arrived, they never left. They continue to appear in front of me now more than ever, especially during healings. I pray to God often and on any day of the week, not just on Sundays—just as Gram taught me—and I pray from anywhere, not just in a church.

But to truly love myself and others, I had to leave part of the religion behind and shift to what I feel is a higher truth. I don't believe a religion should teach that one group or individual is "right" and rewarded while others are "wrong" and punished. I repeat the same question I asked myself in church as a teenager: *How could an all-loving God teach that?*

I know in my heart when and if I've done wrong, and when that happens, I confess that to God directly. Or, I should say, I confess it to my higher self—because I believe that there is no separation between God and us, and that we are all an extension of this infinite Spirit.

For whatever reason, organized religion separated people from the Creator. We got into the habit of looking up at the sky or going into a building, thinking we'd find God there; but really, God re-sides within us, in our hearts. And we are all gods and goddesses and have our own, higher selves to account to.

I DID A LOT OF THINGS IN MY LIFE (that I also described here in this book) that I'm not proud of. I had to learn to forgive myself for those actions and find my own redemption, and both came from within me. If anything, my goal in writing this book is to open people up to their own capacity for healing, love, forgiveness, and redemption. And to show you that no matter what happens in your life, those events are not what define you. How you react and how you face the events and people in your path and how you move through them, *that* is what counts—that is what defines you. And the great news is that you can choose to be either a victim or a victor.

For those who need religion to help them move through, go to it. In general, I embrace all religions because I feel that each one, used positively, is meant to lead everyone to the same result: love, forgiveness, compassion, and non-judgment. That's what Jesus and other religious leaders and prophets spoke about. That's what a heart feels and sees when it looks at the world through the eyes of an innocent child.

Ironically, once I realized I didn't need to conform to a set of rules or a recipe dictating how I'd communicate with God or Spirit or my higher power, and that I could let go of the tenets that did not feel right to me, I was able to fully open myself up and surrender to God even more.

And that includes opening myself up to love.

I've heard many Catholics say that "love is not a feeling" when debating the same-sex marriage or gay-lifestyle issue. In other words, if your body and heart pull you toward someone that the Church says you are "not permitted" to be with, you should ignore those feelings. But if God gives us free will, that would include the free will to feel what we feel and love whom we love, would it not? And if it is God Who allows us these feelings, then you might say it's "God's will" that we love whom our hearts desire. I would, anyway. *Love is not a feeling?!* In reply to that, I paraphrase Jesus—and the immortal words of John Lennon—"All you need is love."

The year before I wrote these words, same-sex marriage became legal in the state of New York, just across the river from me.

Then a few weeks ago, President Obama made a historical statement to the world, saying, "I think same-sex couples should be able to get married." As soon as his interview hit the airwaves, my cell phone buzzed with my mother's familiar ringtone.

"Ri! Did you hear what the President said? We need to vote for him! The other guy is against it, but not Obama!"

I was elated and amused by Mom's reaction, but not surprised by it, or by the President's announcement. I've always felt he was an evolved soul here to help our country shift to the next spiritual level, like Martin Luther King, Jr., and others before him who had the perception and courage to publicly declare a universal truth that will lay the groundwork for change. The President's words are a sign that our world is moving a step closer to unity. After all, the goal is to be inclusive, not exclude people because of their differences. I will repeat it: *We are family.*

Once Mom busted out of the beliefs she'd been trapped in, we could grow even closer together as mother and daughter, in a healthy way—in the way of Good Josh Gold and his angelic mother, and of Mr. and Mrs. Russo and their daughters. With my mother's own new freedom, she was able to embrace who I am and the life I was carving out for myself. She welcomed my healing groups into her home and was therefore pivotal in one of the most important changes in my life.

I MET THE VIVACIOUS AND BEAUTIFUL BOBBIE at Mom's house five years ago when she came for a group meditation gathering. As soon as she spoke, I knew our meeting was destiny.

Two weeks before that, I had attended a Goddess Circle— a night where a bunch of us psychically inclined women get together to eat, meditate, and attempt to receive messages for each other from Spirit. I had received a message from my spirit guide, Clarice, who told me during meditation: "I want you to channel harmony to the earth." I had no idea what it meant, but I figured, as with all things, the meaning would unfold in its own good time and I tucked the message away in my brain.

At Mom's, a group of us were meditating together for an hour, and when it was over, the leader asked if anyone had seen or heard anything. Bobbie shot her hand up. By profession, she's a nurse, but she's always had a psychic talent as well. She raised her hand and pointed at me.

"It was for you," she said. "A woman came through, and her name was Clarice. She wanted me to tell you to 'channel harmony to the earth.'"

I was stunned. She repeated what Clarice had told me, word for word. I thanked Bobbie, but I was too shocked to say any more. At the end of the evening, I went over to where she was sitting on the couch. I knelt down on one knee and put my hands on both her knees.

"Do you realize how psychic you are?" I asked her.

I then explained about my previous Clarice message, and we both were amazed. "I think you and I are going to work together," I said. But I had a feeling even then it would be more. I had known that day in the healing room five months earlier, the day Dad showed up, that I was soon to meet my soul mate and lifelong love. The day I met Bobbie, I felt the clicking sound of the final piece of my puzzle snapping into place. And my getting down on one knee in front of Bobbie that first night we met? Talk about foreshadowing.

Two months ago, after a romantic sunset dinner to celebrate our fifth anniversary, we came home to do an exchange of cards in candlelight when I handed her a big box. Inside was a collage I'd made, filled with photos of all the special moments we'd shared— a photo diary of how we'd fallen in love. On the top of the collage, I'd drawn an airplane soaring across the sky pulling a banner that read: WILL YOU MARRY ME?

Before she had a chance to answer, I dropped to my knee once again and asked her officially. They were words I never thought I'd be lucky enough to say to someone and really, truly mean it.

"Will you do me the honor of spending the rest of your life with me?"

"Yes!"

We kissed, and I got all teary-eyed and choked up. I knew she was going to say yes, but still, we both got swept up in the emotions of the moment. If love isn't a feeling, I don't know what is.

A few days later, I visited Mom and my sisters and told them the news. Ro jumped out of her seat in excitement. "I am so happy for you!" she said, hugging me.

Yo and Mom immediately pressed me for all the exciting details, as moms and sisters do. They all adore Bobbie. A few months earlier I'd taken her to a family wedding, and all of us danced the night away together. We'd come a long way from the days when I had to live a secret life. And ironically enough, since meeting Bobbie I have learned to embrace my feminine side for the first time. I grew my hair out of Dad's shorn, slicked-back look and am never mistaken for a boy anymore. Confident with my own inner self-power now, I can soften that tough-guy suit of armor I created as a child for strength and protection. I don't need it anymore.

Today, Bobbie and I are planning our 2013 wedding, and there's one detail we know for sure: our honeymoon will be in Italy! I want to visit Naples, where my grandparents were born and grew up. I want to see the streets Gram walked as a child in Santa Lucia and visit her father's pharmacy, which is 108 years old and still stands on a little cobblestoned street.

Even Dad approves of my new love. He showed up a few years ago to introduce himself to Bobbie and welcome her to the family. She and I were chatting in the car one night when she was suddenly mute, staring at me with wild eyes.

"What's wrong? Are you okay?" I asked.

"Your father. His face is on top of yours! He says he came to meet me!"

His visits continue on with my friends, especially if he's got something important to say and can't reach me. For example, on the morning of his birthday in March, three weeks after Bobbie and I got engaged, my friend Natasha called me up to tell me that she'd dreamed about him.

"He was holding up a wedding photo of you and Bobbie, saying 'Look, my daughter is getting married. Tell her I'll be there!'"

Again, something I thought would never happen. To see my father dance at my wedding, now *that* would be a miracle. I'll have to play a little Elvis for him.

As I CONTINUE TO SHED PAINFUL LAYERS from my past, memories of my father that I buried as a child rise to the surface. At first, like the time I remembered my violent altercation with Sal, these memories affected me so intensely, emotionally and physically, that I'd be down for the count. But as I've gotten stronger over the years, I've learned to address them without the drama and debilitating emotion connected to the original incidents.

It was only a few months ago, while in session with my client Marina, that I was jolted by the childhood memory of my father beating a man viciously on Gram's kitchen floor. After Marina's session was over, I sat down alone and identified the memory, acknowledged it, put it into context, took a few days to process it emotionally, and then—I let it go. The child within me knows that I'm now strong enough to handle the painful memories, and the adult in me knows that I'm now ready to say good-bye to them so that they won't hurt me anymore.

Part of the reason I'm able to do this is because my relationship with my father is so different now. In the years since we've been in touch between two worlds, I've come to understand and have more compassion for him. Not to diminish the harm he inflicted on others, but I do believe that he got caught up in a world he wanted to get out of yet didn't know how. During his final year in jail, my family was able to see a softer side to him. To them, he expressed regret about being in the street.

"I messed up," he admitted to Ro during one visit.

And during my ongoing communication with him, he continues to try to explain his regretful actions.

"He wants you to understand that as a boy, he felt he couldn't rely on anyone except himself," my friend Brenda told me last month during a channeling session in which my father came through to her. "He didn't feel safe. He didn't feel he was able to be innocent. He felt he had to be one step ahead, mistrusting, like 'You won't be able to get to me because I'll get to you first.' He was afraid he'd be squashed; it was a survival instinct. And his belief isolated him. Now he's saying, 'I want no more blood on the hands of this family—I want it to end. I want my children's children to start with a clean slate.'"

She smiled when she told me the next part. "He sees that you have taken his willfulness and self-reliance and transformed it into the light. When you dig in your heels, he smiles and says, 'She gets that from me!'"

Had my father chosen another path at a critical time in his life, he may have been a different man. The early years my siblings shared with him, when they were a real family, and the cherished moments he and I shared dancing to the King or when I saw him help people—to me, they show a side of him that was very real. Had that side been allowed to flourish, it would have been the "real" Vincent Gigante, son of Yolanda and Salvatore.

Like my mother, I always wanted to see the good in him. And I see it even more now since he's crossed—he's let go of that other persona that he had to create, the one of ego and power.

ALONG MY OWN SPIRITUAL JOURNEY, I bring my family with me so that we can hopefully heal together. I love my family, no matter what. Because of them, I learned the lessons I needed to learn and am able to share my story with you now. Today, I thank them for playing their roles perfectly so that the manifestation of this book could happen. We have our spiritual contracts with each other, and although we are a work in progress, we are indeed making progress.

I hope this book can be a space of grace for them and for you, too—a moment of stillness and energy exchange that heals the body, mind, and spirit.

One lesson I try to express to my family is that we should and can face the past honestly and still love our father and each other. We can take the past, embrace it, learn from it, and make a new and better future from it.

Not long ago I was walking down Sullivan Street, passing by all Gram's old favorites like Pino's Meat Market and Joe's Dairy, and I was shocked when I passed Dad's old café. Gone were the blacked-out windows and nondescript, unwelcoming exterior. In its stead was a bright, New Age–style tea and spice shop! I couldn't believe my eyes. I went in and looked around. Where the bar used to be was an array of organic dried leaves, gourmet coffee, and garlic-infused salts. Where Dad used to sit and play cards, I now saw potted herbs and handmade soaps. God, did I laugh. To me it was so symbolic of Dad's own personal transformation, as well as of how any past can transform into a different future if you have the will and vision.

When other remnants of my painful past show up, I acknowledge them with love, not fear. Last month I was completely stressed to the max about something, and I picked up a pair of socks to put on and thought, *Nope, can't wear these!* And then I picked up another pair and thought, *Okay, this feels good.* The old grooves show up once in a while, but instead of panicking, I say, *Well, hello, my old friend! To what do I owe this visit?* The little visit tells me I'm over-stressed and need to slow down a bit.

EVERY MONTH OR SO I BUMP INTO SOMEONE who recognizes my family name and they'll ask, "Hey, are you related to . . . ?" and I'll say yeah. There was a time when I hid from my family connection, but not anymore. I want to live the truth.

I think that in his way, my father yearned to do the same; that even though his mind could pretend or compartmentalize brilliantly to rationalize some of his actions, he knew the truth, and his soul was urging him to speak it.

Not long after he died, the jail sent a box to my mother of the personal items he'd kept in his locker. In the box were a few pairs of underwear, candy, a prayer book, and a bundle of all the letters I had sent him over the years. That last forgiveness letter I had sent him was worn and faded, as if he'd taken it out and unfolded it and read it hundreds of times.

But there was one item in the box I'd never seen before. It was a square, white, laminated card he apparently carried with him all the time, for years.

The card read:

> Truth is cold, sober fact, not so comfortable to absorb. A lie is more palatable. The most detested person in the world is the one who always tells the truth, who never romances. If a lie is told often enough even the teller comes to believe it. It becomes a habit. And a habit becomes a cable. Each day another strand is added until you have woven a cable that is unbreakable.

No one in the family knew where he got the card from or how long he'd had it, but later on I did a bit of checking online and found it was a quote attributed to a man named Joseph "Yellow Kid" Weil. Weil was born in 1875 in Chicago and was known as one of the smartest con men of his era. Dad's card was missing the first line of the quote, though, which is:

> A lie is an allurement, a fabrication, that can be embellished into a fantasy. It can be clothed in the raiment of a mystic conception.

That was dad, in his pajamas! But what was he trying to say, carrying these words in his pocket, next to his heart? That a lie was better than the truth because it spared feelings? Did it comfort him to know that at least on this 2" x 3" card that he carried, he told the truth about himself? Was he relating to the Yellow Kid, understanding the burden of having to carry so many lies on his shoulders? And finally, was he acknowledging that he was, indeed, good at it and had begun to believe his lies himself?

I'll have to ask him the next time we speak.

Even though Dad got tangled up in his own fabrication of himself, like the quote says, in the end he was able to break on through to the Other Side.

I don't imagine that Shakespeare or Dickens would have thought up such an offbeat story of redemption: *Crime boss comes back in spirit to help his wayward daughter heal the world and make up for his sins.* It's an off-kilter, father-daughter fairy tale with a happy ending.

I grew up in the dark and escaped the dungeon to find my way to the light. In the end, my father was brave enough to follow. There are a lot of different kinds of human-made jails in this world—mental, physical, and spiritual—that have nothing to do with justice or rightness or God. My father and I escaped a few of them and now, we have a lot of work to do together, to help others do the same.

Gram used to say this awesome Neapolitan word when she wanted to get moving, in order to get to church or go shopping and get things done.

Jammuncenne!

It means, "Okay, let's go! Let's do it!" I say it to the gang when we toast at Sunday-night dinner. I also say it to the healing group when we're huddled together like a football team saying prayers, and then we break! Time to go do some healing, time to move forward!

I have my father's infamous Golden Nugget robe hanging in my healing room closet at home. And on the wall, I put up his painting of Saint Rita, with beams of light shooting out to her from God and little angels dancing.

Saint Rita, the Saint of the Impossible. Gram was the first of us to have a direct line to God, and as she predicted, I did do the impossible. I found myself, and I found my father. I found forgiveness, and I found my family. I found love, and I found my calling. I found God, and I found peace.

Turns out I wasn't ruined after all—merely lost. Now I'm found.

Gram would have been proud. I know my father is.

ACKNOWLEDGMENTS

First and foremost, I want to thank Source, the spiritual realm, and Mother Earth for continued love, support, and communion on this project. I am grateful for the opportunity to serve the collective consciousness in hopes that this book may have a positive effect.

To my loving future wife, Bobbie—thank you for your unconditional love and encouragement throughout this challenging process. You are the light that holds steadfast in my heart, and it is an honor to walk this path with you.

Thanks also to Bobbie's son, Joey, who lovingly accepted me into his and his mother's world with maturity, grace, and an open heart.

Thank you to my family, who taught me about forgiving myself and others, the possibility of change, the beauty of compassion, and the meaning of unconditional love.

For my mother, who has been and still is an inspiration to me—I cherish our ever-loving connection. I admire your openness to change and willingness to let your belief system expand and flourish. Thank you for allowing me to share details of your own life in my story.

Thank you, Dad, for who you were and who you became—you played an integral role in showing me my own potential. *Jammuncenne!* Thanks for looking out for me from the Other Side.

Heartfelt love to my steadfast grandmother Gram Crackers—for her courage, wisdom, love, and always speaking her truth. She's the glue that held us all together.

I thank my sister Yo for doing her best to help Mom raise me. She was a lifeline for most of my childhood, and I honor her spirit and soul for that sacrifice.

I thank my sister Ro for being there for me at a moment's notice, for accepting my lifestyle graciously, and for the laughs we continue to share. Namaste.

I thank my brother Sal, who helped me find my strength and taught me that I had to go through the dark to get to the light.

I thank my brother Andrew for sharing Sunday-morning bowls of Cap'n Crunch and afternoon football, *Abbott and Costello,* and *The Three Stooges.*

With thanks and love to all of my nieces, nephews, great-nieces, and great-nephews for their joy of life and for taking our family into a limitless future.

I want to thank Bobbie's family: Mom Sterchele, Eve, Ray, Dominic, Carl, and Billy. You are my new family, who accepted our love and welcomed me home with open arms and a true generosity of spirit.

To my extended family: fellow healers Debbie, Barbara M., Norma, Gerry, Louis, Ellice, Mike, Ro-C, Barbara A., Sal, Anna, Gary, Jenn, Jill, and Peggy; mentors Jinny, Enid, Eamonn, Linda L., and Linda U.; and my clients. You show me every day that we are all universally connected with each other. I love and honor all of you.

Grazie mille to my co-writer, Natasha. You are a kindred spirit who understood and uncovered my voice with compassion and humor. Thank you for gently holding my energy and memories in your hands. You are my new sister and off-the-record secret keeper. Now let's eat!

For my new friend Joseph, who became instant family. Thank you for sharing memories of my father, and for your crucial guidance with this book.

With gratitude and thanks to Joey, Johnny, and Tommy for their collective wisdom and support—professionally, spiritually, and practically.

Thank you to Jeanne for believing in this story, helping Natasha and me make it a reality, and for being part of the home team.

Many, many thanks to the upbeat, unwavering gang at Hay House—Reid Tracy, the incomparable Shannon Littrell, Christy Salinas, Johanne Mahaffey, Richelle Zizian, and Erin Dupree—for your faith and hard work. A special thanks to Jill Kramer, who gave us the green light pronto!

And last but so not least—thank you, Angel (a.k.a. Tripod) and Sara, for your grounding and loyalty; you're the two best "Muhtz" in the world!

And to all the other dear ones whom I love but forgot to list here . . . your names are in my heart forever.

— **Rita**

* * *

Thank you, dear Steve—the kindest, most loyal human being on this planet. xx

Rita—Yo! Thank you, babe, for having the spirit and gut faith that destiny threw us together for good reason. *Fuhgettaboutit.*

To Shannon and the gang at Hay House—you're da goods! (Now, can we have another week's extension, please?)

A zillion hugs to Mom and Dad, who are rooting for me from heaven.

And thank you, Mr. Gigante, for giving us permission to write this book. I look forward to meeting you one day for our big sit-down interview—on the record, of course.

— **Natasha**

*** ***

ABOUT THE AUTHORS

Rita Gigante has dedicated her adult life to healing people spiritually, emotionally, and physically. She has a degree in exercise physiology and is a licensed massage therapist and Reiki master. In 2010 she formed the Collective Healing Network, which conducts monthly sessions in New York and New Jersey. Rita also has a private practice outside of New York City, where she serves clients using energy therapy, intuitive healing, spiritual counseling, sound therapy, and angel readings.

For more information, to attend a group healing, or to book an individual session, please go to:

ritagigante.com
aspaceofgrace.com
collectivehealingnetwork.com

Natasha Stoynoff is a two-time *New York Times* best-selling author with six books to her credit. She has worked as a news reporter/photographer for *The Toronto Star*, a columnist for *The Toronto Sun*, a freelancer for *Time* magazine, and a correspondent for *People* magazine for nearly two decades. She lives in New York City, where she writes books and screenplays.

We hope you enjoyed this Hay House book. If you'd like
to receive our online catalog featuring additional information
on Hay House books and products, or if you'd like to find out
more about the Hay Foundation, please contact:

Hay House, Inc., P.O. Box 5100, Carlsbad, CA 92018-5100
(760) 431-7695 or (800) 654-5126
(760) 431-6948 (fax) or (800) 650-5115 (fax)
www.hayhouse.com® • **www.hayfoundation.org**

Published and distributed in Australia by: Hay House Australia Pty. Ltd.,
18/36 Ralph St., Alexandria NSW 2015 • *Phone:* 612-9669-4299
Fax: 612-9669-4144 • www.hayhouse.com.au

Published and distributed in the United Kingdom by: Hay House UK, Ltd.,
292B Kensal Rd., London W10 5BE • *Phone:* 44-20-8962-1230
Fax: 44-20-8962-1239 • www.hayhouse.co.uk

Published and distributed in the Republic of South Africa by:
Hay House SA (Pty), Ltd., P.O. Box 990, Witkoppen 2068
Phone/Fax: 27-11-467-8904 • www.hayhouse.co.za

Published in India by: Hay House Publishers India, Muskaan Complex,
Plot No. 3, B-2, Vasant Kunj, New Delhi 110 070 • *Phone:* 91-11-4176-1620
Fax: 91-11-4176-1630 • www.hayhouse.co.in

Distributed in Canada by: Raincoast, 9050 Shaughnessy St., Vancouver, B.C.
V6P 6E5 • *Phone:* (604) 323-7100 • *Fax:* (604) 323-2600 • www.raincoast.com

Take Your Soul on a Vacation

Visit **www.HealYourLife.com®** to regroup,
recharge, and reconnect with your own magnificence.
Featuring blogs, mind-body-spirit news, and life-
changing wisdom from Louise Hay and friends.

Visit **www.HealYourLife.com** today!